THE HOLISTIC SMUTS

THE HOLISTIC SMUTS

A study in personality

PIET BEUKES

M.A. (S.A.), M.Litt. (Oxon.)

With a foreword by H. F. Oppenheimer

HUMAN & ROUSSEAU

Cape Town   Pretoria

First impression 1989
Second impression 1990

Published by Human & Rousseau (Pty) Ltd
State House, 3-9 Rose Street, Cape Town
Typography by Patricia Going
Cover design by Wiekie Theron
Painting of J. C. Smuts by Frank Wiles,
reproduced by courtesy of Mr Brian Wiles
and the City and Civil Service Club, Cape Town
Typeset in 10 on 12 pt Times Roman by
Human & Rousseau, Cape Town
Printed and bound by National Book Printers, Goodwood

ISBN 0 7981 2537 3

This book is dedicated
to my wife Helen and to my daughters
Honey, Barbara and Dorothy for their
love and support

The author wishes to record
his deep indebtedness to the late
Sir Ernest Oppenheimer who encouraged him
and sponsored the vital research in England

Contents

Foreword

I was very pleased to be asked by my old friend Piet Beukes to contribute a foreword to his book *The Holistic Smuts*. This is an important and original work which Piet Beukes was particularly well equipped to undertake. He knew Smuts as well as a young man could know a great and, in some ways, unapproachable man of a much older generation. He had grown up to venerate him as a statesman, a scholar, a philosopher and a hero, but most of all, in spite of faults of temperament to which he was certainly not blind, as a unique human personality.

This book concentrates on the religious faith which Piet Beukes convincingly argues was basic to Smuts's life and work. This emphasis will certainly surprise many people; for Smuts was not generally regarded as a religious man. Certainly he was not religious in any dogmatic sense. His character was however highly romantic and a romantic in his nature cannot be a materialist. In his youth Smuts was deeply interested in the English romantic poets, particularly Shelley. This was on the advice of a professor at Stellenbosch who told him that he should make a start with *Prometheus Unbound*. That, in relation to romantic poetry, was surely recommending him to jump in at the deep end! Shelley had been sent down from Oxford for writing and distributing a pamphlet entitled *The Necessity of Atheism*. *Prometheus Unbound*, which he wrote some ten years later when at the height of his power was, in spite of its beauty and originality, generally condemned by the authorities as an immoral and subversive work. Today it may, in a deeper sense, be regarded as a deeply religious poem both in its tone and intent. The relevance of all this to the religious elements in Smuts's nature is plain.

The Holistic Smuts is not a study of holism, but of Smuts's personality as it found expression in his holistic studies and thought. This is the special interest and originality of the work, for no-one previously, as far as I know, has understood so clearly and expressed so forcibly the central part which holism played in Smuts's life and work. It cannot be maintained that Smuts's book *Holism and Evolution* has in itself exercised a major influence either as a work of science or of philosophy. Perhaps it would have been different had Smuts's work as a politician and statesman allowed him time to write the second volume on this subject which he contemplated, and about which the author has been able to give us some fascinating hints based on his study of Smuts's unpublished papers. It looks as though Smuts's mind, in his search for truth, was moving from the study of science to that of mysticism. And might he not have found interest and support in *The Phenomenon of Man* by Teilhard de Chardin? But is it possible to be a party politician, a practitioner of the art of the possible, and at the same time a mystic? In reading Piet Beukes's suggestive book I have come to wonder if this was not Smuts's personal tragedy. For can there ever have been a great man whose career made less of a coherent whole than that of this holistic thinker and idealist? But this is not to criticize Smuts or still less to charge him with any lack of intellectual integrity. It was his misfortune that the environment into which he was born and his own temperament made it necessary for him to work on two time scales. As a holist he thought in terms of eternity; as a politician and patriot, trying to serve South Africa to the best of his ability in turbulent times, he had to think in terms of the next election. It is the great merit of this book, as I see it, that at a time when Smuts's influence and reputation is, comparatively speaking, at a low ebb, it presents his unique personality in a true and splendid light which quite outshines the flaws and inconsistencies in his temperament and career.

I have no doubt that Smuts's life, work and thought will yet exercise a powerful influence for good in the future of South Africa. And in furthering that process Piet Beukes's book should play an important part.

H. F. Oppenheimer

CHAPTER ONE

Introduction

This is not a history or a biography of General Jan Christiaan Smuts. It is an inquiry into his personality and into his ideas and his work, and especially into his religious views and how they influenced his outlook and his statecraft. I have tried to do so on the basis of a new discipline, Personology, which he himself originated and which is here applied in a study of his greatness.

Smuts and especially his Holism were not understood during his own lifetime. Today he is no more with us, but politically his name still is anathema among some of his own people. His memory and his work are still maligned and attacked by those who never knew him and never understood him.[1]

Of one thing we can be certain: neither the petty malice of smaller men, nor the extinction of death can depreciate his greatness. On the contrary, great as he was in life, his greatness comes into fuller and brighter view as death in its mysterious way tears away the body to leave free the spirit which is eternal.

His death has not clouded his living ideas or obliterated his great spirit. Rather it has opened for us the book of his inner mind as the source of inspiration of his greatness.

For what remained closed through all his living years, his inner thoughts and the deep insight which gave him that calm, serene outlook upon all things, is now gradually coming into brighter view. What before was private and personal and hidden is now coming to us through the voluminous notes, memoirs, letters and other personal writings which he left behind.

Those of us who were privileged to know him in his lifetime, who enjoyed and became spellbound by his magnetic personality, can now begin to look deeper into the mind which activated it all. And as we still feel upon us the calm gaze of his steady blue eyes, which looked upon all men and all things so resolutely and so fearlessly, we begin to realize in a deeper and more lasting way our contact with one of the most remarkable men of our time, perhaps indeed of all time.

For, great and noble as the personality Smuts was in his lifetime, his outlook on life, his inner mind with its deep and lasting spiritual quality, is now emerging as something even greater.

Away from the strife and struggle which surrounded his public life, we can see his ethical approach, based on his deep religious convictions, to the great issues of modern times more clearly. At the same time a study of Smuts shows us that his all-embracing mind was even more colossal and more penetrating than we knew when he was with us.

What is more important, we can see the direction of the great ideas and visions which he left behind more clearly. Our perspective is better, for Smuts was mentally far ahead of his time and his generation, and what he believed in and expounded more than fifty years ago is only now coming into view.

But life is like that. It is never static. Like the swing of the pendulum our interests and attention sway in one direction until our entire outlook is askew and lopsided. It is then that the man of genius appears miraculously with that clarity of vision and depth of insight, to bring humanity's mind back to the sane, moderate, middle-course outlook which is basically "common sense", the wisdom of the ages.

Such was Smuts, a nineteenth-century son of a small backward country who somehow was endowed with truly remarkable insight and understanding, so that he saw the whole involved life process simply and straightforwardly, and explained it in living, simple words to his generation and to all generations.

In his thoughts, his words and his actions he rose above the common prejudices, the narrow biased view, the lopsided outlook of nineteenth-century man and his philosophers and politicians. He became one of the first and most representative pioneers of the twentieth century, not only in his statecraft ever striving for the better, greater world, but more especially in his ideas and his great concept of Holism which became the antithesis, the corrective of the hard mechanistic outlook of the nineteenth century which tended to break up life into meaningless parts and compartments.

More than many other philosophers, scientists, statesmen and thinkers of his time – and he combined them all as have few other figures in our modern world – he clearly saw the limitations and the dangers of the rigid mechanistic outlook of the nineteenth century. It was a remarkable insight for one who was part of that intellectual world. In that sense he was of his time, but above and beyond it.

There were many in his and other generations who also foresaw the ultimate futility and self-limiting powers of the rigid mechanistic ideas of modern science and philosophy. But few of them had the knowledge, the mental capacity and the deep insight of this remarkable son of Africa, who in so many ways was more truly European than the Europeans themselves.

And Smuts never made the mistake of most critics of their own times, of bringing the pendulum back to the other extreme. He remained always the master and the great thinker who retained the balance in his ideas, achieving in his Holism a synthesis between faith and reason, science and religion.

Among the complexities of modern thought and the obscurity of scientific and philosophic language, he remained always the simple and straightforward fundamental thinker, as bold and fearless in inquiring as the Greeks, and expressing himself in clear living language.

He revealed his true greatness as a leader and as a thinker by combining his fearless search for truth wherever it might lead with the fine moral and spiritual values which religion bequeathed to all mankind. To Smuts, Jesus of Nazareth was the greatest and the highest Personality mankind has produced, a Light and Fount, who guides our spirits, our minds and our souls in this strange and mysterious and yet good universe of which we are part, but know so little.

What is more, in his own life he combined these ideas and values. His own personality is the symbol and the synthesis of all he thought and believed.

South Africa is a small country far away from the great powers which in their conflicts and interrelationships shape the course of human history. Yet here in an obscure corner of the world, nature saw fit to produce a genius of outstanding qualities, a thinker whose massive intellect and great spirit guided many peoples and many races to a better understanding of themselves and the world we live in.

Smuts belonged not only to South Africa or to Africa. He was a son of the world, a leader of humanity, everywhere. He was born in Africa, but he served the world.

In presenting him here I do not see him as an Afrikaner or even as a South African, but as an examplar of all mankind. Part of this study is how he developed from the one into the other, and in doing so, what he achieved both in the world of ideas and of action for the whole of mankind.

My main emphasis in this study will fall, however, on his religion and how his deeply held religious views and convictions influenced his philosophy and his statecraft. Understandably he was averse to discussing his personal beliefs in public. He preferred to reveal his private self in the many intimate letters he wrote to friends in various parts of the world.

Possibly because of this and especially on the basis of some of the philosophic views he expressed in his *Holism and Evolution*, the idea took root that he was not only antireligious, but also an atheist. In my younger days among the intensely nationalistic Afrikaners of the Orange Free State and before I knew Smuts personally, I also believed that he was an atheist.

There are various reasons why the opinion took hold that he was atheistic, the main reason being that his biographers from the outset created the impression that he did not believe in a personal God. The blame in this regard must primarily go to his well-known biographer, H. C. Armstrong, who in his book *Grey Steel, A Study in Arrogance* misunderstood Smuts's religious convictions completely. In discussing the holistic ideas of his subject, Armstrong wrote: "Yet in his Universe there appeared to be no need nor even room for God."

Armstrong thought that he had summed up Smuts rightly by saying that according to Smuts there might be a permeating influence in the universe which might vaguely be labelled "God" but that in Smuts's views there was no personal God particularly interested in men. "In Smuts's philosophy there was, for the ordinary man, no God," was his conclusion.[2]

This is of course a fundamental misreading of the basic outlook of Smuts. It misses the essential point of Holism and is contradicted by Smuts's personal letters.

Unfortunately Mrs Sarah Gertrude Millin, who wrote two volumes on Smuts in the nineteen-thirties, perpetuated these fallacies of Armstrong's. Being herself a self-confessed agnostic, she could not grasp the validity and the significance of Smuts's religious ideas.[3] Furthermore his own son, Jannie, who also wrote a biography of his father, did not stress the religious aspect of his father's life. His otherwise worthwhile history of his father lacks this fundamental appreciation of religion in the life of Smuts.[4]

Added to this was the fact that Smuts was loath to talk about his religion openly and publicly, and his book *Holism and Evolution*, which is a scientific treatise, did not deal with religion. As a consequence some of the intellectual, and especially the religious leaders made the wrong deductions from the conclusion of his book.[5]

As is well known, the book is a deep and wide-ranging philosophical treatise on the essence of the physical world, in which Smuts discussed the interesting idea of the existence of a holistic principle as part of the upward-striving forces in evolution from lower to higher forms in the development of life. The entire book is in reality a glorification of the miracle of Creation and the upward striving of all forms of life in nature until the glory of the human personality with its immense potential for good or evil is reached.

But is there a supra-mundane Mind or Personality above and beyond the earthly process which produced the human personality?

Smuts in the final chapter of his book states clearly that if such a "Personality" did exist, it would be as different at least from human Personality as this again is from mere organism. "To call such a new Transcendent Whole by the same name as human personality is to abuse language and violate thought alike. There is universal agreement with the well-known argument of Kant, that from the facts of Nature no inference to a transcendent Mind is justified, as that would make the whole still of the same character and order as its parts; which would be absurd, as Euclid says. From the facts neither an organism nor a Mind of Nature can strictly be inferred; still less a Personality constituted by both."[6]

It is possible that those who held the opinion and still hold the view that Smuts was irreligious and even an atheist, obtained that impression from this passage in his *Holism and Evolution*. I will show that the eminent Monsignor Dr. F. C. Kolbe, one of the great intellectuals of South Africa, shortly after the appearance of *Holism* strongly attacked what he called Smuts's "materialistic outlook". He especially singled out Smuts's ready acceptance of Kant's "heresy". He regarded this as one of the biggest blunders of both Kant and Smuts, as according to Kolbe, man discovers God through His Creation.[7]

Although coming from a Roman Catholic source, this was readily accepted by those who differed from Smuts politically and saw him as a traitor to his nation and his country.

There is a second argument used to brand Smuts as an atheist. This is an assumption based on his deep belief in and ready acceptance of evolution. Unfortunately, as I shall point out later. Darwin's overemphasis on the external factor in the evolutionary process exaggerated the mechanical conception of the universe. This led to the false idea in the minds of religious people that evolution is a purely outward mechanical explanation of life and that it by implication denies the inner or spiritual aspect of things. All those believing in and accepting evolution were therefore regarded as atheists, and as Smuts publicly accepted and even glorified the concept of evolution, this was regarded as final proof of his atheism and the denial of God as the Supreme Creator.[8]

In his busy life, with so many issues and events crowding in on his attention, Smuts never took the trouble to deny publicly the accusation that he was an atheist. He was prepared to leave the final verdict, based on his voluminous writings, letters and personal reminiscences, to posterity. No formal biography can, however, do justice to this aspect, the central core of his thinking and his being, but only an inquiry or a study based on his concept of personology and using the methods he recommended.

It is in this context and using his own new discipline of personology as a means to reveal the inner core of a personality, that I propose to conduct my investigation into his religion and the related factors which formed his holistic personality and influenced his philosophical outlook and his statecraft.

CHAPTER TWO

The method to reveal the Inner Man

In his book *Holism and Evolution* Smuts pleaded for a new sort of biography. What is important, he wrote, is not the externals of a life, but the inner growth and development of a personality.[1]

He devoted a great deal of thought to this subject and even coined a new word, Personology, for the new field of study of human personalities. To him it could be a new borderline science lying somewhere between experimental science and philosophy, and he thought it should be applied in the field of biography as a study of noted personalities. He called it a "new discipline" and he regarded it as outside the sphere of psychology and yet containing it. To his way of thinking, psychology as a study of the average individual, with its generalized qualities, is too impersonal to cover the highly individualized personality, which differs in every person. Nor is it possible to study the whole of a personality through the analytical methods of the psychologist, which break up an individual into parts in order to study the parts as a doctor would study anatomy. As such, psychology was to him a preparatory study to the subject of personality without actually grappling with it.

He looked for something more than mere analytical and abstract psychology to understand a personality, which is a concrete reality and should therefore be studied in its wholeness.

James Ward in his standard work, *Psychological Principles* also saw the need for such a new science in the study of concrete individuals endowed with character, and he suggested "Characterology" as a name for it.[2]

Smuts thought that this was too limiting and he also saw the new discipline as covering a much wider field than character, however important it is. Personality was to him much broader than character. In any case characterology did not seem to him suitable as a name for the science of personality and he used the new word Personology, a hybrid word derived from the Latin *persona* (person) and the Greek word *logos* (meaning word) which denotes knowledge or science.

In doing so he pointed out that the Greeks, in spite of their brilliant achievements as thinkers and philosophers and the use of their language in science and philosophy, never rose to a clear grasp of the idea of Personality. There is no term in Greek to express the notion of Personality, which we derived from the Latin *persona*, denoting the legal status of the individual who, according to Roman legal thinking, is clothed with rights and duties in his own right.[3]

When this Roman idea came in contact with Christianity a sense of sacredness, of spiritual dignity and importance was added to the purely legal idea. This brought in a far-reaching ethical quality. Personality thus became a sacred birthright conferred on all human beings through the fatherhood of God.

Smuts in his thinking tried to go a step further and to trace the concept of Personality to its real relationships in the order of the Universe. He went beyond the speculations of the philosophers, the authority of the law and the moral sacredness of religion to ground Personality in scientific reality. To him it became the culminating phase in the synthetic creative evolution of the universe.

As such he thought that it justified scientific investigation and he originated the new discipline which he called Personology to describe its field of study. He thought that this new science should study the biography of noted individuals as expressions of developing personality in each case.

In a remarkable passage in his book *Holism and Evolution* he points out the advantages of his new approach to biographical writings. Such a study will have "the priceless advantage of studying personalities synthetically as living unities and wholes rather than in the analytical manner of psychology and the other human sciences. In biography we have to follow the development of a person as a whole, as a living biological psychical entity, and we are therefore in a position to correct the one-sided abstract generalized results of the analytical procedure of these sciences. The study of biographies as examples of personal Holism, as examples of the development of Personality, will lead to very interesting and important results."

Although the discipline of Personology which Smuts here had in mind has not been definitively stated and it is difficult for me to define it here, he was convinced that it could have decided advantages in the study of personalities. These he outlined as follows:

"In the first place, we shall thus get the materials for formulating the laws of personal evolution. In the second place, these laws will form the foundation for a new science of Biography which will take the place of the empirical unsatisfactory patchwork affair which biography now mostly is. In the third place, the gradual accumulation of biographical facts and data bearing on personal evolution will not only lead to the formulation of the laws of this evolution, but will give the basis for a sound theory of Personality and a proper science of Personology. Personology, as the science of Personality, as the synthetic science of Human Nature, will form the crown of all the sciences and in turn become the basis of a new Ethic, a new Metaphysic, and of a truer spiritual outlook than we can possibly have in the ignorance and confusions of our present state of knowledge. To my mind the basis for all these great developments can only be laid in a new biographical aim and method, which will give us the facts which are vitally necessary for any sound scientific constructions."[4]

It is strange that none of the biographers of Smuts have so far applied this new technique to his own life. That great journalist N. Levi wrote the first biography of Jan Smuts in the form of a character sketch which carried his life to 1916.[5] Smuts was worried about the biography Levi wrote. In a letter to his wife written on August 31 1916 from Morogoro in East Africa he wrote: "It looks as if his (Levi's) book is drawing to a close. I wonder what sort of hodge-podge that will be, for he knows precious little about my life and thought and the cuttings won't make him much wiser."[6]

Levi can be excused for not revealing the inner life of Smuts as the latter suggested, for Levi wrote his biography long before Smuts revealed his real philosophical ideas.

Yet Levi's book is a remarkable study of the evolution of the great individualist which Smuts was, especially in the first formative years of his life.

That well-known international author H. C. Armstrong was the second biographer of Smuts. His book *Grey Steel, A Study in Arrogance*, appeared in 1937, eleven years after Smuts's own *Holism and Evolution*. Not only did Armstrong miss the whole point of Smuts's personality – he tried to force Smuts into a straitjacket of arrogance – but he also concentrated almost exclusively on the externals of Smuts's life. I am able to reveal[7] that his book made Smuts angry and upset. Members of the Smuts family resented the fact that Armstrong never came into personal contact with his subject. As a writer with a preconceived idea, he preferred the easier approach to second-hand material from persons not always friendly to Smuts and who never really understood the latter's ideas.

Armstrong's book is the very antithesis of what Smuts regarded as a modern biography giving a picture of a living personality, because it fixed that personality in a straitjacket of self-invented arrogance even before it started. The living, growing Smuts is not to be found in *Grey Steel*.

And then Mrs Sarah Gertrude Millin appeared on the scene through the friendship of the late Jan Hofmeyr and thereafter by invitation of Smuts himself. Here, if ever, was a biographer who had the most glorious opportunity to study her subject, for she could talk to him in all his moods.

She could enquire even whilst he was shaving, as she said herself. She spent long hours, for many days and weeks and months in his company. She cross-questioned him on all aspects of his career, his ideas and interests. She herself said her book was based on "a personal experience extending over fourteen years; on an admiration increasing with this experience which from fear of excess, may be sometimes unjustly subdued; on his casual and unguarded conversation; and on questions deliberately asked him, never evaded and scrupulously answered."[8]

And yet with all that advantage Sarah Gertrude Millin produced a biography in two volumes on Smuts which is not a living book. Her biography disappointed even Smuts and more so his family and intimate associates.

Mrs Millin's writings on Smuts and especially her later book[9] *The Measure of My Days* which is more candid and therefore more revealing, undoubtedly contain much valuable information on the life and thoughts and sometimes intimate ideas of Smuts. There is a wealth of fact and opinion which is of the utmost value. But Mrs Millin as a biographer of Smuts laboured under two severe handicaps. In the first place she is a self-confessed agnostic writing about a leader who is nothing if not basically and fundamentally spiritual. He himself gave her the advice of turning to religion in her personal difficulties, advice that she never followed, advice which she openly spurned and scorned. As a biographer of Smuts she would be like an atheist trying to understand and write about St Paul.

Secondly, Mrs Millin never grasped the fundamental ideas underlying Smuts's holistic outlook. How could she have, seeing that she was an unbeliever whereas Holism is based on the highest spiritual ideas of mankind? There is in her book also no indication that she had grasped or tried to follow his elaborate suggestions on how to write a biography on the basis of the new science of Personology.

As such her two biographical volumes were a disappointment and her later autobiographical book *The Measure of My Days* did Smuts the great disservice of attacking and vilifying him because as Minister of Justice he did not appoint her husband a judge.

Smuts himself did not think that Mrs Millin understood him. Shortly after the appearance of her book, he wrote to a friend: "I am interested to hear that you have been reading Mrs Millin's book. I shall sign your copy with great pleasure when it arrives. You have to bear in mind that the book is Mrs Millin's view of another person, whom she herself finds somewhat unintelligible, and she is telling the story with a gusto and a flamboyancy which sounds strange to a modest person like myself."[10]

And again in a second letter he states: "There is much divided opinion among my friends about this new Biography. Many intimates say it is not 'me'. Who can tell the truth about 'me' except God himself, and He is wisely silent until the Day of Judgement."[11]

But let me stress again. Mrs Millin has rendered a great service by her faithful recording of ideas and opinions of Smuts which, but for her talks with him would have been lost to the world. For this she deserves unstinted credit.

During the war of 1939-1945 a number of smaller biographies appeared, written from available material. One of these was by Crafford, in both English and Afrikaans. It is again a biography of the externals of the life of Smuts with no attempt to delve into the deeper forces which activated it all.[12]

"Have you read Crafford's biography, Jan Smuts, and if so do you object to anything in it concerning yourself," the publisher C. Kearton of Jarrolds asked him in a cablegram. Smuts's reply was indicative of what he thought of his biography. "Have not read and no time to read Crafford. Friends who have, consider it inaccurate," he telegraphed back on 24 August 1944.[13]

In the same year another biography by Rene Kraus appeared in New York.[14] To this must be added two smaller biographies by R. H. Kiernan and Dorothy F. Wilson.[15]

Of these Miss Wilson's book, although containing no new or firsthand material, is probably the most readable. Miss Wilson's book has the merit that she shared her subject's religious outlook and more than his other biographers she grasped the essential religious basis of his life, as of his thoughts.

"This man is great enough to stand on his own feet. He is great enough to sit very humbly at the feet of Another," was her summing up.

I would like to add here two shorter interpretative treatises. One was in German: *Smuts: Sieg eines Besiegten* (München 1948) in which the author Walter Bargatzsky laid stress on the humility of Smuts and his victory over himself. Bargatzsky has a clear understanding of the Christian religion as the basis of Smuts's greatness, as I shall quote later in discussing the personality of Smuts.[16]

Horace Shipp in his book *Lives that Moved the World* devoted a chapter to Smuts under the title, "The Enemy who became a Friend".[17]

After the death of Smuts in September 1950, his second son, Jannie, produced a remarkable book, *Jan Christiaan Smuts*, which contains much valuable material and in its extensive quotations from many speeches, gives a comprehensive picture of the life and ideas of his father. The book has great merit, but here and there filial prejudices and personal pettiness intrude to spoil what would otherwise be a very readable biography. Of all the biographies, it gives the clearest picture of the ideas of Smuts over the last fifty years of his life. But here again, the author suffers under the handicap that he neither understood the spiritual qualities of his father nor was he able to follow the pattern of the study of Personology to penetrate into the inner development of his personality. But how could we expect this? Can a son ever understand his father? It is essentially an external book but contains a great many living ideas and memories.[18]

We are indebted to Mr P. B. Blanckenberg, one of Smuts's private secretaries, for the extensive record which he kept of speeches, letters, sayings, notes and miscellaneous jottings of his boss and which he published as *The Thoughts of General Smuts*.[19] These extracts cover the very important period from 1933 to 1939 when Smuts was Deputy Prime Minister under General Hertzog in the South African Cabinet. The notes have been carefully sorted out under various headings, and they constitute a wealth of material of a public and private nature. As such some of the notes are most important keys to an understanding of Smuts's inner mind.

And yet those who are privileged to look back as facts recede and the living ideas come to the fore, cannot blame these early biographers for their lack of understanding. They did well in the limits of their own time. Smuts himself was never understood during his lifetime even by those closest to him, nor by those who admired and followed him. Most important, those revealing intimate letters, notes, discussions and recollections which he himself regarded as fundamental for a true evaluation of the growth of the personality, were not yet available to these writers.

By far the most important biography on Smuts, in two volumes, was written by Sir Keith Hancock, the well-known Australian historian, who was invited in September 1950 by Cambridge University Press to compile an authoritative biography of the late Chancellor[20] of their university. Sir Keith, known as a determined and resourceful writer, had to await the availability of the large and unsorted collection of Smuts's papers and their arrangement and indexing. In order to prepare the ground for his writing, he chose Miss Jean van der Poel of the Department of History at the University of Cape Town to collect and prepare the Smuts papers for him. The original idea was that Miss Van der Poel should be seconded for two years for this purpose. How far and how much even a trained historian like Sir Keith underestimated both the volume and the wide-ranging scope of this mammoth task is shown by the fact that it took Miss Van der Poel and her collaborators over twenty years to collect, arrange and index the mass of material relating to Smuts.

Miss Van der Poel in a subsequent revealing article in *The Bluestocking* gave a graphic description of what the work entailed, and with her permission I quote from the main part of the article, as it gives a remarkable insight into the now famous Smuts Collection which is housed at the State Archives in Pretoria, with microfilms available at the Jagger Library of the University of Cape Town.[21]

"The core of the Smuts Collection was at that time rather precariously housed in a low iron shed among tall trees at Doornkloof, the home of the Smuts family at Irene. The owner of the papers, Mr J. C. Smuts, Smuts's son, had agreed that they should be taken to Cape Town and kept in the strong-room of the Jagger Library until Sir Keith Hancock and I should have completed our work on them. So in the early, cold darkness of an August morning in 1952, I set off for the Transvaal to fetch them, in a brand-new three-quarter-ton panel van provided by the University. On the Paarl road the headlights went out and stayed out and I discovered later that the van had been licensed for the Cape Peninsula only!

"The Doornkloof papers, contained in cartons, wooden boxes, old trunks, locked dispatch-cases, filled the van to the roof. On the return journey ash from the driver's cigarette fell on a small bundle of cotton waste at his feet, sending up a spiral of smoke and my heart into my mouth. A desperate telegram to the librarian of Jagger begged him not to lock up until the precious load had been deposited in his strongroom. When we reached the library shortly before closing time a line of porters was waiting to go into action. That was typical of the readiness of Jagger to give us every possible assistance during the years of the Smuts Archive invasion and occupation.

"To the Doornkloof core were presently added papers in the keeping of Henry Cooper, who had been Smuts's private secretary for many years. These, although mostly routine letters, had nevertheless to be sorted for the 5% or so of important documents among them. I gasped when told that the 'Henry Cooper papers' were contained in some thirty ex-Army tin trunks. In fact there were forty-six. They travelled to Jagger in a pantechnicon, fussily followed by my baby Austin, and for many months they formed, piled up, a forbidding grey wall in the basement of the library.

"A third component of the Collection, perhaps the most important, was brought into it by Keith Hancock and myself. We soon saw that the Doornkloof and Henry Cooper papers, though rich in in-letters, were comparatively poor in out-letters, for Smuts wrote a great many letters in his own hand and kept no copies. Clearly it was essential to get those letters into the Collection. We approached owners of Smuts letters and were able to add literally thousands of out-letters, many in the original, to the Collection. Of these additions by far the largest (about 2 000) and most valuable was the letters written by Smuts to members of the Clark and Gillett families – his closest English friends. He wrote to them almost every week over a period of more than forty years and they had the good sense to preserve his letters and the generosity to donate them to the Collection.

"After two and a half years of full-time work on the papers I had to return to my duties in the department of history and could after that give only spare time and one furlough year to Smuts. By now the task had gone far beyond mere sorting and indexing and even that was not finished. For it had been decided (a) to make two microfilm copies of the private letters for use by the biographer and eventual presentation to the Universities of Cambridge and Cape Town and (b) to publish, in addition to a two-volume biography, several volumes of documents from the Collection. I therefore found myself committed to editing what turned out to be seven large volumes of 'Selections from the Smuts Papers'. Of these the first four were published in 1966 and the last three in 1973. Meanwhile the two parts of Sir Keith Hancock's biography – a model of fine scholarship and fine writing – appeared in 1962 and 1968. The Cambridge University Press has clothed this memorial to Smuts in fitting style. They are handsome books.

"The whole enterprise had, of course, to be financed. This was done by setting up a trust to receive and administer the necessary funds. The services of the trustees and their able secretary were honorary. Donations came from funds at the disposal of Mr J. C. Smuts, from the Nuffield Foundation, from the Smuts Memorial Fund in Cambridge, from the Abe Bailey Trust, from the Ernest Oppenheimer Memorial Trust – in all a total of some R50 000. This modest sum served to pay my salary during secondment, the salaries of research assistants for four years, the salary of a full-time typist for fifteen years, the cost of microfilming and of office equipment and stationery. Moreover, when the Trust was terminated in 1973 it was still able to make a substantial contribution to the publication costs of the second series of Smuts Papers. Compared with the lavish sums spent on comparable projects the expenditure on the establishment of the Smuts Collection and the making of the books based upon it have been frugal indeed.

"I have mentioned research assistants. The first of these was Joan Bradley, now Mrs Knapp-Fisher. We worked in a tiny room off the gallery of the main reading-room which was all that was then available in the cramped quarters of the Jagger Library. Known as 'the Black Hole of Calcutta' it remained our only office for twenty years.

"As to our 'modus operandi', the first step was to separate the private papers from the public documents, of which there were a large number, many annotated by Smuts, and to sort the latter into British Government and South African Government papers. Sir Keith Hancock had obtained permission from the British Government to retain their papers in the Collection provided that the same rules of access should apply as in Great Britain. We knew, however, that the South African Government might at any moment claim its official papers, especially as the joint will of Smuts and his wife, which would become operative at her death, had bequeathed such papers to the state archives. We therefore tackled the official papers first, arranging them chronologically into labelled volumes with roman numbers. Each document was then numbered and listed, the lists giving sender, recipient, date and subject. Documents annotated by Smuts were marked as such. In addition we made card indexes referring to the lists. The British papers relate mainly to the war years – 1916 to 1919 and 1940 to 1946, and take 95 volumes. The South African papers cover the whole period of Smuts's political life from 1897 to 1948 and fill 89 volumes.

"Our next task was to sort the private papers into major and minor categories. The minor papers were arranged in volumes with labels indicating their contents, but it would have been a waste of time and effort to index them. The major papers, the cream of the Collection, included not only letters but other documents such as the MSS of Smuts's writings, his memoranda, speeches and broadcasts, his notes, pocket diaries and notebooks, some of which he kept as a student and in the field during the Anglo-Boer War.

"The private letters were arranged in 102 labelled volumes with Arabic numbers and were indexed. The volumes run chronologically, each document being numbered and put into alphabetical compartments according to the surname of the writers. The private letter index contains an extensive special entry on Smuts and indicates which letters were written by him. This index was prepared in triplicate so that the microfilms presented to Cambridge and Cape Town could be accompanied by a copy of the letter index. The other private papers were arranged, listed and stored in 36 numbered and labelled boxes. The Collection also contains a series of press cuttings (plakboeke) about Smuts, collected and dated by his wife and covering the whole of his career from his student days, when she first met him, until his death. The plakboeke are included in the microfilms given to the two universities.

"We never made an inclusive count of all the documents in the Collection. But we did keep a rough tally of those that we listed and indexed. These number approximately 45 000, of which more than half, including nearly 23 000 letters, are private papers.

"When in 1971 all work on the Smuts archive had been completed, the private papers were presented by Mr J. C. Smuts to the state archives in Pretoria. The public papers, both British and South African had, as we expected, been promptly claimed by the chief archivist of South Africa shortly after the death of Mrs Smuts and had been transferred to Pretoria in 1954. It was clearly desirable that the Collection should not be dispersed, but kept with all lists and indexes as a unit in a suitable permanent repository. The private papers were given to the state archives on that condition. There is at present all but unrestricted access to the private papers, but access to the public papers is controlled according to existing rules for such documents in Great Britain and South Africa."

Sir Keith Hancock had most of the Smuts papers available when he completed his two volumes, the first of which appeared in 1962 and the second in 1968. As Miss Van der Poel rightly stated they were both models of fine scholarship and fine writing, with a mass of private and official details of the long and varied life of Smuts. But somehow the Hancock biography also suffers from a lack of insight into the real Smuts. Too little attention is paid to his religion and especially to the profound influence which the Quakers and especially the Gillett and Clark families had on his thinking. When I discussed the task of writing an authoritative biography of Smuts with the then Professor Hancock in England in 1954, he seemed overshadowed by the immensity of the task before him. An authoritative biography by its very nature had to cover all aspects of the life and many-sided activities of the great national and international statesman, philosopher, scientist and politician and it would have been wrong to lay stress on one aspect like his religion or his inner thoughts. That may explain why the writer of such a biography placed little emphasis on an interpretative aspect which is necessary to reveal the inner core of a personality. However, the Hancock biography will remain as the most authoritative record of the part the South African statesman played in the world arena. It is indeed a great achievement, giving a most comprehensive picture of the many-sided personality with the wide-ranging interest and activity which Smuts undoubtedly was. There is a wealth of anecdote and insight based on the Smuts Archive, the great collection of letters and papers assembled by Miss Van der Poel, and from such documents as Smuts's unpublished *Memoirs of the Boer War*, his entries in a penny notebook in 1902 during the peace negotiations to end the Anglo-Boer War and again his intimate letters during the various crises with which his life and statecraft are associated.

In 1975 the well-known Afrikaans journalist Mr Piet Meiring wrote a book, *Smuts, the Patriot*.[22] It is a lively book containing a great many anecdotes of a personal nature relating to various people who came into contact with the General and who fondly remembered what he had said or done at the time. As Piet Meiring was previously associated with Afrikaans newspapers which had at times violently attacked Smuts, his book is somewhat of a revelation as to the deep patriotism of his subject.

Meiring paid a lot of attention to the many private and official letters Smuts wrote: "His letters covering more than half century throw a brilliant spotlight on South African politics. But what is more, they reflect the emotions and the personality of this fascinating, multisided man. They reveal his deepest thoughts and lay bare his inner feelings about his fellow man. They serve as his creed and indicate his philosophical norms. They are the testament of a remarkable man who had great love for many people, excessive vanity and a burning ambition for both himself and his country. His letters provide the best insight there is into Smuts and the Afrikaner, but also into Jan Smuts the Believer," was Meiring's summing up.

Two more recent biographical works on Smuts, *Smuts, A Reappraisal* (1975) by Bernard Friedman, and *Jan Christiaan Smuts. The Conscience of a South African* (1986) by Kenneth Ingham, were published after completion of my study, and I have not taken them into account.

As has been pointed out by Dr Van der Poel, Smuts left behind a tremendous volume of material. He was a prolific writer of letters to friends in many parts of the world. He wrote an untold number of forewords and introductions to many books on a wide variety of subjects. He kept diaries in his student days and during the Anglo-Boer War. He prepared various manuscripts and put his pen to many documents dealing with problems of many countries. And always copies and notes were kept of all his correspondence and speeches.

One gets the impression – one can never be certain on this point – that he almost deliberately followed the pattern of his own recipe for the study of a personality as far as his own life, thoughts and interests were concerned. It was almost as if he wanted to be a true subject, the first real guinea-pig for his new science of Personology, where students with all his letters kept from earliest times could use them to trace the growth and development of a personality from the first obscure confused ideas to the light of knowledge and from there to always fuller and fuller understanding of the real core of his existence.

And so we can begin to study Smuts not in the dull externals of facts, of wars and the ups and downs of politics, but as a living, growing personality.

He himself in his *Holism and Evolution* classified three types of personalities as examples to study.

Firstly there is the type which does not seem to undergo an inner evolution. There are many of them. They appear to be fully grown in early manhood. They reach a maturity early in life and thereafter they remain static with no further growth as far as their minds are concerned. Smuts thought that Carlyle was such a type, whose first great work, *Sartor Resartus*, was a complete and final exposition of his inner self. No further development of his inner life seems to have taken place after that.

Who does not know this type? Smuts himself says: "We meet it in the case of many persons in our circle of acquaintances who somehow don't seem to grow, but to stand still after arriving at a certain comparatively early age. We meet it again in the tragic case of those authors who write a famous book early in life and thereafter can do no more than repeat themselves with less and less freshness and ever-waning originality. All these instances simply point to arrested development, to the absence of a capacity for inner growth. As Personality is best studied in its generic development, as its plastic inwardness is best seen in the successive phases it assumes in a continuously growing, expanding human being, it follows that the exceptional stationary or early maturing personalities afford less favourable material for the study of human Personality as a whole."

The second type of personality is also not interesting for the purpose of our study. Smuts classifies these as those persons who do not seem to have much inner self at all, whose interests and activities are all of an external character, who live not the inner life of the spirit, but the external life of affairs.

In a striking passage he describes this type as follows: "We often notice this feature in the lives and characters of public men, men of affairs, administrators, businessmen and others, whose whole mind seems to be absorbed by the practical interest of their work. In them the capacity for the inner life seems to have shrivelled and atrophied under the pressure of external duties and activities. They may be able, competent, conscientious men, they may even be brilliant men of affairs, with great gifts of leadership. They may be striking and impressive personalities and seem to be specially endowed with that indefinable attribute of Personality for which we are searching. And yet they are lacking in that inwardness, that inner spiritual life which is the most favourable medium for the study of Personality. Their lives are generally an affair of externals, of incidents and achievements, sometimes of pomp and glory, but largely devoid of real deep personal interest. Their biographies are usually dull and uninspiring, and the record and recital of activities, successes and failures soon pall on the reader. The fact is that the real indefinable quality of true Personality is inward and is not reflected in the life of unrelieved externality which such people live. They usually carry on the affairs of the world with great competence, but they are too much of the world. What is worse, they often consciously suppress the life of the spirit; the still small voice is no asset to them in the prosecution of their worldly affairs. And they are far too cautious and reserved to give their inner selves away and to afford the outside world glimpses into the world of real motives influencing and guiding them. For them any self-revelation would be something to be shy of, would be like wearing their hearts on their sleeves. The result is that the inner fires are securely banked, and the flame of the spirit can only fitfully smoulder under the ashes.

"Even if there is a strong personal life in such cases there is usually no record of it, it remains entirely private and personal, and often unknown even to the inner family circle, let alone the scientific student who is dependent on written records, constituting a continuous revelation of the spirit, for the reliability of his conclusions. They may be and often are people of outstanding personality, but the absence of the inner life and of records of personal development make them unsuitable material for the study of the problems of Personality in its more significant aspects."[23]

The third type of personality is found in those whose lives reveal not only an inwardness but an inner growth and development. They can be studied with advantage to discover the inner sources, the secrets of a true and living human personality. Here Smuts expects us to select those people who had real inner histories, lives of the spirit, as well as a fair capacity for continuous development during their lifetime. Among these, he says, the most helpful cases would be those where the written record is fairly full in the form of writings and diaries and where there was no undue restraint in the process of self-revelation and faithful portrayal of the inner life and history.

This he thinks will lead to a holistic study of a personality as against the old biography which concentrated on the mere externals of dates and facts.

In several passages of *Holism and Evolution* he points out the differences in the appreciation of the two great writers Shakespeare and Goethe in this regard. Both were undoubted geniuses who enriched the world with their writings. Both had an inner life which must have been remarkable. In the case of William Shakespeare his plays reveal behind them a wonderful personality endowed with the highest genius, and moving forward in a continuous grand crescendo of self-development as an artist from beginning to end.

"But while the development is there, the Personality itself is too much hidden behind the dramatic mask, and therefore too much a matter of inference, in the absence of proper personal records," was his verdict.[24]

On the other hand in the case of the German poet Wolfgang von Goethe the personal record is well and fully known. We know through the extensive notes, letters, recorded sayings and other writings left behind, how Goethe developed as a personality. We can see how he absorbed and assimilated all the science, art and literature of mankind and of his time. How he took part in many of the practical administrative activities of his time and place "without finding himself oppressed by a load which must have killed a lesser man", writes Smuts, and then he continues to give this evaluation of Goethe:

"He could, as he described in the character of Faust, gather up into himself not only all the knowledge of his day, but all the richness and variety of experience which make his life one of the most interesting records in this history of the world; he could drink of the deepest fountains of passion and arise to the loftiest heights of ideal aspiration – he could do all this and not only preserve his spiritual manhood unimpaired, but actually deepen and broaden and enrich it in every direction. He could assimilate this vast mass of experience, could make it all his own, and make it all contribute to that splendour and magnificence of self-realisation which has made him one of the greatest among men.

"A lesser Personality would have gone under; could either not have acquired so much knowledge and experience, or could not have assimilated it, and in the end would have become depersonalized, a mere mechanical acquirer and hoarder, at the cost of essential unity and integrity."[25]

As I will show later, Goethe whom Smuts here so penetratingly described, had a profound influence on him in his first formative years. In fact he nearly chose Goethe as the subject of his first unpublished manuscript on the study of personality instead of the American poet Walt Whitman.

I quote his analysis of Goethe here as an example of what he in his secret mind probably thought should be the method of evaluating his own inner life and his development as a personality.

He himself, like Goethe, left volumes of material, personal and official, to allow the student and biographer ample opportunity to reconstruct and recreate his living personality with his vital living ideas.

This study of mine does not and cannot pretend to undertake that great task for the simple reason that I have neither the time nor access to all the material to be able to do it. The task of fully evaluating Smuts in all aspects of his long and varied life awaits a mightier pen. But I feel that I can meanwhile point the way which he himself so clearly indicated, but which so far has been neglected or not grasped by his biographers. This study will try to lay the basis of the inquiry into his inner mind in an attempt to reconstruct the living Personality which was his, and which through his works and writings will always be a gift to all mankind. For Smuts, like Goethe and Shakespeare, belonged to the third category of personalities. All his living years he continued to advance, to grow in the capacity of his mind and character. He was a truly growing personality until the end of his days at the ripe age of 80 years.

PART ONE

Qualities

CHAPTER THREE

His family background and education

There are two factors which interact to form every personality.

The first comprises those qualities with which nature endows us at birth. These are the priceless gifts which in the wonderful process of life we receive without our asking.

The second are those external circumstances, experiences and forces which come from the outside world to blend with our inborn qualities and are assimilated by them in the shaping of our lives.

The peculiar interaction of these two main forces, different in each life, produces the great variety of humans, no two being alike. Every one of us responds in a different way to our experiences on the basis of the character and temperament with which nature has endowed us.

But first of all come the inborn qualities, the gifts of our genetic inheritance.

Those who came into contact with Jan Christiaan Smuts during his long and varied life sensed in him, as Alan Paton wrote, "some quality not ordinarily encountered". In his living presence and even now in the presence of some of his photographs, those who knew him felt a sense of awe and wonder.[1] Instinctively one knew that here was greatness.

And it was a greatness not only manifested through outside deeds. It was from within.

What were the thoughts of Mrs Catharina Petronella Smuts at his birth on May 24 1870?

When she held the small sickly child in her arms she did not expect him to live long. And she could therefore not have been aware that this second son was someone out of the ordinary, someone miraculously gifted by nature with qualities which few in the long life of mankind over the entire earth were destined to receive.

To the humble but respected parents of Jan Christiaan Smuts the mere thinking of such ideas would have been foreign. Jacobus Abraham Smuts, his father, at one time member of the Legislative Assembly of the Cape of Good Hope, was an ordinary farmer from Dutch stock. Although born at the foot of Africa he was of almost pure Dutch extraction, a sixth generation of Smutses who lived and farmed on the black soil of the grain country of the Western

Cape. History shows that the first Smuts to leave Holland to settle in South Africa, Michael Cornelis Smuts, did so in 1692. He came from the Dutch town Middelburg and landed at Cape Town from where the Smuts family later moved to Malmesbury, a town some sixty miles (nearly 100 km) into the interior.

A stocky round-faced man with a broad forehead, Jacobus Abraham Smuts was in no way outstanding nor did any of his Dutch ancestors before him show any qualities of greatness.

Nothing in his family history and tradition indicated any outstanding character or quality, but he had a good brain and a mature wit.[2]

Neither was there anything remarkable in the family history of the plump Mrs Smuts, in whose veins flowed about one sixth French blood from the Huguenots who fled for their freedom to the Cape, where they intermarried with the Dutch colonists and were absorbed by them, language and all. A spiritual, cultured woman who studied French and learnt to play the piano, her main claim to notice was the fact that her brother Boudewyn de Vries was educated in Holland and later became a minister of religion in Malmesbury.

To these two ordinary human beings suddenly and miraculously a genius was born as their second son in a family of four sons and two daughters.

When did the sickly young Jan Christiaan first show signs of being different from the other children? Did his mother as a deeply spiritual woman ever discover in the thin, pale and weedy child some great quality, some strength or a sign of greatness absent in her other children?

Neither family legend nor history record any such early indication of outstanding qualities. We only know that in the humble whitewashed barnlike homestead on the farm Ongegund, fifty miles from Cape Town on the broad open veld between the Kasteel mountain and the Great Winterhoek range the young Smuts grew up as a true child of nature.

Later as a man of thirty-two, when he looked back with nostalgia he wrote: "How well I remembered the years spent tending the cattle on the large farm, roaming over all its far expanse of veld, in which every kloof, every valley, every koppie was endeared to me by the most familiar associations.

"Month after month I had spent there in a lonely occupation – alone with the cattle, myself and God. The veld had grown part of me, not only in the sense that my bones were part of it, but in that more vital sense which identifies nature with man.

"Having no human companion I felt a spirit of comradeship for the objects of nature around me. In my childish way I communed with these as with my own soul; they became the sharers of my confidence."[3]

And here we sense the first great quality of this son of the African veld, a spiritual quality, a remarkable outstanding interest and absorption in the things of nature and of the spirit. During his entire lifetime this was perhaps the most outstanding element in his make-up.

There are those who would deny the validity of this spiritual quality with which some are gifted and some are not. Those who have it know and experience it and find their fulfilment in it. Those who have it not cannot grasp it, cannot evaluate it in others and may therefore deny it.

It also reveals itself differently in different personalities. In the case of some it shows itself early in life and conditions the entire span of life. With another it remains dormant until some soul-stirring event forces him to become aware of his real self and the powers in him. It is then that his spiritual qualities sometimes take command over his desires and passions, to control and to sublimate them into more fruitful channels.

Smuts belonged to the first group. With him it was an inborn quality which revealed itself from his earliest youth. There is no evidence that he was ever subject to the desires and passions of what is described in theological terms as "the flesh". And there is no indication that he wrestled with his soul or even strove for spirituality. It came to him as a rich and enriching gift from a bountiful nature.

In an understanding of the genius of Smuts I would put this spiritual element first. With him and in him it had a primal quality. It was the basis of his morality, of his life-long interest in religion and in things pertaining to the spirit of man and so became the foundation of his ethical approach, and it stayed with him throughout his long life with all its vicissitudes, its triumphs and tragedies.

In the ultimate evaluation of greatness I would also put this spiritual quality first, for without it no man can achieve that unity of character and personality, that deep and ultimate strength which comes from a feeling of oneness with the greater divine process of life and therefore with God as the ultimate creator.

It also gives moral worth and spiritual value and a sense of ethical living to a truly great man. Without it one can become eminent, capable of great deeds, a mighty conqueror or victor in war, but never truly great in the higher values and purposes of life. Jan Christiaan Smuts had this spiritual quality in its fullness.

This same quality which was at the base of the real greatness of Smuts was also the outstanding quality of two other remarkable modern leaders of mankind.

We find it in the great spiritual leader of India, Mahatma Gandhi, who became one of Smuts's most formidable[4] opponents, and in the other outstanding leader of this century, Dr Albert Schweitzer, whom Smuts admired and venerated.

And yet, important as this element is in the make-up of the truly great, by itself it is not enough. There are perhaps three or four other qualities which in varying degrees combine in the outstanding leaders of mankind to produce greatness.

These are the gifts of superior intellect, massive self-confidence or fearlessness and sublime imagination or vision combined with that human compassion or true humanity which we find in some great men. Some leaders are gifted with one of these attributes. Einstein was a supreme intellectual genius. Some are gifted with outstanding self-confidence or fearlessness. Caesar was great in his high and noble courage and endowed with a remarkable intellect, but he had little moral sense and no humanity. He became a cruel and immoral tyrant. Some have a combination of qualities. Napoleon was a man of limited understanding, but of ruthless directness and self-confidence developing into arrogance, and he had great physical energy.

The few truly great who have walked this earth received all or most of these gifts.

The boy Jan Christiaan Smuts astonishingly and miraculously received more than most from a bountiful nature.

Of these qualities, apart from his great spirituality, his outstanding gift was his truly remarkable intellect.

It is difficult to know precisely when the young son of the veld and the mountains, who started life tending his mother's geese on the farmyard and gradually progressed to watching the sheep and the cattle, first revealed his high natural intelligence.

It was only when he was twelve and after his eldest brother died that he was sent to school to prepare himself at his mother's wish for the ministry. He attended the humble school in the little town of Riebeek West.

There he first started learning English and High Dutch, Afrikaans being the language of his home. And yet within four years he was ready for a University career. Fortunately a letter was kept that the young Smuts wrote in English when he had just turned 16.[5]

It is a remarkable letter both for its contents and his use of the foreign English language.

In that letter he already states his life philosophy that was to remain with him until the end of his days and became the basis of all the actions and ideas of his long life.

"For of what use will a mind, enlarged and refined in all possible ways, be to me, if my religion be a deserted pilot, and morality a wreck?"

But it was at Stellenbosch that he was first to prove the high quality of his intellect. In six days he got a good grasp on the classical Greek language and in the test headed his class.[6]

It was also this quality which astonished his Professors at Cambridge where according to his diary: "I read much, walked much and thought much and when I left the University I had probably drunk as deeply of the well of knowledge as most."

Though he took both parts of the Law Tripos at Cambridge at the same time, he gained distinction in both. In the analysis of the Encyclopaedia

Britannica this is described as "unprecedented".[7]

His exceptional merit in his studies won him many scholarships and attractive offers. His achievements at Cambridge were described as "quite unparallelled".

In a testimonial to Smuts after he had taken Firsts in Part I and II of the Cambridge Law Tripos, the great Prof. F. W. Maitland wrote:

"Will this do? I have seldom written a testimonial with a better heart." He went on to tell Smuts that he had it in him to achieve a task that no German could tackle and no Englishman would ever tackle – that he had it in him to become the great Romanist, the Ihering of English law.

This was written in 1893, when he was 23, eleven years after he attended his first school in the far away town of Riebeek West.[8]

This brilliant intellect with its comprehensive legal knowledge could also understand and remember the names and classifications of thousands of plants.

His son Jannie recounts that his father was not only a well-read botanist, but he also knew the bibliography and history of botany. He was also an authority on the botanical works of the old travellers and naturalists. He knew the botany of Mesozoic Gondwanaland almost as well as the *Flora capensis* and in addition had a considerable knowledge of the botany of other countries. He was in particular a keen student of grasses.[9]

What that meant in intellectual effort, grasp and understanding becomes evident if we take into consideration that South Africa has many hundreds of different species of grasses, and these with their esoteric Latin and Greek names form more than a full-time study. Smuts knew them all.

Add to these many thousands of plants, shrubs and trees which he knew, could name and classify, and his intellectual powers become awe-inspiring.

In botany he found, in the words of his son, a hobby to test his mettle.[10]

But the capacity of his great mind was even wider. He knew and understood science, philosophy, religion and most related knowledge not in a generalized way, but specifically and in detail. His breadth of capacity was indeed remarkable and with the penetrating insight of his great intellect into the mysteries of science and his understanding of philosophy and religion he became a unifier of knowledge as few others in the history of mankind.

"The amazing thing about my father's brain was that it came from a family background that had, so far as we know, never produced anything that might be described as exceptional, far less brilliant," wrote his son Jannie in his book on his father.[11]

Possessing this transcendent brain with its breadth of capacity, its remarkable retentive powers, Smuts in any century and any place would have developed into a leader.

Such an intellect is rare, but it is all the more remarkable when it is combined in the same individual with other great qualities.

In evaluating Smuts's intellect Armstrong in his book *Grey Steel* writes that: "Smuts had the brain of a Jew; not of the Jew who produced great music and art, nor of the Jew who handled the intricacies of small business or of big finance, but of the Jew who pondered over the minutiae of the Talmud and laboured out the erudite dry-as-dust philosophies of Spinoza. Men with hard material outlooks yet with sudden streaks of idealism and great world conceptions, who dealt with facts as cold desert moonlight deals with shadows, dividing light and darkness with a clear line, and not as the warm sunlight, which weaves them into colours that blend and change. Smuts, like the Jews, could understand, even glory in Isaiah, but he could not enjoy a fairy story or laugh lightly at a thin joke."[12]

The mind of this son of a lonely land was especially to dazzle the great leaders in the dark days of the First World War when the best brains of five continents were locked in mortal battle. Smuts shone like a meteor in the night sky. Contrary to all precedent Lloyd George coopted him on the British War Cabinet next to Curzon, Milner, Carson, Bonar Law, Barnes and himself.

In doing so Lloyd George was motivated in the first place by the desire to retain the great intellectual gifts of Smuts in London for the prosecution of the war.

In his *War Memoirs* Lloyd George evaluated the mind of Smuts, whom he called "the gifted and versatile Dutchman who could be safely trusted to examine into the intricacies of any of the multifarious war problems and unravel and smooth them out".

"General Smuts was one of the most remarkable personalities of his time," he wrote, "that fine combination of intellect and human sympathy which constitutes the understanding man. His rare gifts of mind and heart were strengthening elements in this hour of savage temper and pitiless carnage."[13]

Winston Churchill himself, like Lloyd George a genius with an energetic, resourceful and courageous mind, called him at the time "the only unwounded statesman of outstanding ability in the Empire". President Woodrow Wilson lauded his "clear thinking" and in describing him F. S. Oliver writing from London to his brother, placed him, as far as pure intellect went, superior to his colleagues on the War Cabinet. He explained that by intellect he did not only mean the power of understanding what is written – but a curious and rarer quality of seeing into the very heart of a subject, coupled with the further and still rarer quality, in combination with the foregoing, of being able to state clearly what he had seen.

With his alert attention and his great mind Smuts applied himself to the great tasks of the war effort, to astonish those working with him.

"I had no time for anything but work," he said later. "There was no end to the work they wanted me to do. I have never worked so hard in my life. My hair became white."

He distinguished himself no less during the Second World War.

Viscount Chandos compared Smuts's brainpower in the military field with that of Marlborough and Napoleon. As Sir Oliver Lyttelton, before he became Viscount Chandos, and as Minister of State and member of the War Cabinet resident in the Middle East, he set up and presided over the Middle Eastern War Council of which Smuts was a member. Smuts in his opinion had "that extra ten per cent" which made it possible for him to see the military and strategic implications in a given situation almost immediately.[14]

What was further remarkable was that although he was not a trained scientist, yet such was his intellect that he could master a number of scientific disciplines. His presidential address to the British Association at its centenary celebrations in September 1931 on "The Scientific World-Picture of Today" impressed his scientific audience. Thirty-three years later ten highly competent men of science submitted his lecture to a rigorous examination. All ten gave him credit for descriptive accuracy in the wide field of his scientific interest. Some of the ten scientists found his lecture just as much alive in 1964 as it must have been on the day of its delivery in 1931.[15]

In a brilliant short analysis of the personalities of Smuts and Hofmeyr, Alan Paton points out that even the diffident like Hofmeyr can have greatness. But the final greatness seems to be reserved for those masterminds, already having an outstanding intellect, also possessing what he calls the "self-confidence of maturity to a sublime degree". These men, or women for that matter, command the confidence of others by being sure of themselves and therefore able to lead.[16]

And that was another great gift that Smuts received in an abundant way from life. His self-assurance, his self-confidence was colossal.

If there was a flaw in his character it was probably that he was too sure of himself. He had that unwavering faith in the rightness of his cause and in his mastery of events.

At some periods of his career he suffered from overconfidence, as was the case before his final defeat at the hands of Dr Malan in May, 1948.

On other occasions his complete self-assurance created the impression of conceit and even of arrogance, which his biographer Armstrong misunderstood as his permanent characteristic.

Again in some instances when his supreme belief in his own powers overshadowed his simplicity and his humility, it led to a form of vanity. It was overconfidence amounting to vanity which led Smuts in 1918 to suggest himself to Lloyd George as the commander-in-chief of the American expeditionary forces in Europe.[17]

There were other occasions in his life when his overweening self-assurance led to ruthlessness, although one may argue that events or the too stern following of the path of duty forced him to such a policy to preserve what he regarded as right. It also made him impatient and even contemptuous of lesser men.

But those instances as flaws in his character and as the outcome of his supreme self-confidence were the exception rather than the rule.

Besides his great spiritual quality and his extraordinary intellect this self-confidence was another of his outstanding qualities.

And the remarkable aspect of this quality was that he possessed it throughout his life. It revealed itself in his utter fearlessness.

Smuts was, like Julius Caesar, without any fear. He never knew physical or moral fear. Even as a young man climbing mountains or in the Anglo-Boer War days when he led a ragged Boer commando right through enemy territory for over a thousand miles, when he saw his men shot down, wounded and killed beside him, he never once wavered, never once showed the least trace of physical or moral fear. And he combined with it the tireless physical energy of a Napoleon when he drove his men as he drove himself, to astonishing feats.

Other great men have had moral courage which came from their religion or their belief in the rightness of their cause. Luther had outstanding moral courage. All the great martyrs of all religions were fearless through their moral convictions. They were prepared to die for their faith.

But Smuts was fearless in a more fundamental sense. He had the fearlessness which comes from nature as a rare and splendid gift, as Paton wrote in his analysis.[18]

His intrepidity was not only physical in the sense that he never feared death on the battlefield, on mountain tops or in aeroplanes when storms raged and lightning struck. He was also fearless in a spiritual way. Smuts was fearless in the search for truth. Some searchers after truth are afraid to follow their paths wherever they may lead, fearful lest the foundations of their moral and spiritual beliefs may be shattered by the forces which they lay bare. They compromise with truth or they halt their search when it threatens to overthrow their conventional faith.

But Smuts approached all problems in life and after life with unswerving determination to find the ultimate truth. He was like Abraham Lincoln, "pitiless and persistent in pursuit of truth" although in a more spiritual and philosophical way than the practical down-to-earth compassionate and fearless Lincoln.

It was this intrepid quality which was the basis of his self-assurance and supreme self-confidence. But it was also linked to his great faith in life and the powers of life both in the visible and invisible world.

It was here that his great spiritual quality, the quality which gave him his faith, his morality, his overwhelming belief in God as the final and fundamental Power controlling and guiding all our destinies, combined with his inborn massive self-confidence, his fearlessness both in the acceptance of life and all its dangers and in his unwavering search for truth for the sake of truth and the final Righteousness.

I would add here a fourth quality in the make-up of this gifted man. That is what I would like to call the quality of imagination. Is this a necessary quality in greatness? Is it merely an adjunct to the intellect?

Let me take an example. There are gifted leaders, leaders of outstanding intellect who fail to attract followers. They are brilliant thinkers. They have colossal self-confidence and even a spiritual, moral and ethical quality. But something is lacking in their make-up. They fail to achieve leadership. They remain dry and intellectual, with little spontaneity and less originality. People are not attracted to them.

To my way of thinking they lack that miraculous quality of imaginative vision and insight which is apart and different from the intellect and intelligence, for even the greatest thinker may lack imagination.

Where does imagination come from? And where is its basis in the human personality? Psychologists have not been able to unravel for us the mysteries of the human make-up. But this we know, that a great leader must have imagination, the ability to look beyond the material existing order of things. He must be able to fire the minds and the ideals of men, to make us see our true and higher selves and the nobler world which beckons on the horizon of our consciousness as spiritual beings. Or is this merely another aspect of their spirituality or even a quality in the borderland between the spirit and the intellect?

Call it imagination or call it a vision which miraculously lifts the heart and eyes of some outstanding personality, and with which he in turn fires the imagination of the masses. It is a quality which probably gives that magnetic personality to the great leader, which makes others identify themselves with him and with his ideals and strivings, to become instruments in his hands for the carrying out of his plans.

Smuts had that quality. From his earliest days as a student he revealed a vivid imagination through which he saw life not in the narrow rational and limited way of the materialists of the nineteenth century, but as the great flow of ever grander and nobler stirrings to a higher pattern.

In a way this is the poetic quality in him, a quality which is probably to be found in all great literary figures. Smuts himself, at first at Stellenbosch, aspired to be a poet. As a student he wrote poetry to Miss Sybella Krige and as I will show he was greatly influenced by the poets and writers.

Danie van Niekerk, who went through the files of *The Student*, the Stellenbosch students' magazine, discovered a poem "Love and Life" under the initials J.C.S. in the edition of 1895.

He wrote to Smuts in 1949 asking whether it was his poem. A week later he received a reply from the General stating "my wife assures me that the verses came from me". Smuts states that he had forgotten about them. He wrote them in 1891 when he was 21 years old and on the eve of his departure for Cambridge. They dealt with the separation of two lovers. The first verse reads:

"And in the garden neath the oak far-shadowing

He said his farewell; claspt her arm around him
Her still eyes, large with sorrow gazed bright-glowing
Into his, feeding on the soul within"

The poem then dealt with "the soul's calm water, where no storms e'er wrestle, wherein are mirrored the great Forms to be".[19]

Both at Stellenbosch and at Cambridge he wrote verses in a similar vein, at the same time being greatly influenced by various poets and writers.

He understood them with a profound intuition and as having the same imaginative quality without which there can be no great literature. And yet he was above all a man of action whose life left little time for sentimentality.

There is one more quality which the great should have. That is the quality of feeling, of sympathy, of compassion. It is a quality which is allied to our deepest humanity.

He himself singled it out as one of the most important. "All true greatness ultimately reduces to quite simple terms of humanity. When the position is lost and the pomp and circumstance go; when the pose can no longer impose and there is only the native strength of the soul left, you take the size of the man and you assign to him his rank and place impartially among the great and the simple."[20]

Did Smuts have this quality? It is doubtful if he had it, and if on rare occasions he showed it he did not have it as the conspicuous quality which Abraham Lincoln displayed.

It is remarkable that Lincoln, a son of humble parents and of the prairie as Smuts was a son of the veld, had this great gift which made him the sublime leader that he was, for he had neither the pure spirituality or the comprehensive intellect of Smuts. Was he for that reason a greater or a lesser leader than Smuts?

It is difficult to evaluate greatness by comparison. Smuts lacked the patience, forbearance and forgiveness which Lincoln revealed from his earliest days. He was impatient with others probably because his superior intellect far outstripped those not as clear-sighted and as penetrating as he was. He lacked the deep and abiding compassion of Lincoln probably because his earlier life was not so distressingly unsuccessful as that of Lincoln. But apart from experience the basic quality of deep human sympathy was also absent from his make-up.

And yet he had a deep feeling for some, and especially for those comrades in arms from the Anglo-Boer War days with whom he saw battle, defeat and despair. "He discovered human beings, he says, during the Boer War," wrote Mrs Millin.[21]

When among his old comrades, a new quality showed in him, a tenderness, a sympathy, which livened his entire being and made him a man of compassion. But this was the exception, for as a rule he was cold and distant and lacked warmth and understanding of the feelings of others.

But while not having the deep compassion of Lincoln or of Gandhi, there was a sense in which he shared the veneration of both Lincoln and Gandhi for the common man. As a man who had risen from poverty by his own efforts and had a deep sympathy for others Lincoln placed a very high value on the ordinary people, the common humanity with whom he felt at one. Gandhi with his compassion but deeper spiritual quality almost deified the common man.

Smuts felt an aversion for the "clever" man and he never tolerated weakness or laziness in others.

He could be and was ruthless when occasion demanded. But he also liked ordinary people and felt a great deal for the common man in a rather abstract and intellectual way.

I must give credence to a statement of Alan Paton that humanity was not absent in Smuts. As Paton sees it this quality in Smuts was "part of a miraculous maturity that was the foundation of his self-certitude in that Utopian world which H. G. Wells foresaw and in disillusionment about which he died broken-hearted. All men will mature, if without repressions, frustrations and hidden fears. But in our world, when such a man appears he is a miracle, and men will die for him, recognizing in him the fulfilment that might have been in themselves. Smuts might have held aloof from his men on commando and sat on a rock, reading incomprehensible books, but he could say a word, make a gesture that would quicken men's blood and raise their eyes to God knows what stars."[22]

Paton here sees Smuts as the embodiment of that higher humanity which some achieve who are truly and maturely themselves in the fulfilment of their highest and purest human qualities. That might also be so in the larger and nobler life waiting for the human personality in ages to come, but we are still dealing with an imperfect world and with imperfect human beings and certainly for them as individuals Smuts had no deep affection and probably little real sympathy even though he felt deeply for humanity as a whole.

If there was a flaw in his make-up it was this lack of compassion or humanity.

Here then are the four great qualities and the lack of the fifth with which nature endowed this son of Europe who was born in Africa.

Although lacking compassion he had great spiritual, intellectual, fearless and imaginative qualities. In each of these qualities he was outstanding to an extraordinary degree.

But much more remarkable was the way in which these qualities combined in him to form the unique personality that he was.

Wherever Smuts moved among men he became the centre of attraction. Even the great recognized his greatness and even his enemies stood in awe, reluctantly acknowledging his genius. And this was the result of the way in which all the qualities in him blended to form his unique personality.

I have already pointed out how his spiritual quality combined with his self-confidence to form a unity. Even more remarkable is the way in which his intellect and his vivid imagination blended together, fused with his self-assurance and his spirituality to make him that holistic personality which to him was the supreme achievement of all life.

The combination of his spiritual quality, his self-confidence, his towering intellect and his vivid imagination made him somebody apart. But he was more than a man existing by himself. He was a leader who in the greatness of his mind, the integrity of his spirit, the maturity of his self-confidence and the vividness of his imagination knew and followed the way of life in sublime self-assurance and unwavering faith. Here in the final certitude of his ideas, his values and his personality he became the great leader of men that he was. Others walking this earth in darkness and confusion, in fear because life in its simplicity and grandeur was too much for them, instinctively recognized in Smuts the certain, sure and confident leader who would lead them out of darkness and slavery to the light of life.

And so through the personal qualities with which life endowed him he became one of the greatest leaders of modern times. For all men, even his enemies, recognized his genius and the miracle of his greatness.

At MacClear's Beacon, high on the rocks of the eastern face of Table Mountain overlooking the sea and the earth and the mountains to the north, those who wanted to commemorate his greatness erected a tablet. And on that tablet fastened on to the rocks amongst which his voice rang out in his great "Spirit of the Mountain" oration in memory of those who gave their lives for freedom, these immortal words of another great genius, William Shakespeare, were inscribed.

"His life was gentle; and the elements so mixt in him, that nature might stand up and say to all the world: *This was a man.*" Shakespeare put those words in the mouth of Mark Anthony honouring Julius Caesar. Those who commemorated Smuts on the rocks of Table Mountain at the foot of Africa also applied them to him. They are true except that his life, like that of Caesar, was not gentle.

But there are two aspects in every personality, that which is internal and that which is external. What are the external forces, the people and powers acting on his own inborn qualities, which influence his life and help to shape his personality? In the case of Smuts it was his deeply felt religion, the influence of the poets and scientists and more especially his contacts with the great leader Louis Botha as well as with the Quakers, which helped to form his outstanding leadership and unique holistic personality.

CHAPTER FOUR

His religion

I have already mentioned the spiritual quality, the intense interest in nature and the things of the spirit, as one of the main elements in the make-up of the young Smuts. That it was not just a youthful characteristic, but a lasting and enduring force in his life is evident from a close study of the many letters, articles and speeches which he left behind. There seems to be no single period in his long life when his interest in religion waned or when he became disillusioned or indifferent to religion. On the contrary,[1] as his life developed, as his responsibilities became bigger and as his personality flowered into maturity, his interest in religion deepened and widened. Although no formal regular churchgoer or even a dogmatic believer, judging by his many letters and utterances, religion was never absent from his mind and as the years passed his interest in the Personality and the Divine nature of Jesus grew until in the end the Son of Man became to him the enbodiment, the personification of that final fulfilment and sublime achievement which he saw as the ideal and summit of the human personality in all its glory and potentiality.

Smuts was born into a family and an environment where religion was regarded as natural and essential as breathing and living itself. The substantial, hard-working farmers of the Swartland in the Western Cape "who lived decently in their solid, comfortable houses, enjoyed the regular ministrations of their Church".[2] Smuts's parents were godfearing guardians and especially the fact that uncle Boudewyn, his mother's brother, was the local predikant, brought them into still closer contact with the Church. His father too was well known as a pillar of the Dutch Reformed Church. When Smuts was still a child the family drove every Sunday to the church in Riebeek West and long before he went to a formal school his deeply pious mother taught him to read and especially instilled in him a deep and abiding love of the Bible and the wonderful and exciting stories to be found in Holy Scripture. Endowed with an inquisitive mind and with a deep interest in nature, the religious teachings of his mother and at Sunday school offered him an explanation of his experiences and of the natural phenomena around him.

Hancock in a revealing passage in his first volume described the early effect religion had on Smuts's outlook:

"Had he been left without teaching, he might well have become an animist, discovering in every rock and tree a spirit akin to his own; or a pantheist, believing that God is everything and that everything is God: indeed, he was prone throughout his whole life to lapse into the pantheistic heresy. But from the time that he became old enough to drive with his parents in their Cape cart to the Sunday congregations at Riebeek West, he heard from the pulpit of his uncle Boudewyn a simpler doctrine. The predikant of Riebeek West inclined if anything to the liberal side, but the predikant's nephew received as literal and sufficient truth the whole Bible story, from Genesis to Revelation, of God, nature and man. Perhaps he absorbed, along with the story, some mental habits which Calvinist teaching tends to encourage; the habit, for example, of posing the most tremendous problems and of seeking the most sweeping solutions."[3]

In his early youth, along with his friends at Riebeek West he gave his heart to the Lord when the great Dr Andrew Murray undertook a mission of religious revival throughout the length and breadth of the Cape Colony and also visited Riebeek West.

The little Jan at the time was destined to be a farmer with little education, as his eldest brother Michiel was to receive schooling in order to prepare him for the ministry as was the custom in those days among the Afrikaners. But in 1882 Michiel died suddenly and it was decided that Jan should take his place at school and train for the ministry.

This was the first turning point in Jan's spectacular educational career. He was soon top of his class and was also put in charge of a Sunday school class, where he had to instruct the younger boys, including his later political rival Daniel François Malan, in Holy Scripture.

It was also here in Riebeek West that he developed his great love for climbing mountains which to him was almost akin to a religious experience. He was still a small boy when one day he climbed the steep crag of Riebeek Kasteel. Shortly before his death in 1950 he was to tell of the strange intense mystic experience he felt at that early age on the summit overlooking the surrounding wheatlands of the Swartland. Mountaineering, his great love in life ever after, became synonymous with religion to him. In 1923 at Maclear's Beacon on the summit of Table Mountain he delivered his famous "Spirit of the Mountain" oration which stressed the importance of mountains in the history and meaning of religion.

It was in this spirit of deeply felt devotion that the young Smuts went to Stellenbosch to continue his studies. Before he arrived in that town of learning he had written his now famous letter to Prof. C. Murray expressing anxiety that he may be subjected to "moral, and what is more important, religious temptation which if yielded to will eclipse alike the expectations of my parents and the intentions of myself". He then added the well-known phrase: "For what use will a mind enlarged and refined in all possible ways be to me, if my religion be a deserted pilot and morality a wreck?"[4]

To avoid these temptations he became overreligious by attending church twice on Sundays, conducting a Bible class for coloured boys and finding time for prayer meetings during the week. With all his studies he also found time to write a metrical paraphrase of Isaiah XXV and some poems about Love, the Immortal Mind of Man and the Love of God, the "Steersman Great of Nature's Ways", as he described the Almighty.[5]

Meanwhile he continued his mountain climbing, alone or in the company of Miss Sybella Margaretha Krige who was to become his wife. Isie, as she was known, was a pretty young girl with a round white face and black curly hair which formed a crown round her forehead. She had boundless energy, was extraordinarily talented and had been one of the few women students to attend Victoria College.

On her seventeenth birthday on December 22 1887, when he himself was only seventeen years old he wrote her a letter of congratulation in which he told her that it was "our Heavenly Master" who brought them together "that we may help each other onward on the path of Holiness and Love, and that in loving each other we may learn to love Him more intensely".[6]

But he was deeply perturbed about a poem she wrote in which she stated categorically that she had often tried to be a Christian "but I cannot, cannot be, so no hope to live in heaven through eternity I see". This prompted the youthful Smuts to confront her point-blank: "Isie, you are a Christian, are you not?" To reassure her he wrestled with her doubts, expounded the promise of Eternal Life and assured her that she was indeed a Christian.

His years at Stellenbosch were, however, to widen his interests especially through the discovery of the poets and his study of Greek, a language which, through his rare brilliance, he had mastered in six days. As I shall show, the poets and especially Shelley, Shakespeare, Goethe, Walt Whitman and Emily Brontë, had a profound influence which gave him a brighter view than the gloomy outlook of the Calvinistic doctrines, but his religion was strengthened rather than diminished by his love of poetry. So inspired was he, that he wrote long, involved poetry to Isie, some of which was discovered fifty years afterwards.

Shortly after the outbreak of the Second World War, on November 16 1939 after he had become the wartime Prime Minister of South Africa, he found time to write an intimate letter to Mrs Gillett in which he reminisced about the influence of the poets on his religious outlook during his Stellenbosch days. It was after he had again read Shelley's *Prometheus Unbound.*

"I with my Calvinistic upbringing must have imbibed my brighter view of the world from Shelley in my college days. The innate goodness of man, the perfectibility of human nature, the evil in the world which is due to rotten and corrupt institutions – the sudden catastrophic collapse of Evil at the appointed hour, and the triumph of Good and Beauty in the world. It was a nobler, more poetic rendering than the catastrophic revolution of K. Marx and resembled more the 'Second Coming' of the Christians."

As I shall show later in this treatise, his intense interest in religion and in human personality had already led him on the road to his later concept of Holism although at that time he had not yet invented the word.

He was still toying with the idea of "association" as the first law of nature and in the form of love as "the fundamental law of our spiritual nature, or of religion".

It was with this new and wider religious and philosophical background that the young Smuts went to Cambridge in 1891 when he was 21 years old.

That his outlook was still dominated by his religious interest is confirmed by one of his first contacts at Cambridge, a fellow student called John Gregg, who invited Smuts for a walk. Smuts to his astonishment opened the conversation by expressing his views on a text of St Paul, "Sin revived and I died!"[7]

As at Stellenbosch Smuts was a regular churchgoer at Cambridge, worshipping at the Presbyterian Church. He was at this time especially interested in the writings of St Paul and it was in St Paul that he discovered "a fundamental canon of human development" which he used in his treatise on law. How deeply he was influenced by the writings of St Paul came to light during the Second World War when he felt the need to strengthen his faith against Hitlerism. Among the papers from his Cambridge years there is an essay on Christ in History as well as some chapters on the Cosmic Religion which in some ways foreshadowed his study of wholes as a basis of his later Holism.

It was in this period that the American poet Walt Whitman (1819-1892) had a profound influence on him. Whitman, who had died three years before Smuts discovered his poetry, was at the time little known in England and still less in South Africa, but with his enquiring mind Smuts soon discovered in Whitman a kindred spirit, almost a blood brother with the same Dutch blood in his veins and the same devoted mother, although he was still too immature to notice the homosexual nature of the fiery American poet. Having read everything there was in the British Museum of and about Whitman, Smuts saw him as the first and foremost example of that integrated person or personality which embodies his concept of the whole.

In later years Smuts was to describe the influence Whitman had on his religious views during his Cambridge period. "Whitman did a great service to me in making me appreciate the Natural Man and freeing me from much theological or conventional preconceptions due to my very early pious upbringing. It was a sort of liberation, as St Paul was liberated from the Law and its damnation by his Damascus vision. Sin ceased to dominate my view of life, and this was a great release as I was inclined to be severely puritanical in all things."[8]

Smuts was so enamoured of Whitman that he decided to use him to illustrate his views on personality. He wrote his first book *Walt Whitman: A Study in the Evolution of Personality*[9] which in many ways became the basis of his later writings on Holism. Whitman deepened and widened his thoughts on nature, the human personality and on religion. Unfortunately his book was never published and today remains in the obscurity of the archives. Professor W. K. Hancock, analysing the influence of Whitman on the young Smuts, came to the conclusion that in the maturing Whitman Smuts discovered his own zeal for synthesis, his own passionate craving to apprehend and comprehend the puzzling fatality of life as an ordered and harmonious whole.

When a riper and more mature Smuts returned to South Africa in 1895 he had to concentrate his energies on the practical problems of making a living, getting married to Sybella Krige and establishing himself in the complex political life of the time. There is during this period less evidence of his religion but also no evidence that he became in any way less religious.

Smuts had questioned Rhodes's involvement in the Jameson Raid and he was disenchanted with Cape politics. Furthermore, he was eager to marry Isie as soon as possible, and he had been unable to find remunerative employment in the Cape, while his future wife was struggling on a small salary as a teacher. He moved to the prosperous Transvaal Republic, where he soon earned a decent living as an advocate and at the end of April 1897 he finally married his sweetheart of ten years. They were married at Stellenbosch by Professor Marais, "the man who was so good to us", and soon they were back in Johannesburg where one of Smuts's first actions was to buy a piano so that Isie could play and they could sing French and German love songs and Lieder.

After he had established himself in Johannesburg and later at Pretoria where he became the Attorney-General of the Zuid-Afrikaansche Republiek, he was rapidly drawn into the complex political negotiations between President Paul Kruger and the British High Commissioner, Sir Alfred Milner. Smuts with his insight into men and events saw that war was inevitable, and prepared for the worst. Meanwhile he and his wife experienced their first personal tragedy when the twins born to them died soon after birth. Kosie, their next child, who was born a few months before the outbreak of the Anglo-Boer War, died tragically in the arms of his mother in Pretoria while Smuts himself was fighting with the Boer commandos.

Thereafter Mrs Smuts was removed to a British camp in Pietermaritzburg and the Smuts house in Sunnyside, Pretoria was ravaged by British troops. Smuts himself risked his life and his future with his daring raid into the Cape Colony. When he led his ragged commando of a few hundred men in the face of an overwhelming enemy into the Cape Colony, he carried his Greek New Testament in his saddlebag. He also kept notes scribbled on the back of official Natal Government Railway forms giving his personal observations and impressions during his march from the Transvaal through the Orange Free State to the north-western Cape. After the war he expanded these notes into the draft of a book on the Anglo-Boer War, but it was never completed and never published. In one of the chapters is to be found the outline of a remarkable sermon which Smuts delivered to his men at Kafferskraal on the Vaal River on August 2 1901. It was a patriotic sermon on the lines of the Old Testament outlook and it is clear from this that he based his raid into enemy territory on his religious principles.[10]

When the end of the war came he was brought back by the British to take part in the peace negotiations at Vereeniging. There he kept a little notebook, jotting down notes of conversations, quotations, personal thoughts and headings for speeches to be made. He also wrote some letters to his wife and other friends, stressing his sense of duty and his personal rectitude. "A man may lose his possessions, even his home and country, but he may yet remain a citizen of that larger and higher kingdom whose limits are the conscience and aspirations of humanity."[11]

Although the end had come for the two Boer Republics, Smuts retained his deep hope and trust in God. "The war of freedom had been fought, not only for the Boers, but for the entire people of South Africa. The result of that struggle we leave in God's hands. Perhaps it is His will to lead the people of South Africa through defeat and humiliation, yea even through the valley of the shadow of death, to a better future and brighter day."

It was in this spirit of faith, hope and trust that Smuts took up the broken cords of his life. He went through a period of great difficulties in re-establishing himself and his wife, but he retained his belief in the goodness of life. "I accept my fate – that is the only manly course left," he wrote to his wife.[12]

That Smuts went through a period of depression is undoubtedly true, but that he lapsed into embitterment and despair as Mrs Millin characterized his mood during this period is not borne out by the facts. He remained the strong and determined fighter for the rights of the defeated Boers. He was at the same time again continuing his inquiry into the whole as a key to the understanding of the human personality.

Mrs Millin quotes a letter of his written on February 24 1904 to Miss Emily Hobhouse and which Miss Hobhouse gave to *The Times* in London to publish. It was a letter of anger and bitter disappointment at the stupidity of the Milner policy in introducing Chinese labour in South Africa.

"As sure as I write here, there is a God that will judge; now is our dark hour and agony of bloody sweat. But I can already hear the distant tramp of Nemesis, and unless the conscience of England is roused now and she undoes the foul deed of shame, there will be many dry eyes when her hour comes, as come it will," he wrote. For himself he prefers to "sit still, to water my orange trees and to study Kant's Critical Philosophy until, in the whirling of time, new openings of doing good offer themselves".[13]

That was the depth of his depression, but he never lost his religion or his faith in a better future. In fact as I will show, under the influence of Botha's humanity and the deep spirituality of the Friends Society with whom he came in contact during this time, he was nearing the most fruitful period of his life. The influence of both these forces on him will be treated separately as they helped to form both his outlook and his statecraft.

Despite his fundamental religious faith which always remained with him, there is little direct evidence of religion in his utterances in the stormy years which in South Africa led to the formation of Union and in Europe saw the coming of the First World War.

Smuts was essentially a man of action in this period of his life. But in the dark days of the Great War his acceptance of the teachings of the Man of Galilee and his practical application of these on the war and the peace issue shone like a beacon to all mankind. His great utterances during the last years of the war and during the peace conference of 1919 when he in association with Botha pleaded for charity and generosity toward the fallen foe, are shining lights on the path of international politics. Regrettably in the atmosphere of hatred and revenge which prevailed his pleadings were not heeded. He was greatly upset when his advice was rejected and he predicted that the triumph of vengeance would sow the seeds of another tragedy. It was in this period of unremitting toil and continuous political strife when he became Prime Minister of the Union of South Africa, that he prepared and delivered his outstanding "Spirit of the Mountain" memorial address at Maclear's Beacon on the top of Table Mountain, an address which in nobility has been compared with Pericles's Funeral Oration or Lincoln's unforgettable words at Gettysburg.

Religion is the keynote of the entire speech. "The mountain is not merely something externally sublime. It has a great historic and spiritual meaning for us. It stands for us as the ladder of life. Nay, more, it is the great ladder of the soul, and in a curious way the source of religion. From it came the Law, from it came the Gospel in the Sermon on the Mount. We may truly say that the highest religion is the Religion of the Mountain.

"What is that religion? When we reach the mountain summits we leave behind us all the things that weigh heavily down below on our body and spirit. We leave behind a feeling of weakness and depression; we feel a new freedom, a great exhilaration, an exaltation of the body no less than of the spirit. We feel a great joy. The Religion of the Mountain is in reality the religion of joy, of the release of the soul from the things that weigh it down and fill it with a sense of weariness, sorrow and defeat. The religion of joy realizes the freedom of the soul, the soul's kinship to the great creative spirit and its dominance over all things of sense. As the body has escaped from the overweight and depression of the sea, so the soul must be released from all sense of weariness, weakness and depression arising from the fret, worry and friction of our daily lives. We must feel that we are above it all, that the soul is essentially free, and in freedom realizes the joy of living. And when the feeling of lassitude and depression and the sense of defeat advances upon us, we must repel it, and maintain an equal and cheerful temper.

"We must fill our daily lives with the spirit of joy and delight. We must carry this spirit into our daily lives and tasks. We must perform our work not grudgingly and as a burden imposed on us, but in a spirit of cheerfulness, goodwill and delight in it. Not only on the mountain summits of life, not only on the heights of success and achievement, but down in the deep valleys of drudgery, of anxiety and defeat, we must cultivate this great spirit of joyous freedom and uplift the soul.

"We must practise the religion of the mountain down in the valleys also.

"This may sound a hard doctrine, and it may be that only after years of practice are we able to triumph in spirit over the things that weigh and drag us down. But it is the nature of the soul, as of all life, to rise, to overcome, and finally to attain complete freedom and happiness. And if we consistently practise the religion of the mountain we must succeed in the end. To this great end Nature will co-operate with the soul."[14]

After his defeat in 1924 Smuts devoted himself to science and philosophy, but even here religion was never absent from his interests. In his speech as President of the Centenary Meeting of the British Association for the Advancement of Science in 1931, in London, he described science as perhaps "the clearest revelation of God to our age".

His interest in religion never abated. Mrs Millin in her first volume tells how towards the middle of 1934 Smuts in the midst of serious political business and speech-making found time to cut out an article on Emily Brontë which appeared in the *Times Literary Supplement*. The article explained that Charlotte had revised some of Emily's poems – chiefly the punctuation – and it repeated the well-known poem "No coward soul is mine" as Emily wrote it. In cutting it out and keeping the article Smuts explained to Mrs Millin that it was important to him to have the poem exactly as Emily wrote it.

"No, I do not agree that a comma doesn't matter, and the poem did very well all these years as it was. A thing like this belongs to the search for truth – the meaning beyond. It is the soul. You alter a word and you alter the emotional figure – you alter the shape of the torso of the soul."

And to explain what he means he lifts the veil over the deeper religious thoughts in his mind.

"That is why I am glad I can read the New Testament in Greek. Those people were grappling with something beyond their understanding, trying to express unattainable truth. Translate their words, change a shade of their meaning, and you throw them out of the straight line of their quest and what they were just about to touch is lost."[15]

1934 was a particularly strenuous year for him. Yet he found time to deliver two of his most important addresses in which the flowering of his deep religious thoughts came to the surface in penetrating insights into the nature of life as of his own soul.

The first was an address to a meeting of the British and Foreign Bible Society delivered in August 1934. He chose as his subject the Bible. "We are gathered here tonight around the Bible," he introduced his subject, and he called it "the greatest book in the world and the greatest contribution to human culture, human thought and human religion. Let us not forget that this book is the contribution of the Jews to mankind. In these days when one sees again the horrid head of persecution and when the spirit of intolerance is abroad, let us remember that extraordinary little people who, highly gifted, made this supreme contribution to the welfare of the world.

"To me the greatest thing that has happened on this earth of ours is the rise of the human race from ape-like conditions, from the very dust in fact, to the vision of God, which dominated us. All those ideals of truth, beauty and goodness which to-day are the standards up to which we try to live are enshrined in the Bible. The Bible has in my opinion made the greatest contribution to this wonderful drama of the rise of men. There is nothing in the world to compare with it. It is perhaps a pity that the Bible has to be taught in schools as a text-book of religion. The result is that the interest of the children is sometimes blunted in what is, after all, one of the greatest glories of the human race.

"There is nothing in the noblest literature of the world to compare with that expression of the human mind, of human joy and sorrow which we have in the Bible. Is there for instance an Idyll in the world to compare with the book of Ruth?

"As history, the Bible embodies the whole story of mankind. It is a record extending thousands of years into the past – a record which has been confirmed and filled out by all the researchers of science. There is the Bible of prophecy, with its fine ethical ideals pointing the way to all mankind. It is an interpretation of life, filling out the old Greek conception that the pursuit of reason is the way to the truth. The Bible does not look upon the Universe as a world of reason, but more as a world of mystery, a divine world.

"I cannot say which is the correct interpretation of life, but I suggest that the two have to be taken together.

"On the one hand, the Greek ideal of being faithful to the light of the mind, and on the other hand the Biblical conception of faith. Indeed it seems to me that the Jew probably read deeper and saw deeper into the meaning of life than the Greek. There are depths in the human soul that the mind will probably never fathom and the ultimate interpretation of life may be found through a combination of Plato and Paul. The Word has also been interpreted as power, in the light of the immensity of nature.

"In our pursuit of power as nations, we have made havoc of this world. In our pursuit of national greatness, we have trodden underfoot many great ideals of the human race. As against this pursuit of power we have the Biblical view of life, of life as love, as tenderness and as mercy.

"It is this aspect of the Bible that made Nietzsche call Christianity a slave religion, but the so-called slave virtues represent the highest ideals of the human race. The man who saw that, saw further into the nature of the universe. That is why we have made him a God.

"My own belief is that we have in the Bible insights into truth, beauty and goodness, and into the ultimate human ideal, which are not mere fashion, but which are immortal and eternal."

Two months later he was in Scotland where he gave his famous oration on freedom delivered as his Rectoral address at St Andrew's University.

Here we have Smuts revealing in direct and beautiful words religion as the basis of his credo:

"My fundamental impression of Life I can give you in words which most of you know from your childhood. They occur on the first page of the greatest book in the world. They come from the youth of the world, and to-day in its maturity they are truer than ever. The world is good. This is a good world. We need not approve of all the items in it, nor of all the individuals in it, but the world itself, which is more than its parts or individuals, which has a soul, a spirit, a pull, a fundamental relation to each of us deeper than all other relations, is a friendly world. It has borne us; it has carried us onward; it has humanized us and guided our faltering footsteps throughout the long and slow advance; it has endowed us with strength and courage; it has proved a real vale of soul-making for us humans, and created for us visions, dreams, ideals which are still further moulding us on eternal lines. It is full of tangles, of ups and downs. There is always enough to bite on, to sharpen wits on, to test our courage and manhood. It is indeed a world built on heroism, but also for beauty, tenderness, mercy. I have passed through pretty rough passages.

"I have sampled the world and human nature at many points, and I have learnt that it takes all sorts to make a world. But through it all my conviction has only deepened that there is nothing in the nature of things which is alien to what is best in us. There is no malign fatalism which makes fools of us in our dark striving towards the good.

"On the contrary, what is highest in us is deepest in the nature of things, and as virtue is its own reward, so life carries its own sanctions and the guarantee of its own highest fulfilments and perfections. That is my ultimate Credo; and it is not founded in hearsay, but on my first-hand experience in that cross-section of the world which I have lived through . . . I remain at heart an optimist."[16]

Two years later on August 4 1936 he sent his good wishes for the success of the Christian Mission contemplated for the Summer and Fall in the USA to a friend in New York. Here he expressed his ultimate acceptance of the Christ figure: "Christ remains as the outstanding miracle of our human story. And the more one gathers experience of life and sees the pitiable lot of mankind, the more one is drawn to that Figure and the message He delivered and stands for in our human story."[17]

That this was his considered opinion is emphasized by the fact that these very words appear also in a letter to a Bishop written in September 1936.

It is significant that especially in this period his thoughts again took on a more religious aspect and especially concentrated on the Person of Christ. One reason might have been the deep anxiety he felt in view of the darkening clouds on the international horizon, due to the advent of Hitler and his National Socialism. Another was probably due to his own position under General Hertzog and the self-abnegation he had to practise at a time which called for strong and resolute leadership in the cause of humanity and the preservation of the Christian values.

On March 1 1939, when the war clouds were shadowing the horizon, he wrote to Mrs Millin who was very depressed about British policy towards the Jews:

"You are a demon worker and writer. Is that all you have? Please be not so depressed. I believe you are really without religion, without faith in God. I inherited it from the Bible and from early training and it has steadied me more than anything else in life. This is not a Devil's world, although the Devil has had a great hand in it, especially in our day. It is God's world.

"Then there is that second and equally great insight which makes one believe in mercy, kindness, tenderness – in the femaleness of the universe. That was the contribution of the great Hebrew prophets and of Jesus, the greatest of them all. That great faith is even more at a discount in our day than faith in God."[18]

When the Second World War came, and he took over the Government in South Africa, Smuts was again guided by his religion. He became even more religious in his utterances. Amidst the stresses and tensions of the war and the great part he played in it he found time to read two new books about Jesus, one by a Frenchman, the other by a Jew.[19]

In his famous Guildhall speech on October 19 in London he took his stand on the Christian gospel against the "instinct of the animal in us".

Attacking aggression in whatever form it shows itself he maintained "The Christian gospel still fights in vain against this earlier, more deeply founded gospel of our race, which is still upheld in some countries and some circles as the code of honour and virtue for our society. The blond beast, the superman of nature, still hurls defiance at the Christian code with its gentle virtues."

In a revealing letter to Mrs Gillett written from his farm Doornkloof on September 23 1941, he outlined his deeply felt Christian credo in tackling the problems of change and reform in the world. Referring to Toynbee he writes that Toynbee regards human nature as too permanent a factor to change and all we can hope to do is to change and improve the conditions, the social and economic environment for others, so that they may have better opportunities for living a better life.

"I agree with the conclusion but not with the premise – that human nature is so fixed and unchangeable as all that. Nothing is more flexible and capable of change than human nature. All Christianity, all reform is ultimately based on that flexibility. 'Repent ye', as John the Baptist said, as Jesus said after him, change of heart *in the individual* is the basis of real advance. And it was on this fulcrum that Jesus founded His Kingdom."

His son Jannie relates how his father, whilst spending a weekend during the war with the Royal family at Windsor Castle, was asked by His Majesty King George V to deliver the Sunday sermon in St George's Chapel. Smuts confessed to his son the evening before he was to deliver the sermon that it was one of the most difficult requests he had ever had to comply with.

"Yet he delivered a truly amazing sermon," Jannie writes. Smuts compared the war against Nazism to a "great crusade for good . . . There had been many religious wars in the past, but this was undoubtedly the greatest of them all.

"A member of the (Royal) household remarked to me afterwards that it was the 'most religious sermon' he had ever listened to. And yet the word 'God' had been used only twice."[20]

But it was not only in official or public announcements that Smuts spoke of his religion. In private conversations with friends he revealed the inner working of his mind even more clearly, indicating the power that religion held in his make-up and his ideas.

Miss Lucy Bean, a journalist colleague, has feelingly described the scene at Maclear's Beacon on Table Mountain when Smuts spoke to a few friends during one of his walks up the mountain.

"As we rested on the grass at his feet he leant on his tall stock, his eyes gazing over the blue bay (Table Bay) to the grainlands where he was born."

And then Smuts with a rock as his pulpit and the spaces of the great Table Mountain as his cathedral, gave this definition of truth:

"Truth," he said, "is a vision. Mary Magdalene saw that vision in the garden on that first Easter morning and on it we have built a whole civilization."[21]

And that vision and the martyrdom of the Founder of Christianity must also have been in his mind in his hour of defeat in May 1948 at the hands of the people he had served so long, so well and so faithfully.

"They have crucified me, they have crucified me", was his cry of agony, but his anger and despair and mortification did not last long. He was once more persuaded to continue his work and in the end he agreed and worked harder than ever for the cause of unity and co-operation.[22]

It was at this time of his life in 1948 when he was 78 that life dealt him its cruellest blows. Not only was he rejected by his own people in South Africa, but on October 10 1949 his elder son Japie, after an illness of only a few hours, died suddenly of an acute attack of cerebral meningitis.

Jannie, the younger son, had to break the sad news to his father. "He seemed incredulous. But it was true and it was a staggering blow to him, for

Japie was the brilliant one of the family and our cornerstone. The event aged my father and made him work harder than ever," writes Jannie.[23]

What he does not tell is that Smuts in this dark hour of defeat and personal tragedy was comforted and sustained by his religion.

Soon after Japie's death he went to the Rev. Johan Reyneke of the Dutch Reformed Church in Pretoria. The minister often visited the Smuts family at Doornkloof and was always a welcome guest. "I visited General Smuts in his last days of his illness and also in his grief when Japie died. Often we knelt together and prayed, and we discussed religion and Holism a great deal," he told me later.

The Rev. Mr Reyneke was diffident about discussing the private feelings of his flock with me with a view to publication. But I think it is necessary in the interest of truth and for the sake of posterity that I tell here what he told me. When he visited Smuts soon after Japie's death at Doornkloof, they knelt together in Smuts's book-lined study. Mr Reyneke said a prayer and when he spoke the Amen, Smuts, still kneeling down, repeated "Amen, Ja Amen".[24]

A year later, for the first time in his life Smuts experienced severe pain in his leg. He told Mrs Millin that it was the greatest pain he had ever known. And eventually the great pain moved to his chest,[25] the beginning of the thrombosis which killed him on September 10 1950. Next to him on the table beside his small iron bed was his New Testament in Greek from which he had obtained comfort and peace since his Stellenbosch days.

In February 1950, a few months before he died, he wrote to Mrs Millin: "You incline to put me on a pedestal, which I don't like. I prefer to be what I am – a poor errant soul forever seeking and seldom finding – a pilgrim of the world and of life."[26]

Towards the end of his life, according to Queen Frederica, he became interested in mysticism. "Although in his writing and every-day discussions he ignored mysticism and religious speculations, in the evenings when the world was silent and he could sit relaxed on the front porch of Groote Schuur he mused beyond logical thought into a realm of dreams. Why did he admire Evelyn Underhill, the famous writer on mysticism and give me her books to read? Maybe somehow he sensed that this is 'A world that dreams are made of' and the true reality lies beyond our senses, still to be discovered."[27]

Queen Frederica who knew him well and whom he regarded as the most understanding pupil of his holistic ideas, quotes his last letter to her in her book, *A Measure of Understanding*. The letter, written on May 7 1950, shortly before his heart attack, glows with religious mysticism. Describing a beautiful day after good rains on his farm he wrote:

"Is it at such times that one becomes aware of the Divine, not as something beyond, but as the soul and essence of nature and oneself... The mystic whole is all the time with us and in us, but we understand it only in flashes of high experience."

CHAPTER FIVE

Influence of poets and scientists

Although religion was the main formative power in his life, Smuts never withdrew from the world of reality. In fact the beauty and variety of existence in all its manifold forms and shapes interested him throughout his long life.

With his imaginative poetical nature and his quality of fearlessness he continually sought after truths and he found and experienced truth in many different ways, sometimes in the wonderful works of the great poets, sometimes in the writings of philosophers and more often in the experiments and revelations of the great scientists in the world.

For his sensitive and almost intuitive self these revelations of truth were like strokes of lightning which break through the darkness of human existence to light up the path of life and progress.

But amidst all the studies, searchings and interests, his wide and extensive reading, his fearless search for truth, he always retained his sense of ultimate values. I cannot find any evidence of a single writer or scientist who entirely dominated his thinking. Even in the case of the great Shakespeare he could lay bare the one fundamental flaw.

Smuts's first contact with the poets came when he was a student at Stellenbosch. One of his professors had asked him how he occupied his spare time. "Have you ever thought of reading poetry?" the professor asked him and then suggested Shelley to him.

"You might begin with *Prometheus Unbound.*"[1]

And Smuts began with *Prometheus Unbound*. He recited Shelley to the veld as he wandered over the mountains surrounding this picturesque town. Shelley opened for him a new world of knowledge, insight and beauty and so became the door through which Smuts entered the world of literature, philosophy and science. Jannie tells in his biography how his father read Shelley's poetry as a diversion whilst memorizing his Greek books for his matriculation examinations.

"He became deeply engrossed in this young poet and throughout life preferred Shelley, in whom he found more of the philosophy, to other poets."[2]

He later went on to Keats, Milton and Shakespeare and other classics, though of these Shakespeare is the one in whom he sustained the greatest interest. In later life he was to develop a special passion for Shakespeare's tragedies which as a group, he considered the greatest fictional work in English.

Smuts, many years later, wrote that these five years which he spent as a student at Stellenbosch were probably the happiest of his life.

"I read much and widely, but especially the poets and philosophical writers. I had not yet any definite channel of thinking or feeling. My mind was simply dazzled and attracted by beauty in all its magical forms. My passion for nature made me spend most of my free time in the mountains, along the streams and in the innumerable winding valleys."

Carlyle was another writer who influenced the young Smuts.[3] In October 1936 he related in a letter to a friend how he came in touch with Carlyle's work when he had *Past and Present* prescribed for some examination. He then proceeded to read Carlyle's *Sartor Resartus* which in his own words "made a profound impression on me, as I had passed through personal experiences which made me susceptible to his views as therein set forth".

But Carlyle's influence was temporary and he had to make way for Goethe "which carried me a good distance away from Carlyle, who remained uninfluenced by science and with a moral outlook which did not take cognizance of the universal scope which science had opened up".[4]

It was during his student days at Stellenbosch that Smuts also mastered German and in that way came into contact with the German writers Goethe and Schiller. Especially Goethe made a very deep impression on him and his interest in both Goethe and Shakespeare remained with him throughout his life.

In his book *Holism and Evolution* he discussed both Goethe and Schiller as personalities which could form examples for the study of the human personality. Goethe to him was one of the supreme personalities which the world has produced.

I have already quoted his summing up of Goethe as a personality and it is clear from the quoted passage that he was especially attracted by the comprehensive knowledge, the deep insight and the wide capacity of Goethe in many fields of learning and knowledge. What is interesting here is that he himself revealed in his own make-up many of the qualities which he saw in Goethe and which made this great German poet such an absorbing study for him. It might be that his own genius saw in the genius and the many-sidedness of Goethe, a kindred spirit.

One of the reasons why Goethe had such a profound influence on Smuts was undoubtedly that he was not only a great poet, but also a true scientist who regarded the scientific part of his intellectual existence as not less important than the artistic one.

What further appealed to Smuts was Goethe's living approach to reality. For like Goethe, Smuts regarded the world and the universe not as a void containing inanimate matter, but as a living and growing process.

His interest in Schiller was different. Although early in his life he came into contact with the writings of both Goethe and Schiller, at first he was more deeply interested in Goethe. Afterwards he seems to have satisfied himself as to the true nature and the knowledge and insight of Goethe, but Schiller to him was a mystery, and this mystery remained with him until the end. More and more, and especially in the later years of his life, his interest centred round the personalities of Shakespeare and of Jesus Christ.

Mrs Margaret Gillett, who from the year 1919 until his death selected and forwarded to him books on a variety of subjects in which he was interested, told me that especially in the last ten or fifteen years before his death Smuts became even more interested in Shakespeare, whose plays he read, pondered over and discussed in letters or with friends. He regarded Shakespeare as one of the greatest geniuses which humanity has produced, a genius moreover, who grew in knowledge and insight as an artist, but whose personality behind the masks of his comedies and tragedies remained essentially hidden.

But whilst deeply under the influence of Shakespeare's genius, Smuts revealed the flaw in his writings. To Mrs Millin he stated that Shakespeare's one flaw in his opinion was the fact that he was without religion.

"Shakespeare considered everything except religion. He was a true child of the Renaissance, the greatest of the humanists."[5]

Yet it remains true that the genius of Shakespeare, his deep poetical insight into human nature and especially his powerful expressive language wielded a tremendous influence on Smuts throughout his life.

I have already shown how Smuts during his Cambridge years came under the strong influence of the poetry and world vision of Walt Whitman and how Whitman's supreme freedom and enquiring mind helped to liberate him from extreme Calvinism.

As such, Whitman influenced his religious outlook. But Whitman's poetry also had a profound influence on him in another way. There are many indications that Whitman's poetry, his powerful rhythm and the wonderful potentialities which he saw in every human being touched the young Smuts like a flame of inspiration. It was also Whitman who helped to give him the kernel of his later idea of Holism through his concentration on the potentialities of the human personality.

To understand the powerful influence of Whitman on his young impressionable mind we must bear in mind that already as a young student Smuts sat in awe and veneration before the wonder of personality. Psychologists may be able to explain that he might already have felt in himself the stirrings of his own genius. We do not know, but one can conceive the young Smuts lifted up by Whitman to a vision of the potentialities in his own gifted make-up.

Something like this might have occurred to the young Smuts during his Cambridge period. It might have been his own awakening to the fact that he was a genius, but it may also have been the result of the discovery of Walt Whitman's book of poetry, *Leaves of Grass* when through Whitman he saw what a human being with all his powers and potentialities could be.

For that in essence was what the poetry of Whitman taught him. Whitman as the modern American poet, probably the first poet in the world who not only saw the living process and all existence as a whole, but also freed his outlook and the whole of life from the bonds of forms and formality, matched his freedom of ideas and expression with a free rhythm and the rejection of all conventional poetic formalities. Called by Thoreau "probably the greatest democrat that ever lived", Whitman like Shakespeare was the fearless searcher after truth. And he found the supreme truth in himself in his deepest being where he discovered the many possibilities which existed in himself and all other human beings. "Most of the great poets are impersonal," he said. "I am personal, in my poems all revolves around, centres in, radiates from myself. I have but one central figure, the general human personality typified in myself. But my book (*Leaves of Grass*),[6] compels, absolutely necessitates, every reader to transpose himself or herself into the central position, and become the living fountain, actor, experiencer, himself or herself, of every page, every aspiration, every line."

And because he saw the reality of life in himself as a living unified personality, Whitman combined in his outlook all the aspects and facets of life in a living whole. He revealed himself in his poetic biography, in language and rhythmical declamations. His vision and power stirred the imagination of the young Smuts and made a lasting impression on him.

Like Whitman he began by sitting at the feet of the world's greatest masters of song and what impressed him more than anything else was that in Whitman there was room for nature as well as God, united on the basis of "an implicit belief in the wisdom, health, beauty of every process, mystery, every concrete object, every human or other existence, not only considered from the point of view of all but of each".

It is here that Smuts felt the ideas of Whitman to be identical with his own fundamental outlook. Even as a student in Cambridge he rebelled against the narrow mechanistic or materialistic outlook which was current in the nineteenth century and where mind and matter were separated with the emphasis on the material world.

So deeply was he inspired and influenced by the noble thoughts of Whitman that in 1894 when he was only 24 years old he wrote a treatise *Walt Whitman – A Study in the Evolution of Personality*.

It is clear that Whitman's poetry stirred him to his depths. He tried to delve into the underlying theory of all existence, and through the study, the principal features of Whitman's mental development, to throw "a new light on some of the darkest problems of life and thought".

In this treatise which was never published, the young Smuts showed how he was attracted by the individualism of Whitman which was probably his most outstanding characteristic. He wrote:

"Every individual form of life is a unit, a centre of activity dominated by one fundamental property. It is this ultimate internal unity that shapes the innumerable products of life into an orderly and harmonious whole."

Continuing, he added:

"In every individual form of life this fundamental property produces according to its own laws and forms. By studying the mental life as a whole we shall soon get beyond the range of the pure psychologist."[7]

In studying Whitman he studied his own personality and in trying to reveal Whitman he revealed himself. The significance of Whitman's influence on him is that by studying his idea of personality the young Smuts found his own intellectual and philosophical feet. Whitman was the first outstanding personality who helped to form his own personality.

Later in this treatise I shall go more deeply into the question of how Smuts in the light of Whitman's ideas first developed his great vision of Holism as a key to the mystery of knowledge. For purposes of this chapter it is sufficient to state that Whitman came into the life of Smuts at a time when he was deeply stirred by another great thinker of the second half of the nineteenth century. This man was Charles Darwin.

Darwin (1809-1882), well known as the father of the theory of evolution, wrote his great work *On the Origin of Species by Means of Natural Selection, or the Preservation of Varied Races in the Struggle for Life* in 1859.

With his theory of evolution Darwin opened the door to a new world of thought, a world which is not static as was previously thought, but which is continuously growing and developing. It is a world of movement through the twin forces of variation and natural selection to ever higher forms.

In the history of human thought Darwin appeared on the world scene at a time when science opened up new vistas to the human mind. From 1830 to 1836 he made his long voyage on the *Beagle* as a naturalist and in 1837 when he was 28 years old he published his observations on the relation between animals on islands and those on the nearest continent, and between living animals and those most recently extinct and found as fossils in the same country. He discovered that they were related but not the same. As a result of changing circumstances there were different qualities which came about through changes, adaptation and development. Even then this led him to reflect on the modification of species, and eventually from these and other observations his revolutionary idea of evolution was born, an idea which came to open a new world of thought and vision and which during the past hundred and twenty years has contributed a great deal to the ideas and outlook which we have today.

Darwin's ideas already began to penetrate when Smuts was a young student at Cambridge. It was here that he first came into contact with this revolutionary theory. And how profoundly he was influenced by Darwin he himself reveals in his book *Holism and Evolution*.[8]

Smuts showed that Newton's law of gravitation was one of the turning points in the search for knowledge. Newton with his law of gravitation gave an acceptable explanation of all physical movements in our world and in the universe as a whole.

The great German thinker Kant, himself one of the kings of the world of ideas, regarded this Newtonian system as final. Just as Newton formulated the laws of movement and the material world, he expressed the hope that one day a thinker would appear to discover and formulate the laws of life. Smuts, in evaluating the place of Darwin in the world of ideas, then states:

"Beyond all doubt Darwin fulfilled that vision, not perhaps in the sense intended by Kant, yet in a way which has made him perhaps an even more epoch-making figure than Newton. Newton proved epoch-making for science while Darwin has become epoch-making in a far more fundamental sense. He has changed our whole human orientation of knowledge and belief, he has given a new direction to our outlook, our efforts and aspirations, and has probably meant a greater difference for human thought and action than any other single thinker. But even he is not final. He, even less than Newton, is final. He has pointed the great way, and on that way we are already travelling beyond his great vision.

"Let me first state Darwin's law, which was just as simple as Newton's, and much more easily intelligible. Among living beings there is a tendency to vary and to over-multiply; in consequence, a struggle for survival becomes inevitable, and in this struggle for existence the fittest survive. This explains the origin of species and all organic differences in the world. The tendency to variation is a fact patent to everyone; so is the over-multiplication of individuals under favourable conditions and in the absence of external restraints; the resulting struggle, which Darwin calls Natural Selection, is well known to everyone who has the least knowledge of animate Nature. These are the simple bricks of fact with which the Darwinian theory is constructed. Surely as striking a case of Columbus' egg as was ever presented. The genius of the Master was shown by the vastness of the structure he produced from these simple materials of common-sense and common experience. From these simple commonplace facts he explained the infinite variety of the forms of life which occupy the earth, their geographical distribution both in the past and in the present over the face of the globe, and the marvellous closeness of their adaptation to the physical and other conditions among which they live – adaptation to land and sea, to fresh and to salt water, to conditions of soil and climate embracing the extremes of heat and cold, to the widest range of wet, arid and desert conditions, and to all the innumerable facts and situations which lead to the inter-weaving of the mysterious web of life.

"The whole Darwinian theory is summarized in the last sentences of *The*

Origin of Species with a simplicity and beauty of statement worthy of the simple, but profound genius of the Master, and they raise before us in a few touches the great Darwinian vision. They have often been quoted, but will bear repeating here:

"'It is interesting to contemplate a tangled bank, clothed with many plants of many kinds, with birds singing in the bushes, with various insects flitting about, and with worms crawling through the damp earth, and to reflect that these elaborately constructed forms, so different from each other, and dependent upon each other in so complex a manner, have all been produced by laws acting around us. These laws, taken in the largest sense, being Growth with Reproduction; Inheritance which is almost implied by reproduction; Variability from the indirect and direct action of the conditions of life, and from use and misuse; a Ratio of Increase so high as to lead to a struggle for life, and as a consequence to Natural Selection, entailing Divergence of Character and the extinction of less-improved forms. Thus from the war of Nature, from famine and death, the most exalted object which we are capable of conceiving, namely, the production of the higher animals, directly follows. There is a grandeur in this view of life, with its several powers, having been originally breathed by the Creator into a few forms or into one; and that, whilst this planet has gone cycling on according to the fixed law of gravity, from so simple a beginning endless forms most beautiful and most wonderful have been and are being evolved.'

"I am free to confess that there are few passages in the great literature of the world which affect me more deeply than these concluding words of Darwin's great book. They have a force and a beauty out of all proportion to the simple unadorned phrasing. They are the expression of a great selfless soul, who sought truth utterly and fearlessly, and was in the end vouchsafed a vision of the truth which perhaps has never been surpassed in its fullness and grandeur."[9]

It is clear from this how profoundly the young Smuts was influenced by Darwin's great system of thought. Here again I shall show in later chapters how Darwin's ideas were assimilated by Smuts in the development of his own concept of Holism.

Through Darwin and through his interest in Botany he entered the world of science and thereafter for the rest of his long life he took an active interest in the vast panorama of science. His scientific interest is remarkably deep for a man who was not professionally a scientist. His interest in science complemented and supplemented his interest in literature, philosophy and religion. Walt Whitman had a great influence on his attitude to life, broadened his human interest and turned it to the contemplation of the goodness of life. Whitman sharpened him, opened his eyes. When he came to Cambridge he had the Calvinistic outlook from his religious background. Whitman started in him the immense liberation of the spirit which a fourth external factor, his contact with the Society of Friends, eventually completed. His scientific interest on the other hand gave him that width of capacity and the objective spirit which was essential in his search for truth.

In order really to appreciate the extent to which Smuts was interested in and influenced by other writers and thinkers one has to see his personal library, which has now been transferred from his study at Irene to Johannesburg. Throughout his long and varied life he found time to read and to study and there is no doubt that many authors, scientists and philosophers continually influenced his thinking.

He himself placed the influence of the poets first in helping him to discover Holism. "When I was young I saw a light, and I have followed that light ever since," he explained to the students at the University of the Witwatersrand in 1927. Elaborating on this he said that as a young man at Cambridge he had turned more to poetry than to philosophy for guidance. Wisdom seems to be with the poets. There was more wisdom with the poets than with politicians. Poetry brought out the fundamentals of reality and it was as a student of poetry that he first saw the light.

Continuing, he stated that he had admired Goethe and Walt Whitman most, and in studying the works of these two poets it had seemed to him that there was something greater in them than in their works; there was something greater behind their works and in their personalities than in their works.

It was in studying their personalities that he had come on the concept of the whole; the personality, *sui generis*, underlying their lives and their works; a whole that had its own laws of development.[10]

CHAPTER SIX

Louis Botha's humanity

Of all living people with whom Smuts came into contact the Boer leader, Louis Botha, made the deepest impression on him. I would place the influence of Botha as the second most important force in his life.

Eminently endowed with that great quality of humanity which Smuts to some extent lacked, Botha showed him what a feeling for others and an understanding and love of one's fellowmen could and should be. And although Smuts could no more change his own nature than Botha could become an intellectual, the vision of Botha remained with him all his days and helped to mellow him and to make him more human as the years passed.

Louis Botha, born in 1862, three years before Abraham Lincoln was assassinated, was indeed the South African leader who came closest to Lincoln in his deep compassionate humanity. And like Lincoln he not only had a heart for others, but also never deviated from his course once he made up his mind on an issue. Smuts learnt his South Africanism from Botha.

Already during the Anglo-Boer War and especially towards the end when the ultimate defeat of the valiant Boer commandos seemed inevitable, Botha pondered deeply the causes of division which brought about the war and which led to so much bitterness, misery and destruction.

In his own mind he found the answer in the division and conflict between the Afrikaners and the English. And as he wrestled with the problem in the veld among his loyal burgers, gradually the light of understanding lit up his mind, the light of sympathy which saw the Afrikaners and the English in South Africa as brothers in the great task of building up a united South Africa where peace, and not dissension, would be in the hearts of all South Africans as in their country.

When the Anglo-Boer War came to an end on May 31 1902, Botha could already say: "I feel my inner struggle to be a thing of the past."

Botha had resolved the struggle in his own heart and he was ready for the great sacrifices which a policy of conciliation would demand. When saying farewell to his staff officers at Skaapkoppie in the Eastern Transvaal he said to them: "You can now go and rest a little. As for me, my real work only begins at this hour. The day when rest will be mine will be when they lower me into the grave. The sacrifices we had to make were terrific, but we are going to see a Greater South Africa."

And shortly after the commandos had surrendered their arms he said to Mr J. P. Jooste at Wakkerstroom:

"Tomorrow begins our great task of building a South African nation."

It was clear that Botha had found his soul and his task. His task would be to try to give to the whole of South Africa peace and unity on the basis of the brotherhood of Boer and Briton.

Smuts himself in describing Botha's conciliation policy later said: "Botha's line remained absolutely consistent. No one else in South Africa could have stuck it out. You wanted a man for that, very broadminded, large-hearted. People may say that he went too far in that direction, but it is a policy that helped South Africa over its worst stile. It was quite on the cards that, after the Boer War, the bad old policy would revive. Botha managed to wean the people off that."[1]

Smuts at this stage was still uncertain of the road ahead. More intellectual and less intuitive than Botha, he had to think out for himself what the honest and wise policy for the future had to be. For Botha the light of true South Africanism in which Boer and Briton would co-operate as equals to build up a greater united South Africa shone bright and clear. Nothing that happened after that, not the malign attacks of embittered politicians, the tragedy of rebellion, the threats of strife and war, would divert him one iota from his chosen path.

What is remarkable here is that Botha, although living amongst the Black races of Africa and being served and sustained by them on his farm and in the towns never once considered them as part of the South African nation. Here was the great flaw in his attitude, his outlook and his statecraft. And here the lack in his leadership which also influenced Smuts to disregard the Blacks as part of the social and political scene.

And with his great heart and warm humanity, his strong sense of duty, he gradually became the centre of Boer leadership after the war. As such he began to influence the thoughts and outlook of Smuts, and precisely how he did it and what it meant to Smuts, is happily recorded by Smuts himself in one of the most penetrating analyses ever written.

I shall quote it here in full because in analysing General Botha, Smuts reveals himself and also throws light on the way in which General Botha influenced him. He begins by asking that he be allowed to give a brief personal impression of a friend "whom I knew well for twenty-one years, during most of which we were associated in our work and our lives in a way which cannot but be rare among men.[2]

"I knew him not only in the ordinary ways of living and working together, but far more intimately. Together as friends and comrades we passed through the gravest crises of our lives; together we had to take the most fateful decisions. I saw him under the most severe tests that can be applied to a human being – tests which would have revealed and brought out any flaws in his inner composition. And it is the way he stood all these tests and showed real greatness of soul that has made him quite outstanding in my memories of the great men whom I have known and worked with. I am not going to discuss here the intimacies of his inner life, but to refer very briefly to some of his qualities which flowed from that inner greatness and struck the world at large.

"His natural tact was very beautiful, and indeed struck everybody with whom he came into contact. But in his case tact was not mere superficial form or manner. With him it was the expression of an innate sympathy which was probably the deepest and richest element in his make-up. I have never in any other man seen such a fine power of sympathy. His sympathy made it possible for him to get extremely close to others and to read their minds and divine their characters with marvellous accuracy.

"It almost amounted to a gift of divination as far as character was concerned. It gave him intuitive power of understanding and appreciating men which was very rare. I remember many an occasion when he sized up a person in a way which at the time struck me as somewhat forced or fanciful, but which the experience of after years showed to have been perfectly right. Sympathy with him sprang from unusual intuitive insight into the character and motives of those with whom he came into contact, and his reading of men was in many ways the surest I have ever seen. He read friends and opponents alike as an open book. This is a very uncommon and precious endowment. Great men are often wanting in knowledge of human nature and are taken in by quite commonplace scoundrels. Much of their work is often spoiled by a trust in those who are unworthy of it. I never heard of anybody taking in Botha; and this not because of any analytic power of dissecting motives and qualities, but because of his sympathetic insight, which seldom proved wrong. His knowledge of human nature was as profound as his sympathy, and sprang from it. But it was more than knowledge. It had that emotional touch which made him truly human, and endeared him to his friends, and gave him his personal magnetism. With him you felt instinctively at ease; he inspired those who surrounded him with confidence and devotion. And this sympathetic bond gave him a power over men much greater than any other form of superiority could possibly have given. To understand and love as he did, to evoke love and trust as he did, is indeed the finest power which can be wielded by men. This power he had, a power which reached the very souls of people and did not merely affect their superficial behaviour.

"This sympathetic power not only meant great power, but also great pain to him. It meant that he was abnormally sensitive. He had not that thick hide which is supposed to protect the public man against the rebuffs and insults of his unpleasant profession. Politicians should be pachyderms. Public life for him meant not only the supreme enjoyment of achievement, but the continual agony of misunderstandings, of differences with friends and associates, of hideously unfair and wounding critism, of which he had an abundant measure. On those whom the gods love they lavish infinite joys and infinite sorrows. He had his full measure of both. His place is in the most select list of the great statesmen and men of action that South Africa has produced. In that list he will in future probably be accorded the first place. Great as a soldier and as a statesman, the leader of the Transvaal through the Boer War, the architect above all others of the Union of South Africa, the saviour of his people and its honour in 1914, his achievement is indeed unique. The simple Boer boy of the veld who rose by sheer power of personality and performance to be one of the foremost figures at the Paris Peace Conference has indeed established a record which would be hard to beat. But this great man of action had the tenderest feelings and the most sensitive soul. He combined the strength of a man with the extreme sensitiveness of a woman. A stupid letter of a friend would cause him sleepless nights; an undeserved criticism or insult would inflict pain far beyond what was probably intended. His power of sympathy was not only a powerful weapon, but it left him unprotected and exposed to a degree which would be considered almost unbelievable. It was this blending of great power with extreme sensitiveness which made him a supreme friend. Great as soldier, greater as statesman, he was greatest as friend by right of his sheer humanity and sympathy.

"What was the religion of such a man? What could it be, but the religion of all truly great men? He had his roots deep in the invisible. The human sympathy which bound him to his fellows was one with his deepest contacts with the unseen. All great spirits live by the same fundamental Faith. Most difficult of all to formulate and express, it is yet the truest reality of their lives. Botha certainly never attempted to express it. He observed the ordinary forms of religion, and was in every respect irreproachable in his moral and social habits. But there was always something more which his intimates were conscious of. He did not wear his heart on his sleeve, and seldom spoke openly about religious matters. But in the background was this fundamental faith, and on certain testing occasions it revealed itself visibly in his behaviour. One was at Pretoria the Sunday after the signing (late on a Saturday night) of the Vereeniging Peace Treaty which ended the Anglo-Boer War. He was labouring under almost uncontrollable emotion which it was most painful to witness, and yet through the storms and the wreckage of war and the despair of the terrible ending there was heard the still small voice speaking of simple faith and trust in the Providence which invisibly guides the fortune of men. Then there was another occasion at the beginning of the great War, when the rebellion among his Boer comrades was on the point of breaking out, and he, with myself and a couple of friends, was striving far into the night to persuade General De la Rey to keep out of the mischief that was afoot and to use his great influence against it. General De la Rey – one of the whitest and noblest souls that ever lived – was labouring under a deep religious impulse which made him hear the call of God for the release of the Boer people from the bondage imposed upon them at Vereeniging. The argument with him therefore necessarily took a religious turn, and it went on for a long time, until Botha at last said to De la Rey (calling him by the affectionate name which we all used for him), "Oom Koos, it may be the will of God that this nation shall be free and independent. But nothing will ever convince me that it is the will of God that this shall be brought about through treachery and dishonour." And more to that effect; his language at the time reminding me of one of the greatest passages in the Book of Job. Then there is the third and last occasion when, at the signing of the Versailles Treaty on the very day when the Vereeniging Peace had been signed, his memories of that awful moment blended with pity for the Germans at the Punic peace which was being imposed on them, and he penned those well-known lines which in their ruggedness and intensity of feeling are almost untranslatable, and which now hang in the Prime Minister's room at the Union Buildings in Pretoria:

"'God's laws shall be imposed on all peoples with justice under the new sun, and we shall continue to pray that they will be applied to mankind in love and peace and Christian charity. Today I think of May 31 1902.' At that moment when jubilation filled all hearts, he heard the undertone of the ages and felt only the deepest pity for the fate of human kind. He felt the present whole with the past and the future, and he saw the vision of God who in His infinite mercy and pity washes out for ever the sins of this poor world and writes forgiveness over it all. His attitude that day was a revelation of what was deepest in him, and also of what to me seems to be the essence of all religious feeling.

"There are men whose largeness of soul forms a solvent for the pettinesses of the world; who in their breadth of humanity and sympathy reconcile the differences which divide their fellows; creative souls who, out of the rough material of the passions and self-interests, the party cries and sectional strivings of those who surround them, achieve the comprehensive synthesis of a larger national life; who really make a people, place fresh view-points before them out of the bitterness and sufferings of the past into the warm, glad light of larger ideals and visions.

"These are the rare God-like leaders, and of such was Louis Botha. What South Africa owes to him it will only gradually realize with the years, as the creative seed he has sown sprouts and bears fruit in the coming of the united nation for which he poured out his soul."

That was written by Smuts in February 1929, ten years after Botha's death and when he was in a position to look back upon the first stormy quarter of the twentieth century.

It is again here evident that not once did Smuts in his evaluation of the great humanity of Botha towards Afrikaners and the British and even to the Germans in the hour of victory over them, apply this great sympathy and this deep feeling for others to the Black races of Africa. Here again the typical South African, indeed the overwhelming white outlook of the time, ignored the fate of millions of fellow human beings of different colours. Neither were the white leaders conscious that this was a lack, an omission which flawed their outlook, their statecraft and even their personalities.

Having himself revealed how Botha influenced his thinking and the development of his own personality, let us now trace in broad outline the circumstances which brought them together and the way they co-operated and complemented each other.

The main point here is the way in which Botha's policy of conciliation between Boer and Briton came to be accepted by Smuts and the majority of their fellow South Africans.

The instrument which Botha used to this purpose was the "Het Volk" party which was formed on May 23 1904 in the Volkstem building in Pretoria. Its main aim was to protect and promote the interests of the Boer nation.

Botha became the leader and followed a policy of wise moderation with conciliation as the cornerstone. Smuts himself at first stood apart and aloof. He was still not prepared for his great task, being content, as he wrote to Emily Hobhouse, to "water my orange trees and read Kant's Critique of Pure Reason".[3]

That was the case during 1904 and 1905, but gradually Smuts also came under the magnetism of Botha's humanity. The seeds of true South Africanism were sown in his heart and towards the end of 1905 Botha persuaded Smuts to undertake a trip to London to see the British leaders privately.

That visit became the turning point of Smuts's life, the door to the fulfilment of his real self. For what made that trip so interesting and significant was that what he found in the hearts of the Friends and the new Liberal leaders in England corresponded with the conciliation policy of Botha.

In South Africa Botha worked for unity and co-operation between the English and the Boers. In England that part of the people who in some way had been against the Anglo-Boer War, came strongly to the fore. Most important of all was the leadership of Sir Henry Campbell-Bannerman. Already during the Anglo-Boer War he created a sensation when he denounced the methods employed against the Boers – "this stupid policy of farm-burning, devastation and sweeping of women and children into camps".

On June 14 1901, he spoke even more strongly against the unnecessary war.

"When was war not war? When it was carried on by methods of barbarism in South Africa."[4]

From the outset Campbell-Bannerman maintained that peace in South Africa must be based on the restoration to the Boers of the right of self-government and on co-operation between the two white races in South Africa. And during 1905 it was clear that the electorate in Britain swung towards

Campbell-Bannerman and his Liberal Party.

When Smuts went to London at the behest of Botha these two movements of conciliation and humanity came together and flowed together as one stream. Apart from the revolutionary results of this for South Africa and through South Africa for the eventual Commonwealth of Nations, it was a supreme moment in the life of Smuts himself.

It is now history that Smuts in January 1906 with his arguments persuaded Campbell-Bannerman of the goodness and the rightness of a policy of faith in the Boer leaders and the Boer nation.

In later years Smuts told his biographer Sarah Gertrude Millin how the miracle of self-government for the Transvaal and the Orange Free State came about as a result of his visit to Campbell-Bannerman.

He first saw Churchill, who was sceptical, then Morley, who was afraid, and then Campbell-Bannerman himself.

"I went on explaining. I could see Campbell-Bannerman was listening sympathetically. Without being brilliant he was the sort of personality – large-hearted and honest – on whom people depended. He reminded me of Botha. Such men get things done. He told me there was to be a Cabinet meeting the next day and said: 'Smuts, you have convinced me.'"

The next day Campbell-Bannerman addressed his Cabinet and afterwards Lloyd George told that great journalist, Lord Riddell, that the speech which lasted only ten minutes had moved at least one member of the Cabinet to tears. The former Boer republics obtained self-government.[5]

Botha's trust, conciliation and humanity paid off handsomely and Smuts was the chosen instrument to bring it about. When he returned to South Africa elated in February 1906 he brought the great news of responsible government.

"They gave us back our country in everything but name. After four years. Has such a miracle of trust and magnanimity ever happened before? Only a people like the English could do it. They make mistakes, but they are a big people."

Smuts ever after regarded this as the most important achievement of his political life, as it undoubtedly was. But it was important not only as the basis of the great things which resulted from it and were built on it, but more especially as a living proof to him of the rightness of the cause of human trust and faith.

In March 1906 Botha and Smuts went to Bloemfontein in the Orange Free State to inform President Steyn, General Hertzog and the other Free State leaders of the great generosity of the new Liberal Government of Britain. It was probably here that the first seeds of suspicion and envy or even jealousy were sown.

The Free State never liked to be led by the Transvaal and the Free State leaders and especially General Hertzog did not like to take a back seat in such an important matter. But for the moment this was of little importance. The Orangia Unie was formed in Bloemfontein in May 1906, two years after the birth of Het Volk in the Transvaal. Six years later Hertzog was to split South Africa again, destroying the Botha and Smuts vision of unity.

But nothing could ever separate Botha and Smuts, or dim the vision of unity and trust which Botha had, and imparted to Smuts. In his book *General Botha* Dr F. V. Engelenburg stressed the wonderful way in which Botha and Smuts complemented each other. Germany had her Goethe and Schiller. The German nation had commemorated them in a joint monument at Weimar showing them hand in hand.

Such a monument would be fitting for Botha and Smuts in front of the Union Building in Pretoria. For although Smuts was eight years younger than Botha, exceptionally endowed with intellectual gifts as against the intuitive insights of Botha, they formed a unique duumvirate.

Smuts was the intellectual master, but in Botha he found a natural matter-of-fact capacity, strength of will, a readiness to sacrifice for the good of his country and a profound altruism towards all men. "As a statesman, Botha was not quite so careful although equally far-seeing. What Smuts was able to accomplish, thanks to his trained intellect, Botha achieved by sheer intuition," states Dr Engelenburg.[6]

In her book *General Smuts*, Mrs Millin gives credence to the general view that Botha was the warm magnetic personality and Smuts the cold and powerful brain. "Every newspaper said it. His associates said it, and say it still."[7]

Although differing in so many ways, they co-operated unselfishly and without ever any trace of envy or jealousy.

Smuts was one of the first to be taken into Botha's confidence as regards the policy of peace in South Africa and who at once understood it and promoted it in his own unique way.

In describing their contrasting social life Engelenburg throws new light on their outlook and personalities.

"Socially there never was much intimacy between the two men. Each had his family, his domestic interests, his business to attend to. Botha, by way of recreation, liked a quiet game of bridge. To Smuts such pleasures appeared an unimaginable waste of valuable time. It was his habit to pore over books and documents for hours at a stretch. Botha was fond of a chat. He regarded his landscape with the eye of a cattle farmer; Smuts looked at it as a naturalist. Botha's policy of conciliation was an expression of his philanthropy; Smuts's League of Nations Covenant was the creation of a virtuoso in the sphere of constitutional law."[8]

And so they complemented each other, two different personalities, but always co-operating, interacting, influencing one another. Together they built the Union of South Africa, weathered the supreme crisis of the Rebellion of

1914 and saw the young united South Africa through the storms and stresses of the First Great War.

Together they felt and protested against the injustice of the vindictive and unchristian Peace of Versailles which repeated the tragedy of the Peace of Vereeniging unmitigated by the magnanimity and the generosity of Campbell-Bannerman's gift of 1906.

After the Peace Conference Botha returned to South Africa to die of sheer exhaustion and disappointment in August 1919.

It was Smuts's task to bury his friend and leader, and when he stood by the open grave, these words welled up from the depths of his soul in memory of his friend:

"He (Botha) had no equal as a friend. We have worked together intimately for 21 years without intermission. We came together with a closeness seldom vouchsafed to friends. This entitles me to call him the greatest, cleanest, sweetest soul of all the land – of all my days. Great in his lifetime, he was happy in his death. To his friend is left the bitter task of burying him, and to defend his works, which were almost too heavy for him to perform."

And in the Assembly six days later, after he became the second Prime Minister of the United South Africa which Botha and he had created, Smuts added:

"To the strength of a man Botha joined the loving-kindness, the tenderness of a woman. He was extremely human as regards sympathy and character. Massive sympathy is what he felt for his fellowman."

It was this massive sympathy which Smuts himself lacked as the one flaw in his greatness and which he therefore appreciated so greatly in Botha.

How high Louis Botha figured as an international statesman in the opinion of Smuts can be seen in the following anecdote which the late Major-General Frank Theron remembered. Theron was at first the private secretary of Botha, and after his death in 1919, of Smuts. One day during the Versailles Conference Smuts said to him: "Wie reken jy is die grootste figuur hier op die konferensie? Ons eie oubaas Louis – daar is geeneen van hierdie mense wat by hom kan kers vashou nie."[9] (Who do you consider is the greatest figure at this conference? Why, our own Louis – there is not one of these people who can hold a candle to him.)

What was the reason that these two great leaders, both deeply Christian, both democrats, both endowed with sympathy and loving kindness ignored the Black races around them? Why did the great British Liberal statesman Sir Henry Campbell-Bannerman in granting self-government to the defeated Boer nation, not also stress the fact of the existence of millions of Blacks under their control or even suggest that Blacks should also be made part of that self-government?

CHAPTER SEVEN

Margaret Clark and the Quakers

There is a moment of truth in the lives of all great men when destiny steps forward, touches them on the shoulder and reveals to them their true paths in the service of their fellowmen.

Such a moment must have come to Smuts in January 1906. And it probably came to him in a little church or rather a meeting house of the Society of Friends in the little English town of Street in the county of Somersetshire in the south-west of England.

It was there in January 1906 that the spirit moved him to get up among a number of English Quakers whom he had just met and to speak words of wisdom which almost miraculously became the foundation stone of all the great and good work he performed during the next 44 years of his long and varied life.[1]

I am convinced that that was the great change in his life. The Smuts before January 1906, the brilliant intellectual of Cambridge and the intrepid leader of a Boer commando into the Cape, was still not sure of his true path; he was still uncertain whether to be an embittered Afrikaner or a co-operative South African. But after what must have amounted to his vision in the little meeting house in Street, he never looked back. He became the force which shaped the destiny of South Africa for 44 years and in a remarkable way also helped to create the Commonwealth and two world organizations, the League of Nations after the First World War and the United Nations after the Second World War.

Historians who study these things tell us that usually there comes a turning point in the lives of most great men at about the age of 40. It certainly was the case with our own Louis Botha. It happened to Henry Ford, and the late President Franklin Roosevelt was also an illustration of this. Abraham Lincoln was another.

Smuts was 37 when he arrived in England in January 1906 on what he said was "a private visit". That journey was historical. It was as if everything that happened before to shape his outlook and personality there flowed together in one supreme moment of truth when his real destiny and the task awaiting his genius was revealed. The three forces of his life, his religion, his deep interest in the writings of the poets, scientists and philosophers and the influence of the mellow humanity of Botha on him, here met a fourth, the spiritual power and might of the Society of Friends, and blended with it to create the real Smuts. And as so often happens, the story of this great moment in his life was kept a secret, never before revealed. I am happy to be able to tell it here.

When Smuts travelled to England in December 1905 he did so in the company of a young English girl of 26 years. This girl, Margaret Clark as she then was, Mrs M. C. Gillett as she became after her marriage, had the key to the inner mind of Smuts, until the day he died 44 years later. She lived in the little town of Street in Somersetshire. This is also where Cato, Smuts's daughter, now Mrs Bancroft-Clark, has her home.

To find out what happened on that historic visit to England I visited Mrs Gillett in her home at 30 Portway in Street a few years before her death. Mrs Gillett then suffered from arthritis and she had difficulty in walking. I found her in a wheelchair under a mulberry tree in her lovely garden with green fields in the background. We talked about old times and about Smuts's first visit to Street. She showed me some notes and books and later also extracts from a diary her mother had kept.

And gradually the pattern of destiny opened up before me, the pattern of small beginnings which led to such great things for our country, for the Commonwealth and mankind as a whole, the pattern which united the lives of the Boer Leader and this English family, the Clarks and later the Gilletts, and which became the symbol of Afrikaner and English co-operation in South Africa.

Margaret Clark was the daughter of William Clark, a Quaker who built up the shoe factory in Street. Her mother was the daughter of John Bright who, with Cobden, fought for the Corn Laws and also led the campaign for the extension of the suffrage to the working classes in England. She was brought up in this atmosphere of radical liberal tradition where the main interest was always centred on the underdog.

John Bright, one of the great parliamentary figures of nineteenth-century England, was the first member of the Society of Friends to enter the British Parliament. As a Friend he was against all wars and he opposed the Crimean War. More than 20 years later he resigned his seat in the Cabinet because he objected to the Egyptian Campaign. In doing so he stressed the importance of the moral law founded on religion as the basis for all individual and political action.

He uttered these historical words: "The House knows that at least I have endeavoured from time to time to teach my countrymen an opinion and doctrine which I hold, which is, that the moral law is not intended only for the individual life, but is intended also for the life and practice of states."

On this basis it was natural for the Clark family also to resent and oppose the Anglo-Boer War, and to be branded pro-Boer by the rest of the community.

Margaret had been at Newman College in Cambridge towards the end of the nineteenth century where among others she had Mr Hendrik van Zyl of Cape Town, who was later to become a judge, as a friend. She was 26 years old when Emily Hobhouse came to Street in 1905, three years after the end of the Anglo-Boer War. Miss Hobhouse had been to South Africa on an errand of mercy to help the stricken and impoverished Boer women. In 1905 she came back to England to address meetings and to raise funds for the continuation of her work. She stayed with the Clark family in Street and after her meeting young Margaret asked: "Can I help you in this?" "Oh, come with me to South Africa," was Miss Hobhouse's ready reply. Margaret said: "Yes."[2]

That remark changed the life of Margaret Clark and opened the door for her to a strange and wonderful future where she and later her husband became the most intimate and dear friends of Smuts. She became possibly the only person who knew the inner secrets of the genius that he was.

Margaret became private secretary to Miss Hobhouse and learnt spinning and weaving, and in 1905 they both travelled on the same boat – a German boat – to Cape Town. On board were also President Steyn and his wife and two daughters, Hanna (later Mrs Fichardt) and Gladys (Advocate Gladys Steyn). There was also Dr D. F. Malan returning from his theological studies in Holland, and destined to deal Smuts the greatest political blow of his life in May 1948 when he succeeded Smuts as Prime Minister of South Africa. Dr Malan taught Margaret her first Afrikaans during the voyage. Mrs Jacobs, a granddaughter of President Kruger, was another passenger.

"So that was my introduction to South Africa," was her comment to me 49 years later.[3]

There was a great reception when the boat reached Cape Town. On the wharf to meet the ex-President and his family were General Louis Botha, General De Wet, Mr Jaap (later Chief Justice) de Villiers, Mr Abraham Fisher and Smuts.

Miss Hobhouse introduced her new secretary Margaret to Smuts. Margaret stayed in Cape Town with Mr and Mrs Hendrik de Villiers. It was the hottest time of the year and after a few days in Cape Town the party left by train to the north. Always at all the stations there were crowds. At Noupoort, Percy Fisher and Gordon Fraser got onto the train to welcome President Steyn. Margaret was very intrigued to find out that they were in the Boer party who had blown up the bridge over the Orange River during the Anglo-Boer War. They all got out at Springfontein in the Free State. There old Mr Fraser, Mrs Steyn's father, came with a spider to take the President to Philippolis. That was where Miss Hobhouse and Margaret went too.

That was her first personal experience of the ravages and cruelties of war. "I remembered the broken homes and the bones of the cattle where they were slaughtered. I saw the broken farms and we immediately started helping the women. Miss Hobhouse started a workshop for spinning and weaving through the helpfulness of the Rev. Colin Fraser. Then we organized people to teach the women home industries," Mrs Gillett related.[4]

Later she and Miss Hobhouse moved to Langlaagte and then to Pretoria where she visited the Smuts family at their home in Sunnyside. She stayed with them. "They made their home like a home for me." Margaret and General and Mrs Smuts became firm friends and through her and her family, Smuts learnt to know of the new forces emerging in England.

The political atmosphere in England had undergone a vast change after the Anglo-Boer War. The war party was on its way out and the Liberals were coming strongly to the front. When the Unionist War Government of Joseph Chamberlain resigned on December 4 1905, Campbell-Bannerman, who from the beginning had opposed the Anglo-Boer War, and his Liberal Party, took over the reins of government. Botha thought the time expedient for a new approach to the liberal leaders and when Smuts left for England, he was accompanied by Margaret Clark who wanted to visit her people at Street.

They were travelling in the German ship *Herzog*. Mrs Helen P. Bright Clark, of Street who with her daughter Hilda went to Dover on January 5 1906 to meet her daughter Margaret and General Smuts, kept a diary and I quote some excerpts:

"Jan 6. Rough – doubts as to time but suddenly word that the *Herzog* was just coming in, so we rushed in a mighty wind to the end of the pier as she turned in. Hilda went in the tug but I thought it best to wait. Finally the tug went to the other pier so I had another struggle and met Margaret and General Smuts on shore – he quite young very simple and friendly. In great joy we got our lunch at a very nice and moderate place and then came away about 1.30, travelling in great comfort 2nd class and much attended by porters. Parted in London with our Boer friend . . . and then came home, thankful and all very pleased.

"Jan 10. Margaret went up to London to see Miss Hobhouse's friends and on Jan 12 she brought back Mr Smuts whom we all adopted warmly."

It was just at this time that Campbell-Bannerman went to the country to test public opinion and the Clarks and all the Liberals were overjoyed at the great Liberal gains. "Our guest (General Smuts) watched our excitement and joy with interest," reads a statement in the diary of January 14.

It was then that the Friends of Street, who had always opposed the Anglo-Boer War, met at a "time of thankfulness" that same Sunday of January 14 1906. It is the custom in the meetings of the Friends not to have a preacher or a formal sermon. Members simply get up when moved by the Spirit of God and contribute what they think to be worthwhile in their thoughts of experiences. And it was then that Smuts, sitting amongst these good people – the other England which produced an angel of mercy like Emily Hobhouse and the pro-Boers – was moved by the Spirit to rise to his feet and to say what was in his heart and on his mind. He spoke words of goodwill and goodness.

In her diary Mrs Clark made the following notes:

"Our guest spoke a few touching words of gratitude to English friends – very curious – and I think acceptable to most – alluding to passing thro the valley of shadows and to the effect to do the best thing so far as one could know the best."

In a side note next to a transcription of this passage about "English friends", Mrs Gillett had written "meaning those who had been dubbed 'pro-Boers' and those who had helped to improve the camps." Against the passage "acceptable to most", she had noted: "One or two present (at the meeting) had been supporters of the South African War and a little shocked at hearing a Boer speak to them."

It is recorded in the diary that Smuts left for London on the 10.30 of January 15. He was, however, back again on February 3 when he took long walks over the green countryside of Glastonbury – the legendary burial place of King Arthur and also of Joseph of Arimathaea who prepared the grave for Christ – and also visited the Cathedral of Wells nearby.

But between these dates, and after his impromptu speech to the Friends that Sunday morning in Street, Smuts had seen Campbell-Bannerman. I have not been able to ascertain what influence, if any, the Friends of Street, influential as they were in the financial and political life of the Liberal Party, had behind the scenes in preparing the ground for Smuts's talks with the Prime Minister. That is still a chapter in his life which remains to be investigated. But his mission was successful. The faith and humanity of Botha was matched by the generosity and goodwill of the pro-Boer elements in Britain and Smuts was chosen by destiny to unite them in a miracle of trust and magnanimity such as the world has seldom seen.

It was a deeply grateful and also proud Smuts who came back to the Clark family on Saturday, February 3, and who went for long walks with Mrs Clark and her two daughters. They "sat and talked till suppertime" and again that Sunday night "we sat talking". "Our attractive friend left us at 10.30 on February 5 much to general regret."

On February 10, the Clarks went to Waterloo in London to see Smuts off to join the *Carisbrook Castle*.

Smuts returned to South Africa with a new vision of unity and co-operation. After he came back to South Africa, Howard Pim, the accountant of Johannesburg who lost his position with the mines when he opposed the importation of Chinese labour to the gold mines, wrote to a Friend in England: "You know Smuts has changed a good deal. I think it did him good to meet the Quakers."[5]

The change was that he finally and irrevocably became a One-Stream South African instead of a Two-Stream leader. Botha started him on the golden road, Emily Hobhouse influenced him further by bringing home to him the sense that there was another England beside the jingo England. But it was the Friends, and especially the Clark and Gillett families, who confirmed and sealed his undying loyalty to the cause of goodwill and co-operation. For the rest of his life he maintained his contact with the Friends, on various occasions spoke in their meeting places, adopted their form of silent worship, although he never became a Friend himself, preferring to call himself a "Bush-Baptist".

Margaret Clark went back to South Africa and spent the year 1907 with Miss Hobhouse, living in Pretoria. There she constantly visited the Smuts family, but she travelled a great deal to places like Ficksburg, Winburg and Kroonstad helping the Boer women and educating the girls in the work of rehabilitation to be done. She returned to England towards the end of 1907 and became engaged to Arthur Gillett. They married in 1909 and settled first at Oxford and later, on the retirement of Mr Gillett from banking business, in Street.

Smuts himself was back again at Street in 1909 and this time he had the fruits of his earlier visit in his pocket in the form of the South Africa Act for a united South Africa. He became friends with Mr Gillett and afterwards Mr and Mrs Gillett were his lifelong friends, with whom he kept up a correspondence lasting until his death in 1950.

During the First World War, when he was a member of Lloyd George's War Cabinet, he spent most of his weekends at Oxford at the home of the Gilletts in Banbury Road, which became a second home to him. Mrs Gillett later became helpful to him in another way.

When he was a student at Cambridge Dr Wolstenholme, a don lecturing there gave the young Smuts a great deal of stimulus and help. Dr Wolstenholme took a special interest in Smuts, realizing his exceptional abilities, and after Smuts left Cambridge he selected current books and had them sent to Smuts in South Africa. This he did up to the time of his death in 1919 when Mrs Margaret Gillett decided voluntarily to take over this service to Smuts. When I visited her she showed me the little book with the names of all the books alphabetically arranged which she sent to Smuts from 1919 to April 1950. It was by an arrangement with a firm of booksellers that Mrs Gillett selected the books, knowing what he was interested in, and sometimes he sent her lists of what he wanted. The accounts were sent to him in South Africa and he paid personally for all the books. However, sometimes books were sent to him as gifts.[6]

A short inscription marks the frontispiece of the notebook: Catalogue of books supplied to J. C. S. by M. G. The first entered is Alexander: *Space, Time, Deity*, which was sent to Smuts in 1920 at a cost of £1.16.0. The second book was Ali's *Short History of the Saracens*. Then followed books on international affairs, science, literature and religion. Mrs Gillett states that the books reflect what she thought Smuts would be interested in, and she kept a careful list of all the titles, authors, prices and dates. Looking through the list it is obvious that his main interest concentrated on religion, philosophy and science and especially on the borderlands where the fields of religion, science and philosophy touch one another or overlap and it was precisely here that Smuts was to produce his outstanding contribution to a world where knowledge had become separated into watertight compartments in a large over-specialization by the experts. He wrote back discussing the books, giving his comments and his own views on a vast number of subjects.

It is the notes and memories of the Clark and Gillett families and these letters of Smuts which they have carefully kept, which today form the most important legacy of his real thoughts and which give the key to the wonderful inner mind where the great idea of Holism as a new master-key to knowledge was continually brooding and developing. In looking through the list of books, I came upon a small scribbled note in Smuts's handwriting asking for the following books:

The New Testament: A Reader's Guide, by C. A. Alington (G. Bell and Son). Then followed two scientific texts, a book on the *Legacy of the Ancient World* and the *Divine Personality and Human Life* by Professor Clement Webb. This was followed by Moffat: *Introduction to Literature of the New Testament*.[7]

Important as this personal service of Mrs Gillett was to a busy man like him, in widening his interest and keeping him informed of the intellectual developments, far more important was the wider influence which the contact with members of the Friends Society and especially their spirituality had on his thinking. His own spiritual values and his interest in religion made him receptive to their ideas. Through them he learnt to worship in places aside from churches and cathedrals, and through this the Friends helped the development of his sense of the spiritual in nature, a quality which came to him spontaneously, as he had already discerned it as a boy when he identified himself with the world "around me as with my own soul".

In discussing this aspect of his life with me Mrs Gillett remarked: "As life went on it was clear that he was finding spiritual stimulation in his communion with nature. It wasn't only for exercise that he went for walks. He found something deep and spiritual in nature. That was where he worshipped. That comes out in his letters.

"He was continually writing about the mountain, about the bush and about sleeping under the stars, which revealed his interest in the sense of the inner life, the sense of the spiritual in nature, and it was along those lines that he was continually developing his holistic ideas. This was evident both in his private conversations and in the letters which he wrote."[8]

But there was another sense in which his lifelong contact with the Society of Friends enriched his thought. The Friends have no rigid creed, no established preachers and little formal religion. They believe that Jesus the Spirit of God speaks in the human heart. They believe that Jesus Christ did not die, Christ did not die, but speaks in the spirit through human beings and is alive now and everywhere.

Smuts liked the Friends's way of worship based on silence. Although he could never become a member, rejecting their objections to war as an instrument of the state, he learnt through the Friends to get away from formal religion and he made the idea of the indwelling spirit of God in human beings his own. He worshipped with the Friends at Street and later at Oxford, but he learnt mostly to worship in the freedom of nature.

He never formally embraced Quakerism and never became a regular attendant, preferring to remain free and drawing upon that which corresponded with his own ideas and which he found valuable. And although in accord with most of what the Friends believed, he remained more philosophical about it than most of the Friends were able to be. In this connection he was especially at home with James Rendel Harris (1852-1941), director of the Friends' Settlement at Woodbrooke and afterwards curator of manuscripts at the John Rylands library at Manchester.

It was also in this way that his experience with the Friends proved valuable to the widening of his interests and the shaping of his outlook as a world leader. Before 1906 Smuts was a South African seeing the world from the narrow vision of the South African veld and kopjes. He fought for the freedom of his own people, and Botha eventually influenced him towards a greater South Africa embracing all South Africans.

But the Friends widened his horizon still further. They taught him that God is in all men and that His indwelling spirit pervades the whole world and the entire universe. And so through the Friends and his lifelong spiritual contact with them he became a true human being, regarding all human beings irrespective of race, creed or country as members of one great brotherhood, to be guided and governed as one family.

After 1906 he was ready for his task as a universal thinker and an international statesman. And it was as such that he eventually helped to shape the Commonwealth, the League of Nations and later the United Nations.

The remarkable aspect of his contact with the Friends and their influence on him, was, however, that even they did not and could not overcome his inborn neglect, call it his racial prejudice against the Blacks of Africa. The indwelling Spirit of God which pervades the entire world and all humanity somehow did not include the Black races, probably in the current perception because they were so low on the scale of civilization. They were the White Man's burden rather than God's children. His South African outlook in this regard remained in spite of the Friends.

CHAPTER EIGHT

The holistic man

"Morrison, it is a great thing to be a man – a great thing."

When unveiling the Sir Jacob Epstein memorial of Field Marshal Smuts, Mr W. S. Morrison, the Speaker of the House of Commons, recalled that these were the last words Smuts spoke to him on his last visit to England in the summer of 1948.

And they sum up Smuts's attitude not only to himself, but toward his fellowmen of all nations and creeds. To him not race or nationality, not learning or beliefs mattered, but manhood. Being a man, a whole man with all that that implies in courage and character, dignity and freedom to follow his own inner conviction, was to him the epitome of all existence.

In his own life, in the power and richness of his own personality, he revealed the same qualities which he looked for in other harmonious personalities.

Yet he did not attain his ultimate maturity easily. There are some who like to boast that they have never changed. They hail it as an achievement that they have never departed from their views or deviated from their way of life. They are the self-confessed static personalities.

Smuts was not one of these. His was a growing, living, developing personality, different in various periods of his life, yet always retaining the essential characteristics and always becoming fuller, mellower and richer as life moved on.

In the days of his youth this slender boy with a hereditary background of diabetes in his family attracted little attention as a personality. His intellectual capacity was notable, but neither at Stellenbosch nor at Cambridge was he regarded as a leader or an outstanding personality.

His son Jannie, in an excusable excess of filial admiration, has denied the description by various biographers of his father as gaunt and taciturn, as hollow-faced and serious, or physically feeble and unsociable. He describes his father in youth as a slender young man, 5 foot nine inches tall with blue eyes, fair wavy hair and a transparent skin. "Photographs show him as attractive in appearance," he writes, "with certainly no hint of gauntness. Perhaps his high and slightly prominent cheekbones might suggest that; maybe his over-developed orbital bosses, the forehead bumps above his eyes, would tend to make him look formidable. In build he was slender though the sloping shoulders belied their breadth. His chest was big and deep.

"I think my father must have been a presentable and comely youth, fair and clean looking, and serious of countenance. Not for nothing did those blue eyes of his develop the surrounding deep puckers that denote a sense of humour.

"Old friends of his, especially my mother, deny that he was unsociable or unfriendly. They did not even notice that he was overserious, for in the sleepy God-fearing hamlets of the Boland of those days, it was the normal demeanour of the people. The gaiety of Cape Town of the earlier days of the British occupation so well described by Lady Anne Barnard (1750-1825) never touched the more serious hinterland to the north. Farms were too far apart and people too hard-working to indulge in an extravagance of pleasure."[1]

Jannie is prepared to concede that his father took life a little too seriously, "yet in every other respect he was a pleasant person and a good companion".

But good as they are, these attributes are not what made him the magnetic powerful personality that he was. We must penetrate deeper into the mystery of his life to discover the secret of his personality.

Here we come to the fundamental change, of which his family and especially his children were probably not aware, that came over him and shaped his outlook and his personality. We must remember that Smuts in his youth was essentially an Afrikaner with the characteristics of the Boer people, their God-fearing seriousness, their insularity, their hard Calvinistic outlook instinctively part of his make-up and tradition. Endowed with great intellect and having absorbed the open-minded attitude of a true student and the liberalizing influences of the wider world, he returned from Cambridge in 1895 prepared for a wider friendliness and co-operation with his English fellow-countrymen. He had already as a student at Cambridge written an essay of 35 pages on "*The Condition of South African Literature*" in which he expounded his basic idea that the English and the Afrikaners must work together to form one nation. Once the nation had been made, he argued, its literature would grow to maturity in and perform the work of nation-making.[2]

That explains why in October 1895, when he made his debut as a politician in South Africa, he turned his back on the parish pump politics of the ultra-conservative Boers and took his stand on the side of Cecil John Rhodes with his dreams of a greater unified Southern Africa. He himself later explained that he began "to dream of a great South Africa in which the English and Boer peoples would dwell together in happy concord."

He therefore framed his first speech to "set forth the general principles of a broader common political platform on a reconciled basis for both the white peoples of the Cape Colony".[3]

That was his ideal, learned from books and culled from youthful dreams. But the reality was different.

Smuts was to have this outlook tested by betrayal, by hardships, by personal and national suffering on a scale which shocked the whole civilized world. During the next ten years, from January 1896 to January 1906, the events of the struggle between Boer and Briton, the hatred and sorrows, the ruin and devastation of the land and of men's souls caught his sensitive spirit in a maelstrom of events of which he was quite often at the centre. On many occasions he stared death in the face. He suffered grievous personal loss in the death of his young son during the war.

He was separated from his wife for two long years when she was in a British refugee camp at Pietermaritzburg. He undertook the most arduous military expedition with a handful of ragged Boers into the very heart of the enemy country in the Cape Colony and he saw his men, dear and faithful comrades, shot and wounded and killed next to him. He himself miraculously escaped death in battle, but he nearly died of plant poisoning when, in hunger, he ate "Boesmans Brood" (the fruit of the poisonous cycad *Encephalartos altensteinii* which looks like a pineapple). Afrikaner and Boer that he was in his deeper marrow, he had to experience the utter depths of humiliation which comes from the defeat of a small people fighting for its freedom and its soul. After the war, when ruin and tragedy surrounded him and his people, he had to watch while the new masters added injury to insult and humiliation by introducing Chinese labour to the gold mines of the Rand, to disturb still further the troubled sea of racial differences in South Africa.

Smuts in a letter to Emily Hobhouse referred to this as "more disaster" for the Boer people. "Do you think it likely that, if the Liberals get into power, they will stop Chinese importation? If they don't, God alone help us! There is more to be feared from the despair than from the hopes of brave men . . . I see no ray of light in the future."[4]

Suffering and tragedy, ruin and despair formed indeed the crucible which shaped his character and tested his theory of South Africanism expounded with such ease in October 1895. Failure and ruin were written large over the promise of his youth and early personality.

Under these powerful conflicts and stresses the easy theorizer reverted in many ways to the narrow nationalism of his people. He wrote a powerful treatise against British rule in South Africa under the title *A Century of Wrong*.[5] It was the Afrikaner's indictment of British Imperialism, and when he invaded the Cape with his brave band of 362 men (against a British force of fully 35 000 men) he exhorted his men like a patriot from the Old Testament. To him nationalism and religion were one. He was the true pure Afrikaner who fought for his liberty and his country. How was the great change brought about?

He himself, in a remarkable analysis of character many years later in discussing the life of his great friend, Dr Frederick Charles Kolbe, pointed out that tragedy, when it comes to a deep and sensitive soul, may end either in spiritual death or in second birth, in being reborn in the spirit.

Kolbe, son of a strict Protestant family and one of the greatest intellects that the Afrikaner nation has produced, was touched in the core of his being by a love affair in Europe which to his sensitive soul became an overpowering experience. When his beloved became a Catholic and finally took the veil, Kolbe broke with his Protestant past, became a Catholic and decided to become a priest even at the cost of what had been dearest to him.

With keen insight into the spiritual and mental change which this must have meant in Kolbe, Smuts gave this significant analysis of the deeper psychological forces which came into play.

"Here is the Rubicon of the soul, the passage from one life to the other, the region which forms one of the sources of the higher religions. The renunciation became for Kolbe the new beginning, the new love and ambition, the dedication to the highest.

"What suffering he must have endured, what depths he must have sounded before he reached the summits of the new life of the reborn! It is the sort of drama of the soul which no pen has written or can write, but which the select spirits of the world pass through in their experience of the great passage. The new man emerges from the chrysalis of the old. I am using the language of religion and science for something which in itself is essentially indescribable."[6]

Did Smuts have a similar experience of national and personal tragedy from which his soul rose phoenix-like from the ruins of Afrikanerdom to true South Africanism and ultimately to true and all-embracing humanity?

As one who himself has crossed the Rubicon of Afrikanerdom to a broader South Africanism, who has made the passage not without much mental suffering and renunciation before spiritual acceptance became possible, I venture to suggest that Smuts here described an experience which he himself knew.

The conflicts and tragedies of the Boer War and its ruinous aftermath touched him in his deepest soul. And this brought the great change in his life, the casting off of his old self, the development from the Boer fighter and thinker into the greater, fuller, richer South African personality with his acceptance of the truth of all existence. "I learnt to bow my head to the inevitable," he said in effect many years later.

To me this is the crucial change in his life and personality.

I have already discussed the external forces which influenced him during this period of growth and change, especially the influence of General Louis Botha and of the Friends in England. It was fortunate for him that life in this period of tragedy and despair brought him into contact with these forces for good.

Without them he might not have made the great passage so smoothly and so quickly. And yet with his fine intellect and his deep spirituality the change in him was inevitable. Smuts could never have remained in the narrow confines of the nationalism of his own race.

Thus we find the new outlook and the new personality emerging from the personal and national betrayals, tribulations and tragedies which rocked South Africa in the decade after 1896.

Dorothy F. Wilson, in her *Smuts of South Africa: Soldier, and Peace-maker*, tells how she first became interested in Smuts.

One evening she was in the Australian animal sanctuary at Badger Creek, Healesville where she met the honorary curator, Mr R. C. Eadie, another world wanderer, a man who knew the world and its wonders.

She asked him what was the most wonderful thing that had ever happened to him. "This is what he told me. He had been born in South Africa, not Australia, and he was a young man when the Boer War drew to its close. The thing he would never forget was the night when the Boer leaders met in a tent by the Vaal River to make their final decision whether they would accept peace terms or not."

"The place was strictly guarded," said Robert Eadie, "but I was determined to get near and hear all I could, sentries or not. It was getting dark and a mist came up from the river to help me. I crept along on my stomach, without making a sound, for I was trained in bushcraft. At last, with heart beating fast, I got to the tent – I lifted a flap. Most of the men there were half-starved and in rags. A few wanted to fight at any price, but most knew it couldn't be done and they were broken men. Then came what I think was the most wonderful moment of my life."

"My host's face lit up at the very memory of it," writes Miss Wilson. "If ever there was love and hero worship in a man's face, it was in his. He described how in the midst of these broken men a young man with golden hair and erect carriage 'stood up like a young god' (Eadie's words) and spoke such words of courage, truth and faith; of realism and inspiration that the whole atmosphere was transformed; broken men lifted their heads and squared their shoulders, the issue was faced, and the decision was taken which ended the war. 'The speaker was Smuts. 'Oom Jannie,' said Eadie, and went on murmuring the words softly and lovingly under his breath, 'Oom Jannie, Oom Jannie'."[7]

What Smuts said at this historic occasion to the Boer delegates and what swayed them to negotiate for peace, was inspired by his grasp of the implications of the events shaping the destiny of South Africa.

He felt it was better to negotiate an orderly peace than to be crushed later and have harsh terms thrust upon them.

"The great danger before this meeting is that it will come to a decision purely from the military point of view . . . If we consider it only as a military matter, then I must admit we can still go on with the struggle . . . But we are not here as an army. We are here as people . . . Everyone here represents the Afrikaner people . . . Burghers, we decided to stand to the bitter end. Let us now, like men, admit that the end has come for us, come in a more bitter shape than we ever thought. We bow to God's will," he told the assembled men.

We have another vivid insight into his hurt and humiliation in an anecdote which Mr Ramsay MacDonald related in the House of Commons in 1917 when Smuts was honoured as a member of the British War Cabinet. MacDonald told how in 1902 he found himself one night under the roof that had been battered and broken and smashed by the British Army. It was Smuts's home in Sunnyside, Pretoria.

"He took me by the hand when I went inside his house and, almost broken-hearted, pointed out to me how his books had been used during his absence, and how the leaves had been torn out and left charred and burned, having been used for lighting pipes and cigars by soldiers.

"My heart was full of indignation because in those days I was called pro-Boer and I had suffered the humiliation and indignity of having meetings broken up, and his heart was full of indignation because he had been leading against us in the field and had been one of the most successful generals against us and his cause seemed lost."

It was no wonder that the young, overserious, proud, aloof Smuts of those days of tragedy and defeat was described as the Job of the Afrikaner people. Like Job he might have cried out: "My soul is weary of my life, I will give free course to my complaint, I will speak in the bitterness of my soul."

But like Job, after years of brooding and despair, he learnt to accept the will of God, he bowed to the inevitable and God in His time rewarded him with greater gifts of friendship, understanding and personality.

It is this acceptance of a higher purpose, of God's will, that gives us the clue to this great change in his life, to the rebirth of his spirit, the rising of his personality out of despair to new heights of wisdom and nobility.

The German author Walter Bargatzsky has grasped this truth in his analysis published under the title *Smuts, Sieg eines Besiegten* (Smuts, Victory of a Vanquished).

Bargatzsky saw the greatness of Smuts in this ability to conquer himself and to lift himself out of defeat to triumph through humility and piety.

He quotes Smuts as saying: "*Ich habe in diesem Leben gelernt, dass Demütigung und Ungnade mitunter notwendig sind, um der Öffentlichkeit einen grossen Dienst zu erweisen.*" (In this life I have learnt that humiliation and unpopularity are, from time to time, necessary to be of great service in public life.)

He himself sees the victory of Smuts in this self-sacrifice and self-conquest. "*In dieser Selbstaufopferung, in dieser Selbstüberwindung sehe ich seinen Sieg, der einzige und wahrhafte Sieg, der dem Besiegten verbleibt. Sie allein geben ihm die Macht, Frieden zu stiften, und sie allein geben ihm den Frieden, wieder mächtig zu sein.*" (In this self-sacrifice and this self-conquest I see his victory; the only true victory that remains to the conquered. This alone gives him the power to establish peace and only this gives him the peace to be powerful again.)

Bargatzsky grasps the crucial point that this can only happen through religion, through piety. "*Nur der Fromme kann die Demut finden seine Niederlage einzugestehen, und den Mut, sich von Neuem emporzurichten.*" (Only the pious can find the humility to admit their defeat and the courage to rise above it.) "'*For I am a Chirstman,' sagte Smuts,*" and Bargatzsky adds his own addition "*denn ich bin ein Christ*".[8]

It is in this sense of victory through defeat, of victory over himself through tragedy, of humility through humiliation that Smuts revealed his true greatness. This is where he differed from others and where he finally became the great personality with a message to a world in conflict.

He took his stand next to the truly great. Walt Whitman wrote of Abraham Lincoln after the catastrophe at Bull Run when the Union armies were defeated and humiliated:

"If there was nothing else of Abraham Lincoln for history to stamp him with, it is enough to send him with this wreath to the memory of all future time, that he endured that hour, that day, bitterer than gall – indeed a crucifixion day – that it did not conquer him – that he stemm'd it, and resolv'd to lift himself and the Union out of it."

This is the acme of true greatness. If Smuts had done nothing else in life, if his career had come to an end after 1906, this capacity to rise above the humiliation and defeat, the personal sorrows and tragedies of the Boer War and its aftermath, would be sufficient to stamp him with greatness, for out of the ashes of defeat he and Botha brought victory and freedom. And not only victory over and freedom from the victorious enemy, but what is more important, victory over himself to enter a new life of service and to carry a new light to his devastated country.

We get another clue to the change in his life in a revealing passage in his book *Holism and Evolution*. He wrote of the tremendous effect of the "moral awakening" in the life of a person when he first hears the trumpet call of duty. It is then that the still small voice of the inner life comes to the fore, and conscience and duty take over to bring moderation, self-control, tranquillity of the soul and finally that peace of God which passes all understanding. It is then that a person learns to be himself with perfect honesty, integrity and sincerity and "earnest men find that to gain their life they must lose it, that not in self, but in the whole (including the self) lies the only upward road to the sunlit summits".[9]

Only one who himself has had such an experience can describe it and draw a lesson from it.

Smuts, like Botha, in this inner transformation lost his Afrikaner outlook to gain a new South Africanism, lost his self as a Boer warrior to find his duty in service to his country and to all mankind, lost his enslavement to hatred of the enemy to find true freedom as a personality. This was the great change in his life, the foundation of his inspiring personality, for in bridging the gulf between self and sacrifice, between egotism and duty, between nationalism and humanity, he entered the larger and more rewarding world of the spirit. And having found the freedom of his personality growing, not according to selfish interest, social usage or patriotic convention but according to the dictates of his inner conscience as a human being, Smuts found his true and higher self.

Later in his *Holism and Evolution* he was to explain the changeover in the life of a personality.

"Learn to be yourself with perfect honesty, integrity and sincerity; let universal Holism realise its highest in you as a free whole of Personality; and all the rest will be added unto you – peace, joy, blessedness, happiness, goodness and all the other prizes of life. Nay more: the great evils of life – pain, suffering and sorrow – will only in the end serve to accelerate the holistic progress of the Personality, will be assimilated and transformed in the spiritual alchemy of the Personality and will feed the flame of the pure and free soul."[10]

That was what happened in his own life.

I have purposely stressed this aspect in the evolution of his character, for I do not think sufficient attention has so far been paid to the importance of the breakaway of a person from his race or group to embrace a wider loyalty. It entails high sacrifice and demands character and discipline. The transformed person must learn to suffer insults and misrepresentation, and having discarded the emotional and sentimental appeal of group feelings, remain true to the dictates of his higher conscience and of his reason. It is a hard and difficult path which only exceptional characters can follow.

These personalities to my mind and in my experience are the happiest, freest, most enlightened and most dependable in the great conflicts and crises of life. They are rare souls who, having been lifted above the traditional loyalties of their tribe, group or race, achieve that which is ideal, their true humanity. Such a one was Smuts, above and beyond tribal and racial loyalties, strong and sure to be himself, to brave and ignore the attacks and insults of his own people, and to live out his full humanity.

Did this victory over circumstances and over himself come through a struggle or without it?

Alan Paton assumes that Smuts attained his sublime certitude on life "as a gift and not as a reward or a consequence" of struggle.[11] I cannot agree and I think events and his letters of the period support my view. Like most of us, Smuts was the victim of external events. He knew despair, he knew struggle and inner conflict.

He faced squarely up to it all and in the end he was vouchsafed a spiritual victory which was in tune with his great natural qualities and which helped to form his serene, majestic personality.

He himself in unveiling a monument at Frederikstad on July 19 1905, spoke what must have been in his soul: "It is the man who has been cleansed in the fires of adversity by whom a nation's greatness shall be built up." And to stress his acceptance of the higher powers moving him like a Job, he added these words: "God hath taken our liberty from us – God is great."[12]

Henceforth the new man, cleansed and purified, appears on the scene, reborn and with his spirit set free to reveal his truly remarkable personality and his leadership of men.

I have dwelt at length on this transformation in the life of Smuts because to me it is the key to his greatness. It is only by grasping this change in the deep core of his being that we can fathom his true personality. This is what gave wholeness to his character and to all its manifold facets. N. Levi, his biographer, must have had something like this in mind when in 1917 he asked for a comprehensive work on Smuts to take the place of the procession of disjointed images. "Alas, the artist who will create this has not yet risen among us. It will require a Thorvaldsen – nay, a Rodin, a modern – to draw with tentacles of intuition the innermost out of Smuts; to visualize for others, less gifted, by the aid of delicate sense and robust craftsmanship."[13]

Levi himself gave this summing-up of his subject: "His is a clear-cut personality, in spite of the antinomy that seems to exist between the different parts. His great master, Kant, demolished time and space, but the good people of Königsberg set their watches by the little professor's clock-like appearance in their streets. So you will discover in Smuts a contempt for amateurs and theorists, a strong predilection for empiricism, coupled with a genuine belief in pure science. He is surely the most practical idealist, the most martial metaphysician that ever lived. He indulges in day-dreams, but rises in the dead of night to turn them into facts. The subtle lawyer in him has not made him a legalist. Chockful of sentiment he knows no sentimentality. In Parliament he once spoke of conscientious objectors as 'the salt of the earth'. Outside, he peppers them. He is as old as the hills, and as young, as fresh."[14]

But these are externals of his personality, however interesting they are. The core of his being, the secret to his personality came through his religion and his development from an Afrikaner to a South African to a universal man. Here he grew into the ever larger whole as a personality which eventually became the pattern of his Holism. Thereafter his rise to fame was as rapid as his personality revealed itself in its full flowering. He bore the fruits of his conversion. How harmoniously and gloriously his own personality evolved out of this is revealed in a pen sketch we have of him which I discovered in a dusty reprint from *The Church Family Newspaper* of June 1 1917, published at Cambridge.

As a member of Lloyd George's Supreme War Cabinet, Smuts visited his old college at Cambridge in May 1917 during the stalemate on the Western Front. The Master of Magdalene College, Mr A. C. Benson, who was present at a luncheon at which Smuts was a guest, gave a rare and delightful picture of Smuts who was 47 at the time. He described him as a "strangely youthful-looking figure".

"I doubt if I should have guessed the General to be much over 30. His light curling hair and beard hardly concealed his features. He looked about him with a boyish air of animation and curiosity and pleasure, and his blue eyes glanced quickly this way and that. He talked gaily and eagerly to those next to him. He seemed to take everything in and to enjoy everything. There was not a trace of care or weariness about him, though his days of late must have been full of serious consultations, social engagements, public speeches, hard official work.

"He did not look quite like an Englishman, but still less did he resemble my idea of a Boer. It came into my head that if I had been asked to guess what he was, I should have imagined that he might be a Scandinavian by race, while his wholly unembarrassed air, his responsive courtesy, the entire absence of any trace of self-consciousness under many curious and enthusiastic glances, would have made me think he was a prince of Royal blood, travelling more for recreation than on business.

"Then Smuts rose. He looked around the hall with an alert and friendly glance of pleasure and amusement, which instantly put him in close touch with his audience. Then came another surprise. He began to speak in a quick, natural voice, with a slightly foreign accent, hardly seeming to exert himself, yet perfectly audible all over the room. It was not an oration at all, but more like a friendly conversation. It seemed, as he did it, to be the easiest thing in the world. But it was a triumph of hidden art. His points were clearly made, but not by an accumulation of intricate sentences. Indeed the sentences were short and concise, with emphatic little repetitions of important phrases, but all in the simplest terms, while his mood varied swiftly from serious to humorous. The emotion was never tense nor contrived, always genuine and sincere, while the humour gave no sense of preparation, but was as if it just overflowed out of a mind at ease.

"It really seemed like a man thinking aloud and doing it with a natural grace and beauty; indeed, the grace and restraint of the language indicated a mind of a high order, with a poetical touch about it, and in complete command of its resources. It was not literary and still less academic, but it had a perfect artistic appositeness and appropriateness to the exact occasion. It did not give a feeling of calculation, but rather as being the unconsidered utterance of one who knew well what he desired to say, and trusted to the sympathy and inspiration of the moment.

"It caught the spirit of the hour, and seemed more like a confiding interpretation than a diplomatic utterance, and with just the right touch of lightness for a social gathering. Most striking of all was the total absence of the sense that he was undertaking a serious responsibility, of course, yet all was said with a lively enjoyment as if in a holiday mood, and yet wholly without levity – indeed with touches of fine emotion.

"He did not speak as though he were a man with weighty affairs on hand, or as if he were the object of general interest. He spoke with great and vivid emotion, not mournfully, but hopefully of the service of liberty as the greatest cause the world had ever seen.

"What was the special charm of it all?

"It was the charm of contrast. One knew of the General's daring and brilliant strategy, of his amazing feats of warfare, of his hairbreadth escapes. One knew of him as a profound and learned lawyer of varied experience. One recognized in him a statesman of marvellous insight and resources. Yet he stood there, a slenderly built and active soldier, without any sign of care or anxiety or endurance with a dancing light of gaiety and interest in his eyes, his small mobile lips uttering these simple and graceful sentences, but without preoccupation, or nervousness, or anxiety as to how his words would be received, and more as if the whole affair had been arranged for some other purpose and as if he had all the pleasure and none of the responsibility of it.

"He seemed to me the embodiment of grace and sympathy and freedom. He had no touch of resentment or suspicion about him. He was not there to conciliate or to ingratiate himself, or to persuade. He was just a friend among friends, entirely trustful and kindly and grateful, full of delight at the familiar scene, and with all misunderstanding and hostility and passion swept away.

"'You came down on a small nation too severely, and laid the Imperial paw on too heavily,' he said at the luncheon with smiling vehemence, 'you used unnecessary force – I thought so then, and I think so still.' But all had been forgiven, and better still forgotten.

"It seemed to me indeed the perfection of civilization to be thus able not only to respect and regard an old foe, but, though vanquished and overthrown, to meet him and greet him, without a single thought of bitterness or spite or vengeance of the mind. It was a beautiful spirit, I felt. It seemed to me to be so fine in its instructive sympathy, and to show a heart that did not need to make a reluctant resolve to be loyal, but that rose nobly and simply into a clearer air, threw the old strife and sorrow away, looked happily at the present and confidently to the future. A reasoned and honest loyalty is fine enough, even if it is reluctantly adopted. But this kind of gay and unsuspicious trust, full of deep seriousness, and yet wholly true and unresentful seemed to me the finest flower of honesty and chivalry and human brotherliness. But how this noble impression, so genuine, so unaffected, so peaceable, was conveyed, that must remain a mystery. I can imagine a man thus presenting himself with a sincere good will, and yet being so afraid of the pitfalls of speech that he could hardly venture to utter it. But General Smuts seemed afraid of nothing, to be haunted by no fears or shadows, but to come with a boyish freshness combined with a deep experience, to sweep away with a quick smile, a natural gesture, and a few sentences of careless beauty and simplicity, all the complications of race and conflict and policy to meet a triumphant opponent of past days with perfect confidence and reassuring good will."[15]

Here we see a Smuts entering that higher sphere of personality where man rises above himself to true civilization and true universal humanity. The foe becomes the friend and sheds all bitterness to taste the full sweetness of life even amidst overwhelming danger.

He became a "universal man" as Shakespeare, Goethe and Leonardo da Vinci were universal men and as Dr Albert Schweitzer was a universal man of our generation. Like these men he grew beyond his own environs and his own race to become a full personality irrespective of time or space. Like them he followed the dictates of his stern, glowing sense of duty and again like these Olympian giants his mind ranged over a wide field of subjects. He shone as a politician in his own country, a statesman for the Commonwealth, a great leader of mankind in general. He became an outstanding soldier in war, a notable student and philosopher who found time to explore the secrets of existence and evolved a new key to their understanding. He grasped and practised religion with humility in his heart, a willingness to apply the teachings of Jesus, and awe before the great mysteries of the universe.

Alan Paton spoke of him as though he partook of some quality of the divine. Jan Hofmeyr, another of the geniuses produced by the Afrikaner nation, regarded him with veneration "stronger than respect and different from love, because of the added component of awe".[16]

What was the power of his magnetism for all who came into contact with him, for kings and the great as well as his lowly burghers and servants?

Paton in his analysis thinks it was the conviction in the hearts of all those under the influence of Smuts that he enjoyed some great measure of immunity in life. "Is it not true that the human world of today is afflicted, more than anything else, by the feeling of so many men that the world is out of control, that events and circumstances have mastered them?

"Smuts gave men the impression that he and event and circumstance marched together, he bowing to their inevitability, they bowing to his creative genius."[17]

Lesser men and women instinctively in the dangers and confusion of life turn towards such a man "who marches with event and circumstance as though he were their equal", and he becomes their leader.

"Many a life," says Paton, "is tragic because a man does not know what he is. He is a man of affairs, but wishes he had been a poet. He is carnal, but wishes he had been religious. Religious, he wishes he had been carnal. So bound by the one and desiring the other, he is nothing at all. But Smuts combined and contained them all, and continuing, so also continent. He possessed them, and was not possessed by them. He was, as we say, the master of himself."[18]

This masterly analysis illuminates one of the most powerful elements of Smuts's leadership. That is his certitude, his self-assurance.

He was not only able to find the way of life, but he had the confidence to take it.

Having resolved his struggle, there were in him no conflicts to confuse his thinking or to paralyse his actions. This final certainty was the outstanding impression he made as a personality. It was this characteristic more than anything else which drew men of all nations and races to him in the knowledge that here was a man who was master of life and not its slave. It was for this that his ragged burghers gave their lives and their all under his command in the Anglo-Boer War.

It was also this mastery of events, ideas and ideals which made him an outstanding leader in two world wars and in the uneasy peace between them. Smuts knew the way and he walked the way sure and serene and majestic.

This very sureness and serenity was also the secret of his almost childlike simplicity. He was content with simple, natural things. He was happiest with his family and on his farm or in the veld or on the mountains of Africa. He loved children and became one with them in playfulness and naturalness. These things constantly renewed him as his personality cast a glow over them.

But he was human and, as human beings are, sometimes inconsistent. He hated telephones and yet once when I telephoned him for a press release and offered to come to his farm at Irene, he pointed out to me the value of telephones to save people trouble. On that occasion he was all for using the inventions of modern science.

Friendly and accessible at times, he became aloof and unpredictable at others. I once took an American friend, George Dunning, to him in his office in Parliament in Cape Town and he forgot the world and all its problems, he forgot time and duty as with glowing eyes and radiant personality he explained to the two of us the wonders of life in Africa. It was shortly after his return from San Francisco, where he helped to form the United Nations. "The problem of modern man is to get away from the pressures of his fellowmen. In America that is their greatest problem. To escape they have to crowd into cinemas, into holiday camps, on the roads in automobiles. But here in Africa man can still sleep under the stars, commune with nature and its primeval forces, for Africa was the mother of all, the first home of *Homo sapiens*." We were spellbound under his words and his personality as he held forth as if we were a crowded gathering or a learned assembly.

Yet his mood could change. In New York in October 1946 at the first session of the United Nations, I sat next to him in the South African section. I plagued him with a few questions whilst the Polish delegate held forth. Suddenly he turned his steely eyes hard on me and said to me: "Don't be a nuisance. Don't bother me. I have work to do here. I must follow the debates. Leave me." I crawled away like a naughty child.

Again in Parliament on another occasion when I approached him to vet an article on his visit to the farm of his birth, he instantly became fiercely angry with me. He resented this prying into his earliest life, his sacred memories. To Sir Alfred Hennessey, who accompanied him to the family farm he pointed out the black burning marks of the fire sparks on the wooden floor of their modest farmhouse on Boplaas. My intrusion into the private world of his youth must have hurt him to the quick. "This is pure nonsense. I have never heard of such nonsense. Get out of here," was his tart and angry send-off.

Yet on other occasions he wasted precious time to explain to me who was of little significance in his scheme of things, the importance of stirring events. The day after Rommel overpowered the British forces at Sidi Rezegh he took me to the huge military map in his office in the Union Buildings in Pretoria and with bright eyes, perfectly serene and composed, he explained calmly and reasonably what General Ritchie should have done to avoid the disaster. It was a great disaster. It could have meant the loss of North Africa, but talking to him, hearing him explain with a smile on his eager face, there was no hint to me of despair or even of disaster. He was sure of ultimate victory. This was a minor setback. His hope, his faith and his optimism were supreme.

In August 1948, shortly after his disastrous defeat by Dr Malan and the National Party, I saw him in his suite in the Mount Nelson Hotel in Cape Town. He was defeated because, among other reasons, he neglected to unite with Mr Havenga, the leader of the Afrikaner Party, and the latter promptly joined up with Dr Malan.

As Editor of his Party organ, I had started a belated movement to wean Havenga away from the Malan group and this brought me into conflict with Hofmeyr, Smuts's deputy, who lectured me about the stupidity of co-operating with "a fascist" as he called Havenga, remembering the latter's close association with the Ossewa Brandwag. In great anger and disgust Hofmeyr sent me to see Smuts. Smuts received me kindly.

"My son, if you knew as much about men and politics as I," he explained with true interest and friendly animation, "you would have nothing to do with a man like Havenga. Havenga is not a leader. You can never depend upon him. He will say one thing when with you today and tomorrow when he is with someone else, just the opposite. Leave him. If it was General Hertzog – ah, there was a leader, a man you could trust to the last. If he gave you his word you could count on it, but not Havenga." I yielded to his reasoning, accepted his arguments and left with a better insight into the nature and character of politics.

I shall always remember the second last time I saw him. He was in pain, his eightieth birthday was nearing when he had a coronary thrombosis. All over the country money was being collected to build him a little cottage on the slopes of Table Mountain near the beautiful garden of Kirstenbosch where he loved to roam. Some of his old burghers from the Free State had donated a tidy sum and they wrote asking me to arrange that one of their sons, a Fouche from Smithfield, who then was a student at Cape Town University, personally hand over the money to Smuts. We saw him in his office as Leader of the Opposition in Parliament in Cape Town. He was deeply, visibly moved. His blue eyes danced in their sockets and his ruddy face glowed with happiness. He was supremely happy to be thus remembered and honoured by his Free State burghers. "You Free Staters are the salt of the earth, the best I have come across," he said. He leaned with his hand against the door post and with his head on his arm, being in too much pain to stand upright. Yet standing there he was the picture of the happiest, kindliest, friendliest being on earth.

In our present state and in our present world when such a man appears he is a miracle, and men will follow him and if need be die for him, recognizing in him the fulfilment that might have been in themselves.

Alan Paton summed it all up in these revealing words: "Smuts might have held aloof from his men on commando and sat on a rock reading incomprehensible books, but he could say a word, make a gesture, that would quicken men's blood and raise their eyes to God knows what stars. Even the great thought that he was great."[19]

Harold Nicolson in remembering Smuts described him as "a splendid wide-horizoned man".

Here was truly a Holistic Man.[20]

PART TWO

Philosophy

CHAPTER NINE

Background of his ideas

Who was the first Holist?

Smuts assumed that he was and there is no doubt that he coined the word Holism from the original Greek.

But shortly after his book on Holism appeared, his friend Monsignor Kolbe traced the holistic idea back to earliest Christianity and Smuts in reply wrote:

"It was a matter of great gratification to me that on the appearance of *Holism*, Monsignor Kolbe at once acknowledged himself a Holist. I hailed him as a convert. There I was wrong, and he has written this interesting Essay to prove that Holism is older than my book, that it is at least as old as Christianity, and that St Paul was the greatest Holist of them all. So be it. I waive all claim to priority before such august competition!"[1]

There are others too who have pointed to a variety of great minds who saw life as a whole. Maurice Morgan, for example, as early as 1777 attributes the greatness of Shakespeare to his wonderful faculty for constructing his characters as "wholes".

He pointed out that for Shakespeare it was not enough to have formed his characters in the most perfect truth and coherence. He also possessed the faculty for compressing his own spirit into these images and of giving animation to the forms.

This was not done from without; Shakespeare must have felt every varied situation from within. Through this ability Shakespeare's characters, which are seen only in part, are yet capable of being unfolded and understood as a whole – every part being in fact relative, and implying all the rest.

"If the characters of Shakespeare are thus whole, and as it were original, whilst those of other writers are mere imitation, it may be fit to consider them rather as historic than dramatic beings, and, when occasion requires, to account for their conduct from the *whole* of character, from general principles, from latent motives, and from policies not avowed."[2]

There are others too who perhaps predate Smuts as Holists. Alfred Adler, the psychologist, was probably one. Although analytical like Freud he nevertheless placed more emphasis on the person as a whole, and upon the appearance of *Holism*, he claimed it as "the key of our science".

Professor Koffka of Berlin with his Gestalt Psychology may be another. Smuts himself acknowledged how he read Koffka's *Growth of Mind* with deep interest and profit. Like Koffka he held that "in some mysterious way structure and pattern are at the very root of the universe and of mind".

Robert Bridges, the poet, declared that his own *Testament of Beauty*, written in 1929, was a poetical version of an almost identical idea.

Similarly the idea has at various times and by various writers, including Smuts, been traced back to Plato, to Aristotle and to St Paul and it will probably help to understand it better if we put it in its proper historical and philosophical setting. This may enable us at the same time to evaluate the place of Smuts in the sphere of knowledge.

H. G. Wells, in his *Outline of History*, has shown that the sixth century BC was the first great century of ideas, when men's minds from the Nile to the heart of China were astir. In that first age of questioning and inquiry we find the Hebrew prophet Isaiah teaching his great moral and spiritual truths to shattered and captive Jewry in Babylon. The Greek thinker Heraclitus (±513 BC) in the same century was carrying on his speculative intellectual inquiries into the nature of the material world at Ephesus in Asia Minor. This was followed by the Jewish moralists, Isaiah, Jeremiah and others who evolved a new system of direct moral responsibility of mankind to the one eternal and universal God, and by the philosophers of Ancient Greece who were tracing the human mind in a new spirit of bold and fearless intellectual inquiry into the universe and man's place in it. Socrates (450-380 BC) became the first great searcher after truth for truth's sake, even though it cost him his life.[3] Plato (427-348 BC) followed by examining systematically the methods of human thinking and man's first political institutions, while Aristotle (384-322 BC) became the father of science with his first systematic collection of knowledge.[3]

Smuts admitted his great debt to the Jewish moralists as to the Greek thinkers. He showed, for instance, in his *Holism and Evolution*, how Plato presented the human soul as an absolute, indestructible and unchangeable whole and used its indivisibility as an argument to prove its immortality. In his preface to the German edition of *Holism and Evolution* in 1938 – 12 years after the first appearance of the original – he again drew attention to this. To Plato the soul was real, and as a reality it was a whole and not an abstract idea. This view Smuts fully accepted. "Somehow it seemed to have escaped notice, but the time is now coming when both science and philosophy will have to adjust their viewpoints and methods to this basic concept of the real," he wrote almost accusingly.[4]

Three centuries after Plato when Rome under the Caesars was supreme, Jesus of Nazareth was born to bring to the world, through His understanding of the nature of man in his relation to his Supreme Creator, the idea of the Fatherhood of God and the brotherhood of all mankind. Here bold intellectual insight combined with supreme moral truth and the highest spiritual values of self-sacrifice on the basis of the eternal law of love and mercy, to give mankind light upon the darkness of its ways and a quickening of its God-given spirit.

It was indeed the highest and noblest life's view with the emphasis on the supreme worth and value and sacredness of each individual personality and for Smuts it was part of his intellectual and spiritual outlook throughout his entire life.

Western civilization as we know it today is the result of these three ideas – the contemplative Oriental outlook, the speculative Greek inquiry and the Roman concept of law and order. The Christian idea combined all three into what Smuts named a new holistic unity. For the new union was more than the sum of its parts, it was creative and it formed a whole of living life-giving ideas.

St Paul had a great deal to do with the creation of this larger synthesis. Hebrew by birth and upbringing, Greek by orientation and a Roman citizen with a Roman's respect for law and order, he became, after his miraculous conversion, all Christian. He was thus, as Dr Kolbe points out, the first great Holist, the man in whom all parts combined to form a truly remarkable personality who was able to leave a lasting impact on the history of mankind.[5]

Smuts himself was a great student of St Paul. In his library there were many volumes dealing with his ideas and his work. He was profoundly influenced by St Paul's epistles in the New Testament.

To sum up, one can therefore say that Smuts derived support both from Greek philosophy and early Christian thinking for this idea of the whole.

But what of Evolution?

As I have already shown, there is unfortunately a tendency among some religious leaders and the public in general to regard the evolution hypothesis as a denial of creation and therefore a denial of God. This may be one reason why some uninformed people hold the mistaken view that Smuts was an agnostic or even an atheist.

The truth is just the opposite. Far from denying God and His creation, evolution to him was a key to explain the great mysteries of our world, thereby opening up the wonder, beauty and grandeur of God's continuous creation.

What is not always remembered is that evolution was not an invention of Charles Darwin. Darwin (as I will show) collated, arranged and marshalled the facts of growth and development to formulate the theory of evolution. But long before him there were thinkers who accepted evolution as a natural process, and amongst them were many great Christian leaders, of whom St Paul, according to Dr Kolbe, was one.[6]

Even amongst the earliest Greek thinkers a form of evolution in the processes of life was taken for granted, but owing to their lack of scientific facts they failed to carry their ideas further and their speculation became barren.

When the Christian idea arose, its first efforts towards self-expression were naturally and necessarily concerned with Faith. But Christianity is a comprehensive idea and it compels thought in every direction. What would it say about evolution? It is advisable to go back to the origins of our ideas.

Dr Kolbe points out that there was a continuity between pagan (Greek and Roman) and Christian intellectual activities. There were universities and Christians studied in them. The question was bound to arise about the origin of the world, and its relations to the Infinite. There was also Scripture to interpret.

According to Dr Kolbe, the deepest minds among the early Church Fathers, like St Basil for the East and St Augustine for the West, adopted the idea of Absolute Evolution.[7]

We must also remember that both Plato and Aristotle had already grasped the idea of the Infinite and to such an Infinite – God in our language – there is no time. A moment or a million years is all the same to Him.

The early Christian philosophy therefore considered that the revealed mode of creation was a poetic and oriental way of explaining incomprehensible truths to people. God's act, simple in itself, is successive and graduated to us. They held therefore that the Creator by a single word, which was to reverberate and actuate throughout the ages, brought into existence a mass of unformed matter and endowed it with the power of forming itself into higher substances, until it should reach even the body of man. The forms of inorganic substances and the souls of vegetable and animal beings were "educated from the potentiality of matter itself". Matter was endowed with *seminales rationes* (creative qualities), said St Basil and St Augustine. The Creator did not need to keep on intervening to supply for insufficiences in His work. It is on this basis that St Paul attributes creativeness to the material world. In his Epistle to the Romans 8:19 he wrote "For the earnest expectation of the creature creation waiteth for the manifestation of the sons of God. For the creature was made subject to vanity, not willingly, but by reason of him who hath subjected the same in hope. Because the creature itself also shall be delivered from the bondage of corruption into the glorious liberty of the children of God. For we know that every creature in all creation groaneth and travaileth with maternal creativeness in pain together until now."

This view of evolution means nothing more than that the Creator in some miraculous way sent matter into existence with all its potentialities, endowing it with some of His own creativeness. In this way we as creatures of the Almighty can grow and develop higher and higher and from form to form.

There can be no quarrel with this view of evolution, which was the view of early Christianity and which the two great Christian philosophers, St Basil and St Augustine, expounded. They saw no "jump" in the visible world which would have called for Divine "intervention" in the way of special creation.

I have dealt at length with these early Christian ideas for the sake of greater clarity and a better understanding of Smuts's own view of evolution which, in many ways, was based on this, avoiding the materially conditioned views of the nineteenth-century thinkers.[8] It is the more necessary to clear our thinking of extraneous formalities and go back to the origin and purity of the great ideas which have moved man's progress, because there has been and still is much deviation and confusion in their application over the centuries.

The basic fact to be considered here is that both the Greek thinkers and the early Christians regarded evolution as natural and as an acceptable explanation of part of the mysteries of the universe.

What caused the later deviation?

What factors led many religious people to reject evolution as from the Devil? And why do they regard those like Smuts who sincerely accepted evolution, as agnostics?

The study of the history of ideas will give us the answer to these vital questions on the understanding and evaluation of Smuts's Holism. Two factors emerge here. The one is that evolution in its earliest forms was merely an idea, a way of trying to explain some of the mysteries of life and development. It was not yet a scientific theory with all the valid proofs which only science could bring. The early thinkers were not scientists and in their time science hardly can be said to have existed. They were therefore not able to verify their ideas or carry them further. It took mankind nineteen centuries before a genius arose to postulate evolution as a scientific theory, namely Charles Darwin.

When evolution appeared again on the human scene it was unfortunately enmeshed in the purely mechanistic outlook of the so-called Naturalists. As such it was unacceptable to those who try to see life as a whole, a unity of matter and mind and with a spiritual content. That is one important fact in the development of this idea which must be borne in mind.

The second historic fact is that darkness and confusion enveloped men's minds as well as the entire civilized world shortly after the beginning of the Christian era. With the decline and fall of the Roman Empire in the fifth century AD barbarism returned to Europe. Men's minds were again enslaved by fear and superstition during the Dark Ages.

It was fortunate for the survival and the progress of ideas that Mohammed arose as a new prophet in the seventh century at Mecca in the Arabian desert. For our study of the history of ideas it is important that those who came after him in Egypt and Spain carried on the method of free enquiry which the Arabs had acquired in their conquest of the Greek seats of learning.

For many centuries the accumulated knowledge and wisdom, the science and philosophy of Aristotle remained safe in their hands. Through the Arab mathematicians, chemists and philosophers of Alexandria, Cordoba and Sicily, Europe once again in the twelfth and thirteenth centuries discovered the wonders and delights of intellectual enquiry.

Roger Bacon, the English Franciscan of Oxford, took up the torch of

Aristotle to light the lamp of science and to inquire into the nature of things. Bacon became the father of modern experimental science as Dante was the founder of modern literature. H. G. Wells gives Roger Bacon a prominence second only to Aristotle. Here was a rebirth of that bold and vigorous spirit of enquiry which led to the discovery of the compass and so of new continents, to science and the steam engine, the industrial revolution, electricity and ultimately to the atomic age.

Unfortunately, the emphasis on reason and rationalism as far as the external world is concerned led in time to that mechanistic, materialistic outlook which was the dominant pattern of nineteenth-century thought.

Smuts even as a student clearly saw the dangers of that mechanistic path, and through Holism he strove to restore the unity of outlook, the whole man in a whole world. In his *Holism and Evolution*, he paid a great deal of attention to the fallacy of mechanistic conceptions. "The science of the nineteenth century was like its philosophy, its morals and its civilization in general, distinguished by a certain hardness, primness and precise limitation and demarcation of ideas. Vagueness, indefinite and blurred outlines, anything savouring of mysticism, was abhorrent to that great age of limited exactitude. The rigid categories of physics were applied to the indefinite and hazy phenomena of life and mind. Concepts were in logic as well as in science narrowed down to their most luminous points, and the rest of their contents treated as non-existent . . . a 'cause' for instance wat not taken as a whole situation which at a certain stage insensibly passes into another situation, called the effect. Everything between the cause and the effect was blotted out and this made it impossible to understand how the one passed into the other in actual causation."[9]

To say this is not to deny the immense achievements of science with reason as its guide, even in the nineteenth century. All that we possess today in our mastery over the elemental forces of nature is due to the application of the fearless rationalistic ideas on our material world. But at the same time this belief in the inexorable rule of natural law relegated the spiritual experiences of man to the backwater of superstition. The result has been that a chasm and a conflict developed between the material and the spiritual worlds. As the material forces became supreme it made the experience and the value of the spiritual more and more inaccessible to modern man. To this we must also ascribe the gradual loss of the influence of the churches in modern society.

The rapid advance of science in the 18th and 19th centuries revived the interest of thinkers in the development of life. Advancement, progress was in the air. As Professor J. B. S. Haldane has shown in his treatise, *Is Evolution a Myth?* the theory of evolution began as a hypothesis like the roundness of the earth. It was held by daring thinkers on incomplete evidence, Darwin's arguments tilting the scales in its favour.[10]

Darwin brought biological and botanical proof and he collated, arranged and marshalled the facts of life to show a definite trend. Out of that he deduced the laws of evolution governing the process of growth. He himself realized his inability to explain all the mysteries of life. All he did was to say that among living beings there is a tendency to vary and overmultiply. In consequence a struggle for survival becomes inevitable and in this struggle for existence the fittest survive. This explains the origin of species and all organic differences in the world.

This is the basis of Darwin's theory, and as Smuts points out, this tendency to variation which underlies Darwin's thinking and observations is a fact patent to everyone. So is the overmultiplication of individuals under favourable conditions and in the absence of external restraints. The resulting struggle, which Darwin calls natural selection, is well known to everyone who has the least knowledge of animate nature.

Darwin's laws may not have been complete, but they were right and natural as far as they went, and they justify us in placing him alongside Copernicus and Newton as one of the great illuminators of scientific thought.[11]

Having opened this new door to mankind, Darwin paved the way for a vast new extension of knowledge in practically every sphere of life. Those who came after him have broadened and corrected and amplified his views, but they have not superseded them. Regrettably some of his followers have given the theory of evolution a much stronger tendency to mechanistic materialism than he did.

Smuts avoided this and he warned against it. To show how Holism fits naturally and logically into the idea of evolution, Smuts refers to the two factors which Darwin saw in all development – an inner factor, variation in the reproduction and inheritance of living beings and an external factor, natural selection, or divergence of character and the extinction of less-improved forms, or survival of the fittest as Herbert Spencer, not Darwin, called it.

Both are essential elements in the theory of evolution, but Darwin's overemphasis of the second or external factor had one unfortunate result in the view of Smuts. It directly and powerfully reinforced and exaggerated the mechanistic conception of the universe. This led to that false idea in the minds of religious people that evolution is purely outward mechanical explanation of life and that it denied the spiritual aspect of things. It arose because Darwin's theory was wrongly identified only with natural selection. The sole cause of organic change and progress was seen to be an external factor operating on organisms from without, in the same way as physical forces operate from outside on bodies. When the scientist began to apply these mechanical analogies, evolution came to be looked upon as something purely physical and with no spiritual or ethical application. Darwin's theory was thus regarded as proof of the material view of life and through it the mechanistic outlook came to be extended from the kingdom of matter to that of life. To the lay mind, man was regarded as little more than the ape and as purely materially and mechanically conditioned. Similarly, the whole of life was simply regarded as a struggle and as the survival of the fittest. In business, in politics and in international affairs this led to incalculable harm, for everywhere the validity of moral values was denied and unethical deeds were justified by the natural law of the survival of the fittest. This view, unfortunately, to a great extent still dominates national and international affairs.

Smuts, whilst accepting evolution and seeing in it one of the noblest advances in knowledge, rejected this overemphasis of the material or external factor. He went back to the original two-sided nature of Darwin's theory and for him the importance lay in the first or internal factor.

"The difficult part of the theory, the aspect of it which even to Darwin had remained a mystery, the inner creative factor of variation, was ignored while Darwinism was in the course of being generally accepted, and accepted in this mechanical sense," he wrote in his *Holism and Evolution.*[12]

He points out that biologists like Weismann and others have also stressed this internal factor, but even in these cases the discussion of the internal factor mostly took place on the basis of the mechanistic outlook. The result was to stress further the mechanical nature of evolution.[13]

Against this he pitted his own view of the validity of the inner factor in the evolution of organisms. In his view the inner controlling, regulating pattern, which he calls Holism, is the real factor in evolution. He thought that there is something wider and deeper at work in evolution than the two factors which Darwin and his successors discovered, something of which those factors are themselves but an expression. The whole and the natural tendency to wholeness in all nature may be this something more.

In this way, according to him, Holism as a pattern in evolution not only reconciles the inner and external factors of Darwin, but also accounts for the creative unity of life. In this view life does not merely become a struggle with survival of the fittest as the end and purpose. It becomes a creative growing unity which makes all the diverse elements of existence the co-operative members and inhabitants of an essentially friendly universe. Instead of stressing the survival of the fittest as a theory and a practice, his Holism came to show the underlying family relationships of all life – all are part of a whole as they are themselves wholes combining their parts in a unique way. And as they are true to themselves and to the deepest forces in all nature, they also achieve order, harmony and beauty.

Take the case of beauty in nature. Survival on Darwinian lines is not sufficient. Beauty cannot be explained other than through Holism. It is a relation of parts to the whole, a blending of elements of form and colour, of foreground and background, of expression and suggestion, of structure and function, of structure and field which is seen and appreciated as harmonious and satisfying.

Similarly, mind cannot be regarded as purely the result of survival. There is no doubt that struggle for survival played a powerful role in its origin and development. But how much more is it than that in its marvellous human efflorescence![14]

In one of his fine passages of inspired writing, Smuts carries the argument further:

"The glories of art and literature, the peace of the mystic's religious experience, the creative ideals which lift life beyond the limitations of its lowly origin – all these experiences and developments have built a new spiritual world on the humble foundation of survival values.

"In the kingdom of life is visibly arising its capital, the City of God."[15]

And he sees the same sublime pattern in the beauty of nature. He sees it in the song of birds, with its primary appeal to sex, but with so very much more in it than sex appeal. He sees it in the glorious forms and colouring of birds and beasts and insects which no doubt arise in and from the struggle for existence, but finally rise above it and rob it of all sordidness and drabness. Above all, he sees it in the wonder of flowers and plants which were meant for the eye of birds and insects, but which contain so infinitely much more than the eye of bird and insect ever beheld or can behold. Everywhere in nature it is the same. Everywhere we see the surplus of the whole.

"So little is asked; so much more given. The female only asks for a sign to recognize the male, and to help her select him and to stick to him in preference to others. And for an answer she gets an overpowering revelation of beauty out of all proportion to her modest request. The pea-hen has no discriminating understanding of the wondrous colouring of the peacock which far transcends even our human powers, but in some inscrutable way something of an emotional nature in her takes it all in and is satisfied.

"It is deep calling unto deep; it is the whole appealing to the whole."

There is evidently more in this than the Darwinian factors can satisfactorily explain, and it would be both foolish and unscientific not to recognize this frankly.

"To me the conclusion of the matter is that the inexhaustible whole is itself at work, that Holism is an active factor interacting with the particular Darwinian factors, that not only its aim, but also its output far exceeds the immediate present utilities and needs of organic evolution, and that its bow is bent for distant horizons, far beyond all human power of vision and understanding."[16]

I have purposely dealt fully here with this discussion of evolution as a landmark in the history of ideas, as I think that it serves a number of purposes. It helps us to place Holism as a new idea, in its context of history. It helps to explain it further and it also serves as an illustration of the deviation of the purely mechanistic thinkers from nature and from truth. It might also help us to bridge the gulf between evolution and religion, thereby establishing Smuts as a bridge builder between different aspects of knowledge.

It still remains for us to analyse more fully his rejection of both conflicting currents of modern thought, mechanism as well as idealism or spiritualism. After that we shall be able to see more clearly his own contribution to the ideas which move the world and also the direction which he pointed for the future.

To do this we must again go back to the origins. Modern thought is based on the Cartesian system of thought. We must therefore go back to the French thinker Descartes (1556-1650) who tried to explain for himself the mysteries of existence and who became the father of the Cartesian system. Descartes was a staunch Catholic, but he rebelled against the sterile dogmatism into which the scholasticism of the Middle Ages had degenerated. In applying his reason and only his reason to existence, he gradually and logically came to the idea of the separation of body and soul. On the basis of his abstract speculations he taught, among other things, that the soul governed the body from without like an engine driver.

In looking back upon the history of ideas, it is clear that the rationalism of Descartes has been the foundation of science and of philosophy ever since. In science this use of reason as the final arbiter came to be coupled with a series of great practical discoveries which made progress the watchword of the modern world. Science and reason became one, a great united force for the advancement of mankind. Through its very success and its marvellous achievements, it came to ignore and deny the world of the spirit and its values. There never was a scientist who envisaged the opposite reason.

In philosophy the ideas of Descartes gave rise to two great systems of thought. On the one hand his successors continued to stress absolute reason as both the instrument and end of philosophical inquiry, and through Hegel's logic and Karl Marx's dialectic, matter and the materialistic outlook came to be regarded as the absolute truth. Out of this originated Communism as the practical application of the purely materialistic rational system of thought.

Against this and again arising out of Descartes's reasoning, there grew the opposite view, of the spirit as the activating force of life. It took the form of obscure metaphysics which, in some thinkers like Comte, was called positivism, in others, like Bergson, intuitive knowledge. Both systems were purely speculative and their application eventually led to the great chasm – the dichotomy between mind and matter. As science and discovery were on the side of matter, the dominance of the materialistic rationalistic outlook in modern centuries became complete. The world and the entire universe were regarded from the purely mechanistic point of view.

It is against this machine-minded materialistic outlook as well as the necessary dichotomy which arose from it, between matter and soul, that Smuts, even as a student in 1893, rebelled. As such he was one of the first of modern thinkers to revolt against the Cartesian system. But it was not until 1926 that he finally rejected it. He then showed how the new creative factor in evolution had already shaken the whole fabric of mechanism to its foundations.

He was not alone in this. There were others too who saw the limitations and the dangers to which Descartes's extreme rationalism had led. They rejected alike the sheer materialism in science and the strange acrobatic feats in philosophy to which the Cartesian system gave rise. Even *The Times Literary Supplement* on September 9 1926 headed one of its articles with the title: "The Dethronement of Descartes."[17] The significance of Smuts's Holism was that it was the first systematic rejection from both the scientific and philosophical point of view of the Cartesian system and all that it stands for in its materialism in science and its dualism in philosophy and religion.

Smuts made this very clear in his presidential address at the centenary meeting of the British Association for the Advancement of Science in 1931 in London. He regarded the invitation to give this address as the crowning honour of his life, especially as it came from scientists and not from politicians.[18] He therefore used the opportunity to state categorically:

"Gone is the time when Descartes could divide the world into two substances – extended substance or matter and thinking substance or mind. There is a whole world of graduations between these two limits. On Descartes's false dichotomy the separate provinces of modern science and philosophy were demarcated. But it is as dead as the epicycles of Ptolemy, and ultimately the Cartesian frontiers between physics and philosophy must largely disappear, and philosophy once more become metaphysic in the original sense. In the meantime under its harmful influence, the paths of matter and mind, of science and philosophy, were made to diverge farther and farther, so that only the revolution now taking place in thought could bring them together again. I believe, however, their reunion is coming fast."

What he referred to here as the new revolution in thought were his own holistic ideas. For he did more than overthrow the Cartesian system of thought. He brought in its place a new idea which not only avoided the dualism which resulted from Descartes, but also brought a new approach to the whole process of thinking. As such it was another landmark in the history of essential ideas.

Professor A. D. Ritchie recognized this when he wrote:

"What seems to me the most interesting part of his (Smuts's) theory is that it is an attempt to mediate between the view that what is new and emergent comes from without by sheer magic and the view that it is imposed from without by a transcendent Creator.

"The second view precludes any attempt at scientific account by introducing something of which science itself is not cognisant. The first seems scientifically absurd. Holism is an attempt at a third line of approach."[19]

How Smuts himself saw this new line of approach and its results for thought as well as science, he made plain in a number of speeches and articles. I shall try to combine them in explaining the significance he attached to the holistic view.

To him orthodox science, like abstract philosophy, has been too exclusively concerned with analysis and the synthetic reconstitution of living and non-living things from their analytical elements. Thereby it has missed a most important part of reality, namely the fact that the whole is always more than the parts.

In missing the whole in its concentration upon the parts, science tended to reduce the world to dead aggregations rather than the real living wholes which make up nature. The result has been that there is a gap between experience of the world and the abstract mechanical reconstruction of the parts. This has led to fundamental mistakes and has falsified our whole world view. For one thing this gap between living reality and abstract philosophy and analytical science has probably been responsible for much of the strain in the world today. There has been not only deep disappointment with science, but also a tendency to regard science as a danger and as a force which may ultimately destroy all life.

In saying this Smuts, in his preface to the German edition of *Holism* written in April 1938, made it clear that he was not arguing against science as a whole. Throughout his life he looked upon science as a most powerful, though not the only, instrument for the discovery of truth. In fact on many occasions he went so far as to state publicly that science was the special revelation vouchsafed to our age.

"In its fidelity to exact fact, in its faith in human reason as the divine light within us, in its liberation of the human spirit from an earlier bondage, in its forging of the technical links which will yet bind the whole human family together in a new age, in its revelation of principles of harmony and beauty pervading the whole universe, it has rendered and is continuously rendering a service which is indeed imperishable. But we must recognize that it is still young, still in its infancy as an agency of truth, still imperfect and partial. Far-reaching reconstruction of its fundamental ideas is even now taking place (as in the relativity and quantum concepts), and there is no guarantee of the finality of even these, the latest, concepts."

It is against this background of the great search for truth that Smuts appealed for a new approach away from the purely analytical and the purely mechanistic or materialistic.

This is the background against which he originated the concept of Holism.

CHAPTER TEN

Holism and evolution

Every great thinker who has tried to explain reality to us started from a simple vision of a natural truth.

Newton saw the falling apple and on that based the law of gravitation which explained the physical world to his generation.

Charles Darwin was 27 when he gazed on the "tangled bank clothed with plants of many kinds, with birds singing on the bushes, with various insects flitting about and with worms crawling through the damp earth", and out of that vision came the illuminating theory of evolution through natural selection which opened a new world of thought, growth and development for all mankind.

Einstein pondered on a man "enclosed in a cage" so that he cannot observe any other body and cannot notice his own motion, and saw in that the vision of a new law, the law of relativity which dethroned gravitation and now rules the universe and the mind of man.

Similarly Smuts had a vision of a natural process – in his case the human personality – which became the foundation stone on which he built his idea of Holism as a new master key to knowledge.

Smuts was only 19 and a student at Stellenbosch when he was first struck by the strange and wonderful phenomenon, the human person and his almost divine personality.[1]

There is no actual record of what led him to this contemplation. It might have been his interest in law with its Roman idea of the person as the basis of all law, or it might have been, and more probably, his contemplation of the great religious truth of the sacred human personality as the revelation of God in humanity.

I am inclined to think that his deep interest in religion with its emphasis on the supreme worth of every person or individual was the first cause of his conception of personality as the most important and highest factor in life. Religion came to him before the law. His legal studies, however, confirmed his ideas in this connection. Already in his Stellenbosch period when he was only 19, he wrote several articles – I will quote some on the next few pages – on religion as the basis of all values including the human personality. But it was only in 1893, four years later, that he wrote his first serious legal article, *Law – a Liberal Study*, in which he emphasized the legal basis of the person as the highest fulfilment of human life. He claimed then that "along the channels of Law are flowing the most permanent currents of human thought and activity. The greatest work that can be done in this world is the harmonization, in accordance with the law of freedom, of the subjective with the objective, of the unit with the whole."

As evidence of the growth in human understanding and development he goes on to say:

"The person is recognized more and more. The rights of Personality become more and more inviolable."[2]

But whatever the first cause of his ideas, it is noteworthy that in his nineteenth year, six years after he first went to school, he wrote an essay called *Homo Sum* which dealt with slavery in its various forms. It was written in High Dutch in *Het Zuid-Afrikaansch Tydschrift* of June 1889 and almost prophetically he declared the Person to be the highest manifestation of Truth.

The profoundest Truth, he wrote, is man's individuality. Science has burrowed deeply in order to work out laws, but the history of Humanity will ultimately convince Science that Personality is above Law, that, in fact, "no law is thinkable without the existence of Personality, law being but the very faintest recognition of the harmonious form in which Personality reveals its essence."[3]

Here the Smuts of 19 had the great vision, the contemplation of the human personality which like Newton's apple, Columbus's egg, Darwin's tangled bank and Einstein's closed cage, became the guiding star of his mind and his interest until his dying day 61 years later.

"When people ask me where and how he got his idea of Holism," wrote Sir Keith Hancock in his Creighton Lecture on the Smuts Papers, "I can only reply that he grew up with it, he grew into it. The idea of it, or at any rate the feeling for it, is already present in the verses that he wrote for Isie Krige on her seventeeth birthday. And it is interwoven there, as it was in all his later writings, with an intense feeling for the worth of human personality."

Sir Keith adds that in 1893 at Cambridge, Smuts continued these ideas in a long paper *On the application of some Physical Concepts to Biological Phenomena*, a paper which showed him purposefully upon the track of his holistic philosophy. It was at this time that the idea of God was continually in his mind. But I think it is wrong to anticipate here his "holistic philosophy". The idea of Holism as a key to knowledge – Smuts never regarded it as a systematic philosophy – came very much later.[4]

What is important here is that he started off with his fundamental interest in the person and the human personality.

And it was only through his study and contemplation of the human personality over many years, always trying in his fearless search for truth to find the mainspring, the inner core, the propelling force in and behind it, that he gradually uncovered his great idea of Holism.

It took many years of thought and study, reading and checking before he felt ready to launch his ideas on the world. At first, in the initial enthusiasm of freshly discovered truth, he wrote a treatise on Walt Whitman, calling it *A study in the Evolution of Personality*. He had hopes that this study would throw new light on some of the darkest problems of life and thought.

It is undoubtedly a remarkable book. As early as 1894, when only 24 years old, he ventured into the depths of philosophy in an attempt to lay bare some co-ordinating principle, some truth which would illuminate the whole human experience.

And inspired by the poetry of Walt Whitman, with his emphasis on the immense potentialities of human beings, Smuts looked for a characteristic activity, distinct in each individual, as the key to Personality. He thought that the unrestrained and natural development of this activity would realize the full promise and potency of that life.

There is something noble in his ideas on personalities, and although never published, this treatise is valuable as an indication of the early flowering of his genius. It contains "remarkable stuff" as he himself stated many years later.[5]

It lacked, however, the ripeness and mellowness of the rich and full experiences of his later life. It is too wordy and it also lacks that clarity and directness which characterizes his later writings. Although in many respects his basic thinking was in advance of his time, it was still not far enough away from the rigid mechanistic outlook of the nineteenth century. Smuts had to undergo the hardships of the Anglo-Boer War, he had to share the goodness and simplicity of Louis Botha, he had to experience the great spiritual influence of the Friends and to delve deeper into the mysteries of science, philosophy and religion before he was ready to write and explain his holistic ideas.

But the key idea of seeing the world, life and the human personality as a whole simmered continuously in his mind. Gradually the idea of the whole as the centre and unity of all matter and of all life came to the forefront of his thinking.

Amidst the enormous burdens of taking a major share in building the new Union of South Africa, he sat down in 1910 and wrote a second treatise on wholes.

He himself in his introduction to *Holism and Evolution* explained how he had outgrown his earlier ideas on personality. "Gradually I came to realize that Personality was only a special case of a much more universal phenomenon, namely the existence of wholes and the tendency towards wholes and wholeness in nature. In 1910 I sought relief from heavy political labours in an attempt to embody my new results in a study called *An Inquiry into the Whole*.[6]

Smuts sent his manuscript to his tutor, H. J. Wolstenholme, in Cambridge. To his dismay it had a very negative reception. Wolstenholme in a personal letter, dated March 15 1912, advised him to regard the proposed book in "its present form" simply as a rough draft to be kept for alteration, expansion and above all for greater precision and definiteness both of thought and expression. Later he took the manuscript and added his derogatory comments to the first three chapters.

Wolstenholme was undoubtedly correct in describing the treatise as "a general undeveloped and unmatured outline, preparatory to a more definite and detailed work". On the other hand, the manuscript contained much that is valuable in the early evaluation of the concept of the whole.

Smuts formulates the whole as "the all, but not in an arithmetical sense. We shall not arrive at the whole by adding up all the items of existence. It is not a sum total of Being or Experience. It includes all this but much more, and it is just that more that makes the difference for the conception of the Whole. A mere summation leads to a mere mechanical totality which is no Whole at all."[7]

He must have been very disheartened by Wolstenholme's brutal rejection of his work, but in a letter shortly after that he made no mention of the subject. However, he refrained from publishing the manuscript and kept it for 14 more years, and in 1924, after his Government was defeated by General J. B. M. Hertzog, Smuts in the quiet of his farm Doornkloof at Irene, outside Pretoria, returned to his earlier treatise. He then found much of the scientific setting to be out of date and that his idea of the whole had also changed in certain aspects.

Out of this emerged his final manuscript which was published as *Holism and Evolution* and in which he explained his concept of the whole as the new master key to open the door of knowledge and wisdom, giving a deep and remarkable insight into truth as we see it in nature and in human life.

Here again we must seek the origin of his idea of the whole as the essence of things, in his religion. As a Christian and a student of the deeper forces of the Christian religion, Smuts noted the use of the word "whole" in the New Testament to denote health, healing, normality, oneness with the Divine Being. Jesus used his God-given power to make the sick whole in body and spirit. But Smuts saw the whole as the condition of things in a wider and deeper sense. He explained wholeness as the fundamental character of every personality as of every form and structure in the universe.

What does it mean?

It means that we live in a world and in a universe where everything, as every life and person, always forms a whole. It is a universe of whole-making in its very essence. Nothing is half-finished, and if it is, it is abnormal and contrary to the purpose of nature as of all existence.

The core of existence in all its forms is the unifying power which makes everything whole.

Smuts began by seeing through the poetic eyes of Walt Whitman the vast potentialities for the human personality, a power bestriding the earth with visions of greatness and goodness, nobility and generosity. But as he thought about the human personality over the years, he came more and more to single out its one main characteristic, its wholeness.

He saw every personality, every individual as a whole and the whole in every case was more than its parts, the personality was more than the body, the intellect, the humanity and all its other attributes. As he thought further and observed more, he found the same quality of wholeness in nature.

He noticed it in plants, in animals. He saw it in the smallest cells of life, in atoms and in the universe. And on that observation he laid down his idea, that this is a whole-making quality where every whole that is formed has more in it than its parts and again combines with other parts to form an even greater whole.

This whole-making is not mechanical or artificial. It is real and organic, dynamic, evolutionary, creative. Thus there arises a progressive scale of wholes, arising from material bodies through plants and animals to man and to his personality and through this to the ideals and artistic creations of the spiritual world. As this whole-making goes higher, so we approach nearer to the ideal of perfection, to the ultimate whole as the end of all creation. But always the structure, the vital process of whole-making as the core of all development is retained.

It is as if the great Creative Spirit in the universe has said: "Behold, I make all things whole," for there are no half measures in reality, only complete wholes.

He saw six stages in this process, ranging from the physical and material world, to living bodies like plants, in the animate fields as in animals, in the conscious world of man, in human associations like communities and states and finally in the world of ideals and values where truth, beauty and goodness lay the foundations of a new order in the universe.

Underneath all this development and the creation of ever new and higher forms of life, lies the creative principle, the whole-making structure of nature as of all existence. It is the scale of wholes which forms the ladder of evolution, and it is not merely mechanical although it has its roots in the material world, for at every step something more comes into play, a new force, a sort of special field where the new whole becomes more than the parts from which it is formed. The whole which is more than its parts has something internal, some inwardness of structure and function, something more. What is that more? It is, Smuts says, the holistic force in the core of all existence, and to express that he coined the word "Holism" from the Greek word *holos* meaning whole.

To grasp it we must think and understand how it can happen in nature as in life that a higher form can grow out of a lower form. How can life develop out of the material world? What new force comes into play to form animate life out of plant life? And how does the human mind develop by itself out of the conditioned animal instincts? Again, how does the glorious human personality with its nobility, tenderness, and mercy develop in the biological field? Somewhere a new vital force must operate, a force which in a creative way brings a new element into play and lifts the process of development onto a higher plane.

In order to understand and explain this phenomenon we must take into consideration two interacting forces. The one is development or evolution; the other whole-making or Holism. The first, which was stressed by Darwin, means growth and development; the second, Holism, means that there is a definite pattern, an inner core which produces ever higher forms in all evolution.[8]

In a remarkable analysis of Darwinism and Holism, Smuts shows how the two are interrelated and how evolution cannot take place without the inner controlling and regulating factor, wholeness and whole-making in the organism. He points out how Darwin traced organic descent to the interwoven effects of variation, which is an inner creative factor operating spontaneously and somewhat mysteriously inside organisms and modifying their hereditary structures and functions in very slight degrees, and an external factor, natural selection, which operates selectively on these slight variations, weeding out those organisms whose variations were less suitable to their environment, and leaving the organisms with suitable variations to multiply and develop. By continuous summation of small useful variations through many generations, definite specific characters would in time be achieved and new species arise.

Darwin, as is well known, laid most stress on the external factor of Natural Selection. He was rather vague and hesitant about the inner factor of variation. In the view of Smuts and others the emphasis should fall rather on the creative inner factor which is the real positive motive force of evolution. "The real secret is in the cell, in the germ-cell or fertilized ovum rather than in the external situation, important as that is."[9]

It is here that the concept of the whole as the basis of Holism gives the key to evolution. Smuts shows convincingly that where modifications and variations take place, they do not come singly, but in complexes involving many minor and consequential modifications and variations. He asks the pertinent question: are they all individually "selected" even before they have any survival value or strength? To his way of thinking it is the organism as a whole, an entity, which selects the variations. "It is the organism that advances on a certain more or less limited front . . . the variation issues from it and is in conformity with its whole trend and movement."[10]

The variation is in other words not single and unsupported, but behind it is the whole force of the organism. It is thus the organism as a whole which in the first instance selects the winning variation or series and confers on it support and survival value.

Here Smuts brought into the discussion a new idea which may help to explain aspects of evolution which had so far not been stressed. This is that there are in evolution not only creative forces responsible for the variations, but also repressive forces which hold in check certain tendencies and features while releasing and pushing forward others. Thus the balanced whole of the type or species is achieved. This repressive aspect of progress was neglected by Darwinism, but Smuts gives it a validity just as real as active variation. He points out that the repressive tendency as part of evolution operates on the organic level, but becomes much more conspicuous on the psychological level where it operates as ethical restraint, so essential to beauty and the formation of the Personality as a moral whole.

Charles Darwin in his study of plant life originated the idea of evolution as a fundamental principle in the universe. It is, as I have pointed out, one of the most important steps forward in man's understanding of himself and his world. But unfortunately Darwin's great vision of the world as a living developing world was soon distorted by scientists, philosophers and theologians. Instead of accepting his simple premise of development and growth in all things as a natural process, they narrowed his ideas down to a mechanistic explanation where men began to argue over static forms and divisions. What resulted was that the process of continuous growth, the regular flow of development, was halted and broken up and certain forms isolated. His followers then tried to explain these in their isolation and began to argue about so-called missing links, whether man was descended from apes, and similar questions. In the process the real grandeur of evolution as a key to the riddle of life, as part explanation of creative life, was neglected and forgotten. This may be one of the reasons why Darwin's noble thoughts never succeeded in ousting the earthbound materialistic outlook of the nineteenth century, and why some religious leaders regarded evolution as antireligious and atheistic.

It remained for Smuts and others to restore the grandeur and the vision of Darwin's theory of evolution. With Darwin he showed that matter, life and mind do not consist of fixed, constant and unalterable elements. He recognized the idea of continuous growth and development, of continuous creation where life and the universe are never static. But he went further. He combined this with a new active factor, the whole, which science and philosophy up to that time had not recognized. He showed that the whole has an influence and an effect on the evolutionary process all of its own.

If we think of evolution as a dynamic growth and variation of patterns, a progressive advance to higher patterns, a new element comes into play, a unifying regulating principle which through inner direction and central control always forms or creates new and higher patterns. This is the element of

Holism or whole-making.

"In other words," Smuts explained in the *Encyclopaedia Britannica*, "wholeness or Holism characterizes the entire process of evolution, in an ever-increasing measure. And the process is continuous in the sense that the older types of wholes or patterns are not discarded, but become the starting point and the elements of the newer, more advanced patterns. Thus the material chemical patterns are incorporated into the biological patterns, and both of them into the subsequent physical patterns or wholes.

"Each series of wholes progresses both in complexity of elements and unity of pattern up to a point, when it more or less suddenly mutates or swings into a new rhythm or type of pattern, which again shows the same holistic development, until it in turn gives birth to a new and higher type.

"While the lower grades are more mechanical, and the higher grades more holistic, the movement throughout is towards more and more wholeness. The central feature or character of the cosmic movement is therefore towards wholeness or Holism.

"Electrons and protons, atoms and molecules, inorganic and organic compounds, colloids, protoplasm, plants and animals, minds and personalities are but some steps in this movement of Holism."[11]

Smuts thus saw two main forces operating in all existence, the one growing and developing – evolution – the other binding, forming and formative – Holism – and between the interaction of these two, the patterns of life are shaped to ever higher forms.

The importance of Holism as an active factor in growth and development as in all creation comes strikingly to the fore when we ask ourselves the question: how can the higher arise from the lower in the scale of evolution? How can the more come from the existing; how can something grow out of nothing? How can a higher form arise from a lower? What of the law of cause and effect? How can the effect be more and higher than the cause?

This problem has baffled scientists as well as philosophers who have found themselves unable to explain the new and generally accepted idea of "creative evolution". Holism seems to provide the key to a logical explanation. It opens the door to the riddle of creative growth toward ever higher forms.

It starts off by stating that through the holistic unifying tendency in all existence, the whole which is formed out of its parts is more than the sum of its parts. The whole is in this sense a creative principle or factor. Wherever parts come together or are driven together to form a whole, something comes into play which makes the combination more than the parts. Smuts explained this in a special note on Holism as follows:

"It is in the very nature and concept of a whole to be more than its parts. The origin of a whole from its parts is an instance of the more arising from the less, the higher form from the lower, in a way which does no violence to reason, but on the contrary follows from reason, because the concept of a whole in relation to its parts is a product of reason.

"Creative evolution is therefore an inexplicable process unless we link it to the concept of wholes, and look upon the creative growing evolving universe as a universe of wholes.

"It is the making of wholes which makes this universe creative, and the creative universe is therefore necessarily the holistic universe."[12]

It is in this sense that evolution (growth and development) is only part explanation of the miracle and mystery of life as of all existence. In order to become intelligible we must introduce one more factor, the controlling, regulating, pattern-building force which lifts each successive growth in the process of evolution to a higher form, and that force is Holism.

This process starts in the earliest material world and follows the pattern of life from the minutest first stirrings of movements and life up to the highest forms as we know them.

The world process which the concept of Holism as the partner and regulator of evolution opens up before us, tends from matter through life to mind and spirit, from the necessity of the material forces to the freedom of life, from the externality of natural elements to the inwardness and selfhood of the highest creations.

He sees this lifting up of the process of life to the highest forms as part of the growth of mankind towards the great values of the spirit. Through Holism the "more" in the upward growth inwardly and miraculously, yet naturally, develops and reveals the existence of the human spirit.

In this sense the world is truly, as Keats said, "the valley of soul-making". But, Smuts points out, we must recognize that souls are only its climax phase, and that the lower wholes of many grades characterize its earlier phases. Whole-making leading up to soul-making would thus be a correct description of the world process.[13]

As this double process of evolution and Holism develops and as ever higher forms come into being, the force of freedom comes more and more into play to make man, as the highest creation, the master of his destiny instead of the slave of the material world. It is here that the spiritual forces born of freedom take over the lives of people to create the great values which guide our destinies. To Smuts right through his life the principle of freedom, both as individual freedom and in the political sense, was a cornerstone. What importance he attached to it I will point out in the next chapter. Freedom resulting from Holism he regarded as the cornerstone of his idea of personality as the final flowering of the holistic universe.

CHAPTER ELEVEN

Freedom

There is a tendency in the world to think only in terms of national or political freedom when referring to the age-old quest for liberty. This is especially so in former colonial countries where the indigenous people had to fight against their conquerors or oppressors for their political or national freedom. To them as to others, freedom is synonymous with their national independence or their political sovereignty or their self-determination as a people.

Where this fight for independence coincides with political struggle and development, freedom is mostly identified with the conflict against an outside power, a foreign conqueror or an alien exploiter and oppressor.

This is understandable. The emphasis falls on the fight against the oppressor, the struggle for rights and liberties to be won from the oppressor. And so the vast force which, since the dawn of mankind, we perceive in the assertion of the right to liberty is narrowed down and confined to a political struggle against an alien foe.

The danger, of course, is that in fighting for liberty against an external oppressor, forces are created internally in the name of liberty which may enslave the people and rob them of that higher liberty, the freedom to live their own lives in their own individual way without social, political, economic or psychological domination or pressure by aggressive leaders or tyrannical majorities.

The Afrikaner's vision of independence from Britain had become a central issue of Afrikaner politics in the late nineteenth century, and Smuts, during his first period, when he became closely associated with the Transvaal Republic, was truly representative of this way of thinking about freedom. First as a participant in the futile negotiations with Milner to preserve the freedom of the two Republics and later as an active commander in the field, Smuts was in essence the patriot fighting for freedom.

In this period of his life, he wrote his famous tract, *Een Eeuw van Onrecht* (*A Century of Wrong*), in which he analysed and castigated British imperial policy in South Africa.[1] It is indeed a powerful indictment of the wrong which Great Britain perpetrated in Southern Africa from the time she first occupied the Cape in 1795. It was natural that the freedom-loving Boers who during the

Great Trek forsook their ancestral homes to brave the unknown further north, resented and fought British rule with a tenacity which still draws admiration.

Smuts the patriot, imbued with an intense nationalism, played his part in the struggle, prepared to give his life for the freedom of his country. But in the period after the Anglo-Boer War, especially after his contact with the Quakers and through the profound effect which the magnanimity of the Liberal British Government of Campbell-Bannerman had on him, his outlook changed. He became less of a patriot and more of an individualist.

At the same time he was more and more drawn into the new political dispensation in South Africa and later into the secret British preparations against a possible war.

The threat of Prussian militarism opened his eyes to the wider danger to freedom not only of nations but of individuals. There are many indications in the letters between Botha and himself of how they were covertly drawn into the preparations of the British for the possibility of a German war.

This may have had a lot to do with the split with Hertzog which developed in 1912 when Hertzog, sensing the direction and import of their policy, came out strongly for a South Africa First policy. This was the beginning of the split in South African politics which was to change the face and the destiny of Southern Africa.

At first both Botha and Smuts were reluctant participants in the British war preparations, especially when they were pressed into the conquest of German South West Africa which led to the rebellion by their former comrades-in-arms from the Anglo-Boer War.[2] By their action as well as their direction in associating themselves with British imperial policy, both former Boer patriots separated themselves from the mainstream of Afrikaner nationalism. For Smuts it also brought about a profound change in his outlook on freedom, especially as it coincided with his deepening interest in the idea of the whole and its influence on human personality. Henceforth he was to see freedom not so much in its patriotic sense as a struggle against the outward oppressor, but as an inward movement of the self towards its full realization, and in his *Holism and Evolution* he tended to put freedom on a pedestal as one of the highest principles and achievements in the process of life.

As I have pointed out in the discussion of his ideas on Holism, he regarded an organism like a plant or an animal as a natural whole with an inwardness of structure and function, some specific inner relation, some internality of character or nature.

To him the important aspect is that organisms come into being not through external causes alone. Nor are their states and characters the effect of external forces only. An organism is in a large measure its own cause and the cause of its own states and functions. External environmental influences are merely the rough material with which it works and builds up its own system. And in the act of building, the material is itself more or less completely changed into the character of the structure built. We say "more or less" because this character of creative mastery and transformation which an organism displays in respect of external influences and materials is itself of a progressive character. In the lower organisms there is much more of passive acceptance and response than in the higher. In this way the whole vast process of evolution largely becomes a continuous growth towards independence and self-regulation.

The important aspect of this inner factor which shapes and moulds the organism is that it is inherent in the nature of things, and it is a free factor not bound by outside causes. It is part and parcel of the very essence of growth and development.

From this it is clear how the idea of freedom, according to Smuts, is rooted in that of the organic whole and therefore in the very foundation of all nature. Freedom and not necessity or external determination is of the essence of things.[3]

This is true in metaphysics no less than in science. In metaphysics we say that the whole is free, the parts bound, for beyond the whole there is nothing external to determine it. It follows its own free way while the parts are necessarily bound by their relation to one another and by the whole which is more than the sum of their parts.

In science and reality we see how an organism maintains itself through its inwardness against external factors and how it thereby reveals its inherent freedom to follow its own path. The external cause, the stimulus which operates on it, is transformed by its subtle metabolism into something of itself. Otherness becomes selfness. The pressure of the external or the other is transformed into the action of itself. The organism shows that it is largely detached from its surroundings and it centres in itself. This means that necessity is superseded by and transformed into freedom.

"The whole, therefore, even in its most humble organic forms, lays the foundation of the new world of freedom," states Smuts.[4]

He goes on to say that we can arrive at the same result by another process of reasoning. In the old system of mechanistic philosophy the effect equals the cause and is therefore completely dominated by the cause. This is the system of blind cause and effect which has never been able to explain growth and development, for how can the new arise out of the old if the effect is never more than the cause? But Holism has shown that in all organisms something more comes into play when a cause is transformed to bring about a greater effect. The effect in Holism as in reality comes to contain the new and it therefore transcends its cause. Smuts sums up this position by stating:

"The element of newness, of novelty in the holistic order of the world, means a release from the complete bondage of matter and its causality and necessity. It means a certain latitude for expansion and growth. It widens the range of possibilities; the straight and narrow path of physics becomes the prospect which ultimately widens into the great horizons of life and mind.

"Freedom broadens out into a world of opportunities. The animal finds that it is no longer imprisoned in its cell like the plant; it begins to move about. Gradually it learns the lessons of direction and self-direction. The great Experiment of life assumes ever-widening degrees of freedom, until finally at the human stage freedom takes conscious control of itself and begins to create the free ethical world of the Spirit."[5]

Here then we see how the beginnings of freedom are laid in the early dawn of life itself, if not earlier. For we must bear in mind that the domain of life is largely distinguished from that of inanimate matter and energy by its greater degree of freedom.

In matter there may be an element of chance, but in life there is the basis of freedom to choose its own course. Life is not entirely bound, even in its most primitive forms. There is variation and creativeness which becomes ever more accentuated in its progress. Evolution as we know it traces this line of freedom from its earliest beginnings and reveals its escape from the prison of matter to the full freedom of the human spirit.

We thus see that freedom has its roots in the foundation and constitution of the universe. Smuts warns against the tendency to look for freedom only in the human will. Freedom did not originate in the human will. It is deeper and more fundamental than that, for it is in one degree or another the grand rule of the universe in an ever-increasing form. We thus find the ever-widening reign of freedom in the gradual increasing self-determination of the universe. And as greater wholes are formed through the process and pattern and principle of Holism, freedom grows with them.

In the human personality this freedom becomes conscious, and the more perfectly a personality realizes itself, the more perfectly free it will be. Here we enter the sphere of higher freedom where it becomes in the life of a person pure self-activity, untrammelled by external influences. Freedom is here spontaneous or conscious self-determination by virtue of which all its actions flow from the pure source of self and are not pressed or forced on it by unassimilated external conditions or causes alien to itself and which have not been transformed into unity with itself. In this way sincere self-expression in men and nations through freedom becomes to Smuts the true ideal of human development and culture.

From this it is clear that freedom according to him is no mere abstraction. It is a real active force. It is part of life and existence. It is at the centre of all growth and development and it is at the same time one with the highest ideals of human development. And as such, it is also the highest attribute of personality, higher and wider than the will.[6]

In what sense is a person really free? In the long controversy about free will, Smuts takes a new line. One group of thinkers, the Necessitarians or Determinists, regard the will as not free. They say it is determined by motives and conditions like all other natural events. They see it as a mere link in the chain of life and according to them freedom is therefore a mere illusion.

Opposed to them are the supporters of the Free Will theory. They maintain that the will may act irrespective of motives or external conditions. The will according to them has a freedom of choice between various alternatives. It may even act in a capricious way.

Smuts rejected both these conflicting views. We do not live in a purely physically determined world, nor in a capricious world. Personality is not mechanically determined, nor is it the outcome of caprice or choice. Freedom as an inherent character of personality is therefore neither mechanically bound nor the result of caprice or choice. Rather it is self-determined, bound by its own laws.

Where a human being is deficient in personality his actions also tend to be a mechanical reflex of impulses and external conditions. In other words, such a person is bound by forces and factors outside himself. He is not free. Where on the other hand he is a full strong personality he follows his own line, he expresses his own character in whatever he says or does, and as such he is a free agent.

It is in this way that freedom becomes also an ethical and personal ideal. Freedom is the full measure of self-realization which each human being by his or her nature aspires to. The freedom of a personality is the measure of its development and self-realization. It is the active power which gives a personality full control of itself, not only over its impulses and rebellious tendencies, but also over its deepest desires, its thoughts and emotions. Smuts summed it all up in these words:

"To be a free personality represents the highest achievement of which any human being is capable. The Whole is free, and to realize wholeness or freedom (they are correlative expressions) in the smaller whole of individual life represents not only the highest of which the individual is capable, but expresses also what is at once the deepest and highest in the universal movement of Holism."[7]

Let us apply this in the case of men and women as we know them. There are some whose lives are dominated by hatred of other individuals or nations. They can never be regarded as free personalities. Hatred clouds their thinking, warps their emotions and eats into the vitals of their existence. They are never able to realize themselves in their grandeur and beauty as free personalities at peace with themselves and with their fellowmen. We know them in our daily lives as sour, embittered, warped human beings, constantly at war with their own higher selves and with their fellowmen. In this category we can also place those individuals who through their greed for money or material things or their ambition to dominate others in an aggressive way, destroy the beauty and dignity of their own lives and become a danger to their fellowmen. Similarly there are the victims of their own passions who through their sin enslave themselves to external forces over which they have little or no control.

They become morally and spiritually debased, the victims of alcohol, drugs or vices.

In all these cases we see the enslavement of the human personality through hatred, passion, greed and ambition, the deadly sins which religion warns us to eschew.

Contrast with them those personalities who live a calm, peaceful life in full control of themselves. They are positive personalities who live a full and active life, enjoying the vast and varied experience of living without ever becoming the victims of excessive hatred or sins. They are that happy band of free individuals who taste life at its best and its deepest in wisdom and understanding and whose judgement is never clouded by external forces because they are able to meet all the contingencies of life. Freedom allows them to blossom in their full humanity as loving, understanding beings. In the words of the Bible, they are "whole", and even where they have fallen they could rise again through grace, love and mercy to become free and at peace with God and with themselves.

It is in this application of freedom of the life of the individual that Smuts saw the ultimate test of his concept of Holism as a great living force.

In his fine rectorial address at St Andrews in October 1934, he developed his ideas of freedom as a coherent concept.[8]

It was at the time when the dictatorships both in Europe and the Far East established themselves and began to threaten the free world. The state became an end in itself, the individual was regarded merely as an appendage, or worse still, as an instrument of the state. In the face of this trend, Smuts declared his belief in the individual as the highest end, and not as a means to an end.

"For me the individual is basic to any world order that is worthwhile. Individual freedom, individual independence of mind, individual participation in the difficult work of government seems to me essential to all true progress."

He saw further than the dangers of wars and dictatorships. He saw in the intolerance of the times a threat to human liberty and was concerned by the decay of the spirit of sturdy individualism which inspired progress in the past and which created all our human values. He saw how men and women, exhausted by suffering, were abdicating their rights as individuals, surrendering to the mass will which leads straight to autocracy. He knew that with individual freedom gone, freedom itself was being endangered.

To him the disappearance of the sturdy, independent-minded, freedom-loving individual and his replacement by a servile mass-mentality man is the greatest human menace of our time.

"Here we reach what I firmly believe is the heart of the problem, the issue round which the greatest battles of this and the coming generation will be fought – if the cause of civilization is to be saved."

This threat to freedom he saw not in the first place as a threat to the liberty of nations, but as the growth of intolerance in the human mind, and hence as the acceptance by the individual of a new tyranny disguised in patriotic colours.

As early as 1934 he was warning against the threat of Nazi intolerance.

"In spite of all our scientific expansion, our essential human rights are contracting. Individuals prostrate themselves before national leaders as before a god. Popular self-government and parliament are disappearing. The guarantees for private rights and civil liberties are going. Minorities are trampled upon; dissident views are not tolerated and are forcibly suppressed. With this there is in the modern world a tendency for intellectual freedom to disappear. Freedom of conscience, of speech, of the Press, of thought and teaching is in extreme danger. One party in the State usurps power, suppresses its opponents and becomes the State. The Press is made to write to order, and public opinion is manufactured for the support of the autocracy. Even freedom of religion is no longer safe and religious persecution again shows its head."

He saw the new dictatorships which enslaved many countries before the Second World War as nothing more than the old tyranny writ large.

"I fear the new tyranny more than I fear another great war. Tyranny is infectious. As Burke said, it is a weed which grows in all soils, and its nature is to spread."

It was against this denial of freedom that he made his clarion call for the re-establishment of liberty in the hearts of men and women.

"Freedom is the most ineradicable craving of human nature. Without it, peace, contentment and happiness, even manhood itself, are not possible. The declaration of Pericles in his great funeral oration holds for all time . . . 'Happiness is freedom and freedom is courage.' That is the fundamental equation of all politics and all human government, and any system which ignores it is built on sand."

His call to all to take up the fight for human freedom has a ringing appeal to our post-war generations when the threat to liberty is as serious as before. It is a call to democracies and to all mankind.

"In these days of widespread backslidings, of lukewarmness or downright disloyalty to our fundamental human ideals, the countries which have always been in the forefront of the historic fight for human liberty have a very grave duty imposed on them. They cannot refuse the challenge of the times. They dare not abandon the cause which our forefathers rightly placed along with religion itself as calling for the highest loyalty and the greatest sacrifices.

"In the long run only the spirit of international comradeship can solve the problems of freedom and of peace. But in the meantime the supreme cause has to be kept going and to be safeguarded from all danger till the new coming of the renaissance of the European spirit.

"The inner freedom and harmony of the soul; social freedom and equality before the law as the foundation of the State; international freedom in the rule of peace and justice; these should be the creative ideals of the new age, instead of sterilizing the repressions of the past and still more sterilizing the tyrannies which are forging new shackles for the human spirit. Creative freedom is the watchword of the new order to the realization of which we should bend our energies. I have no doubt that the present disquieting phase will pass and a new renaissance of the European spirit will follow.

"What a glorious opportunity for our youth today to live in times when the situation is once more fluid and the world is once more in the remaking. Are we going to leave a free world to those who threaten our fundamental human ideals and our proudest heritage from the past? Or are we going to join in the battle – an agelong battle which has been going forward from the dawn of history – for the breaking of our bonds and the enlargement of our range of free choice and free action? Remembering the great appeal of Pericles which rings through the ages, let us seek our happiness in freedom, and bravely do our part in hastening the coming of the great day of freedom."

On a later occasion he repeated this challenge to mankind to make the will to freedom its real motive power. "Creative freedom is the watchword of the new order, to the realization of which we should bend our energies."

For he saw the existence of freedom in the world as the supreme condition for the growth and development of unfettered human personalities, which to him was the highest and most precious creation of all existence.

How necessary freedom is for the full flowering of the human personality we will see in the next chapter.

CHAPTER TWELVE

Personality

The more Smuts thought about the marvel and the miracle of the human personality, the more he recognized its harmony, its wholeness, and also its relatedness to nature and the material world, and its penetration into the sphere of the spirit. Out of that contemplation his interest in the whole arose and on that cornerstone of wholeness he built the pattern of a process which starts in matter, and gradually through a process of ever-increasing and more complicated wholes, emerges in life, mind and personality.

Here then we have the full circle of his ideas. The one word "PERSONALITY" which in May 1902 he wrote in big letters on the last page of his poignant surrender diary – together with a quotation from Lincoln – becomes the beginning and the end, the whole purpose and the aim of his life's work.[1]

How highly he valued personality is evident from the fact that he placed human personality at the pinnacle of the progressive series of wholes in the evolution of the present universe. Other higher orders of wholes may exist elsewhere or arise in the future evolution of this unfathomable universe, but to him, in the present order of things, human personality is the supreme achievement of life. It is an organism with conscious reason and soul and thus the highest embodiment of that spiritual principle which he believed to be at the heart of the universe.

He recognized that there is beauty and order in the universe and in all its manifold patterns. But there is something in human personality so much deeper and higher that it forms a pattern or a whole apart. The ideals which the human personality has evolved as its proper equipment and endowment – the good, justice, right, freedom, love, truth and beauty – remain the highest lights of the world and of this order of the universe.

In making this claim, Smuts in the preface to the German edition of *Holism* – written in April 1938 – agreed that it might not meet with general approval. But he felt it might be of value in the troubled world of today and in the dark perplexities which surround mankind.

"I cannot get away from the conviction – borne in upon me by a lifetime of thought and active participation in affairs – that the way of reform, the way of salvation lies through the fostering, the purification, the enrichment of the human personality. There the Divine Light shines most clearly in the dark world."[2]

This statement points to the cleavage in modern thought and in practical politics. There are those who do not agree with this view. They do not regard personality as the highest end of life. To them the person is but a means to an end and in their philosophy and in practical politics they subordinate him to the group, the community, the nation or the state.

It is, of course, the age-old controversy of the individual versus the state, but in the practical politics of today, a government even in a democracy imposes its will on all aspects of a person's life. It is the central problem of present-day government in most countries in the world, where the state takes upon itself the added responsibility of trying through law to regulate even the moral life of people by applying more and more censorship not only for moral purposes, but sometimes even in the ideological and intellectual sphere. This is based on the theory that human beings are fundamentally weak and must be protected by a powerful ruling class or group.

We then have more than a system of government. We have a system of thought, a philosophy which even in this enlightened age still has many adherents. Even among modern thinkers there are those who think that it is genuinely best for people to be guided and protected, ruled and controlled by the power of the state. Human happiness and progress, they maintain, can only be brought about by rules and regulations, controls and laws which govern every aspect of human life.

The great German philosopher, Hegel, worked this out into a logical, consistent theory of the state as the be-all and end-all of existence, transcending personality. This is the basis of fascism (the corporate state) no less than of communism and also other forms of authoritarian states.

Against this we have the extreme liberal philosophy which denies any validity to the state, regarding it as a necessary evil. The individual is abstracted from the state and from his group and all authority is rejected as oppressive.

Smuts with his holistic ideas poses a middle way out of this conflict. With Kant he agrees that the human personality is a supreme end in itself, but at the same time he gives validity to the state and the community as a vital and necessary organization though not an all-embracing organization as Hegel would have us accept.

On this basis a reconciliation is possible between the state and the person. The supreme aim and object of the state should be to form and foster the highest citizenship. The noblest types of personality should underline the code, substance and striving of the state. In this way the good state will in the end be the good society and every person will find opportunity for the highest and freest self-expression without undermining the authority of the state or interfering in the lives of others.

To understand this difference between those who regard the state as the highest end, and those who, like Smuts, place supreme value on the person, we must take the matter a little further. Fundamentally it resolves itself into how and what we consider the human being to be. And it is a question of how well we know ourselves.

Let us look at different personalities and study their system of direction for their fellowmen. A person who knows himself to be weak and subject to temptations which he, unaided, cannot resist, will naturally favour a system whereby authority is given to some outside force to regulate and control individuals. He sees others as he is, and because of his own doubts and fears – often he will consciously deny these – he is in favour of a system of controls. But such is the irony of life that he himself will invariably strive for the power to control the weaknesses, not those which are in himself, but those which he sees in others. Such are the autocrats of the world, those who know best what is best for others. They are the systematizers who build up great power organizations to force life and all living into fixed channels. They are the dictators, and we find them even in democracies, where they use the power of the people to stifle the free development of the people.

But there are also other personalities, those who in some way have reached maturity or who, through crisis and suffering and hardship, have discovered new and undreamt-of powers and potentialities in themselves. With some, this comes as a gift, and instinctively they know their mastery over events and forces. With others, experience has convinced them that though some persons will inevitably falter along the road of life, the majority have it in them to triumph over whatever life may produce. These persons will mostly wish for others what they have learned for themselves through exposure to circumstances. If they have successfully gone through the mill of life they will know too that human beings can be trusted, that whatever life brings to them or whatever happens to them, in the end their essential humanities will reveal themselves in the goodness inherent in people.

Such a person, and such a thinker was Smuts. He knew people because he knew himself. He trusted human beings because in the fire of life he himself was tested, and he emerged a better, stronger and wiser personality. And what he asked for himself he was willing to grant to his fellowman.

It is in this sense that his own personality is fundamentally the basis of his ideas about personality and it is in this context that we can best understand his Holism as applied to personality. The first great truth he stressed in discussing personality is that there can be no personality without mind or reason. But mind is no abstract organ or external power given to man from outside. It is the outcrop of matter. It is inherent in the material world. If the atom and the cell were the two great departures, in the first upbuilding of the universe, in the growth from material to organic structures, mind is the third great step forward.[3]

Psychologists who try to explain to us the secrets of our being mostly do so by studying mind as a phenomenon by itself. They tend to break up life into parts such as consciousness, feeling, emotion, instinct, will, sensation and other aspects and by studying each one separately they try to give an understanding of the process of life. But this analytical method which led to psychoanalysis destroys the very thing it tries to explain because in isolating mind from its source and its context it kills its life.

The other danger of this method is that mind is pitted against matter as if these two entities are diametrically opposed and in conflict.

Through his holistic outlook Smuts saw mind not as the antithesis to matter as most philosophers do. Mind has its roots in the power of regulation and co-ordination in the lower organisms, which through atoms and cells spring from matter and are themselves rooted in matter. In its individual aspects it becomes a conscious force able to regulate and control the organism itself. In man it pushes to the front as conscious individuality which becomes the identity of the personality.

But important as the mind is as a part of personality it is not the master of a person. It is but the key in the hands of the master which is personality. As such it unlocks the door and releases the new-born spirit from the bonds and shackles of natural necessity. It is the supreme system of control in the hands of personality and it holds the secret of freedom.

Smuts described mind as the eye with which the universe beholds itself and knows itself divine.

"In mind nature at last emerges from the deep sleep of its far-off beginnings, becomes awake, aware and conscious, begins to know herself, and consciously, instead of blindly and unconsciously to reach out towards freedom, towards welfare, and towards the aim of the ultimate Good."[4]

He saw mind in the personality as the creator of that element of intense individuality in the life of every person. On the one hand through its subconscious "field" – the forgotten experiences of the individual and the psychological and racial inheritance – it gives a bias and an individual outlook on persons and things. In this way it helps to form what we call the individual temperament. On the other hand, through its reason which is universal it becomes part of the universal order. Thus in the personality the individual subjective mind is united with the universal or rational mind. Pure individualism thus becomes an impossibility or a misleading abstraction. The individual, alone and by himself as liberal philosophers see him, does not exist, and is an abstract fantasy. The individual becomes conscious in himself only in society and from knowing others like himself. He is himself and yet part of society, and he finds his highest fulfilment amongst his fellowmen, not in a narrow nationalistic sense, but in a universal rational sense where his reason has the opportunity to express its full universality as well as its individuality and where they are in full harmony. If this action is individual and universal at the same time, mind fulfils its deepest purpose.

In consciously willing this purpose, mind becomes the creator of the great ethical values in which it finds its noblest expression, the Realm of Ends as Kant has called it.

Mind in this sense is the most important and conspicuous constituent of personality. But the body is also very important and it gives that intimate flavour of humanity to personality. The view which degrades the body as unworthy of the soul or spirit is unnatural and owes its origin to morbid religious sentiment. The ideal personality only arises where mind governs body and body nourishes mind and the two become a whole where they in mutual support, enrich and ennoble each other.

Holism, in the view of Smuts, gives a new significance to the body which has been degraded by negative diseased religions from the East and which have spread to some parts of the West, and according to which the body is regarded with contempt as the seat of all weakness, evil and sin. Even adherents of the Christian religion often regard the body with abhorrence.

Smuts points out that this degradation of the body is against his holistic view as it is against the Greek and Roman ideal of a healthy mind in a healthy body. It is also not in accordance with the pure spirit of Christianity, which regards the body as "The Temple of the Holy Spirit". The natural and proper view is to look upon the body as clean and wholesome, to rejoice in it as something good and beautiful, to make it the twin sister of the spirit and the source of joy and wholesome pleasure. This view, which is at the basis of Holism, leads to respect and reverence for the body as worthy companion of the spirit.[5]

In Smuts's own life he practised what he expounded and one of the striking aspects of his personality was the unique blend between his optimistic, hopeful spirit and his supple, healthy, energetic body. Holism, where body and spirit become one, prevents the degradation of the body by the spirit or the perversion of the spirit by the body. Through his application of Holism also to the spirit-body relationship he saw arising a new spirit of respect and reverence for natural things and processes, and not least for the human body – a spirit which is far deeper and better founded than the old happy-go-lucky, pagan attitude of the Greek world.

He saw this high regard for the body not as naïve and sentimental, but as an objective scientific attitude.

"It means justice and fair play for the body, as against all theological prejudices and theories based on erroneous views of human nature. And it completely justifies the normal attitude which regards the body as inseparable from the spirit, and as the source of much that is most dear and precious and beautiful and intimate in human existence.

"Natural relations and affinities, instead of being condemned, receive the sanction of science, and under the powerful patronage and protection of science the simple human can once more hold up its head and without shame or regret give expression to the spirit of glad wholesome enjoyment which naturally wells up from its inner depths."[6]

To underline the important synthesis of the spirit and the body in personality Smuts pointed out the notable contribution Christianity has made to the idea of personality. It invested the human being with a character of sacredness, of spiritual dignity and importance which implied a far-reaching revolution in ethical ideas. Through the teachings of Jesus, the Roman legal concept of the person became blended with the moral sacredness and inalienable rights of human beings as children of God. After this, philosophy mainly through Kant raised the idea of personality to the dignity and status of a high philosophical conception.

With his Holism as a unity of science, philosophy, religion and common sense Smuts strove to go a step further and make personality a reality in line with creative evolution as the culminating phase of all development.

There is another aspect of personality which will help us to understand it better as a product of Holism. What is the relation of a personality to our inheritance from our ancestors?

The human person has in addition to his organic animal inheritance a psychic inheritance from his long line of ancestors. While the animal is bound by its inherited instincts, man through his reason has a capacity for educability. He can acquire new experiences. He can learn new ways of acting and reacting and he can adapt himself to new conditions.

What we human beings inherit, above all, is freedom and the capacity for free and self-determined action and development in our individual lives. In our psychic nature we are thus raised above the bondage of organic inheritance.

This means that there is actually something more in every person over and above his inherited qualities. He inherits a body slightly different from those of his parents and ancestors. Likewise he inherits a mental structure again a little different from but generally resembling that of his parents. And added to this there is an individuality which blends the animal body with the mental capacity in its own unique way, and it is in this blending, this combination that each personality becomes somebody unique on earth. The flavour of each human person is uniquely and absolutely individual.[7]

This explains why children of the same parents are never alike however much they may resemble one another physically. In each the inherited characteristics are blended in a unique way to form the marvel and beauty of their personalities.

From this it is clear that the important influence in the shaping of a personality is not the inherited characteristics or the organic or human qualities, but the new blending of them. How and through what is this brought about?[8]

It is here that, according to Smuts, we reach the core of a personality: a new conscious centre which in freedom organizes, blends, combines and shapes all individual and inherited characteristics into the new unity, which is more than a unity because it has creative powers to make it go beyond and above that unity into a still higher and more glorious personality.

This core which combines, shapes, blends, regulates and creates, he calls the pattern and principle of Holism which he sees as a factor in all existence. It operates as the central principle in the atoms and the cells no less than in the highest creation of life, the human personality. Here the central regulating factor with its freedom and creative power rises to a maximum in relation to inherited materials used in the new structures. Our very conception of personality is that it is a unique creative novelty in every human being.

From this analysis he saw three factors emerge which arise naturally from the central holistic core of personality. The first is freedom, the second purity and the third creativeness.[9]

We have seen in discussing freedom how it exists in the very nature of things. It does not deny matter and it operates between cause and effect to make the new effect greater and more than the cause and the whole more than the sum of its parts. Freedom is thus a fact, a power, a force in the universe itself and not a mere capricious power peculiar to the human will. It operates in the lowest categories of nature to help in their upward growth and development and with the coming of organisms it plays an ever more important role until in the human personality it emerges as a vital force to become the basis of self-determined growth and self-expression.

From this it is clear how important it is that every person should be free to form his or her own unique personality and to determine and express what is deepest in him or her in the freest way. No personality can truly find itself and express itself where there is no freedom or where it is dominated by others, by external forces or by internal fears and passions. That is why without external and internal freedom a person cannot find his dignity or his happiness.

In dealing with the second factor, purity, he touched upon this internal freedom to which it is related. Purity, according to Smuts, is essentially identical with freedom, for purity means the elimination of foreign elements which destroy the inner harmony of a personality. No person can truly find his personality if his various inherited characteristics, his body and his mind, or his desires and his ideals are not in harmony. Harmony is the basis of the universe no less than of the pattern and principle of Holism. Where there is no harmony there can be no wholeness and that means that a person lacks purity. Suppose someone is brilliant intellectually and has a very fine body, but lacks direction in his moral and spiritual life. Suppose that he, therefore, abuses his body by indulging in excesses which weaken the body. This will also in the nature of things react on the mind and on the entire personality. A sense of loss, of impurity, of not being true to himself will enter into such a life and thereby the personality will not find its true fulfilment.

What is needed is not only freedom to follow the urges and impulses of the inner self, but also a sense of purity, of control and discipline to see that the new does not introduce extrancous factors which destroy the harmony. Purity then means the harmonious co-ordination of the lower and higher elements in human nature, the sublimation of the lower into the higher and the shaping of the personality through control, through moral discipline.

But this moral discipline must come from within, must arise out of the feeling and desire for purity. If it originates externally it will not enter into the inner harmony and stability of a personality, but will always remain an outside agent. As long as it is applied externally it will tend to make a personality conform in a mechanical way to a rigid pattern, and the moment it disappears it will leave the personality in a worse state than before. That is why personal morality can never be assured by laws. It must come from within, from the purity of the inner life of a person.

The third factor, in his view, is creativeness. If a personality needs purity for its realization and if it has freedom and through freedom creativeness, it must use that to ensure its own ideal state and condition. To do this it creates values. There are rational, moral, artistic, ethical and religious codes based on and directed to the great values of peace, joy, blessedness and goodness. It is thus that through the fundamental holistic pattern which operates in the field of personality, we enter the field of the higher spiritual values which a personality needs for its internal harmony, its basic purity and its fundamental freedom to express itself.

It is here too that a still higher phase of the development of a personality is seen. From the foregoing and from the very nature of matter whence mind arises and where personality retains its basis in matter and mind, the growth and development of a personality is partly conscious and rational and partly subconscious and organic. In inadequate personalities control is largely subconscious, and such personalities emerge as the result of forces and circumstances not clearly understood or controlled. This is the case with primitive persons, but we also find such personalities in our own day and age, men and women who do not clearly know themselves or the forces operating in them and on them to shape their lives.

In the case of these people the elements of thought, emotion, will and passion are not in full harmony. They have not been consciously fused into one whole. Either the personality, through want of creativeness or freedom – inner or outer – lacks direction, or the reason or will is too weak to effect full control. If it lacks direction it will not develop that internal harmony which will bring it in tune with the harmony which is in nature and the entire universe. It will in confusion tend in its own direction, contrary to its basic organic needs, and thus destroy itself. If it lacks control it will not have authority over all its wayward urges and impulses, and it will become the victim of its animal nature, thereby destroying its freedom and its chances for higher development. In all cases it will be in a constant state of inner warfare which will destroy its peace, its happiness and create confusion. When this inner warfare becomes extreme and constant, the danger is that the personality may split into two warring factions, to become abnormal.

In many ways mankind is still in this condition of development where the full personality has not yet emerged. Smuts regards this as natural. He sees personality as still a growing factor in the universe. To him, it is merely in its infancy. Its history is marked by thousands of years, whereas that of organic nature is marked by millions.

Personality as a result, has as yet not attained its ideal or fundamental wholeness. Nevertheless its character and its function are already distinct and clearly visible.[10]

At present, in looking at personality, we see darkly. We are still in the state where in individual personality there is the wear and tear of internal struggle and confusion. There is friction and waste not only in the individual soul itself, but also because of the confused disputes among psychologists, philosophers, scientists and theologians about the human soul and its destiny. Theological thinkers are apt to deny the material and organic base of the personality and regard the flesh as evil. Philosophers have entangled themselves in systems which tend to deny freedom and smother the grandeur and dignity of freely developed personalities. Psychologists have broken up personality into many fragments and busy themselves studying the parts, forgetting the principle and the pattern which united those parts into a whole bigger than and different from the mere aggregate of those parts. Thereby they tend to study the body, after the soul, the life, the unity has left it. Scientists in their study of well-marked manifestations of reality have the advantage of a true approach, but they still stand outside the great secrets of the material world and have not yet approached human personality, partly spiritual as it is, with scientific investigation.

Yet in spite of our confusion, our lack of knowledge and understanding, there is progress in the development of the human personality. We see it in the upward trend in the case of more and more personalities in many parts of the world. We also see it in those rare individuals, great personalities, who arise from generations of the commonplace. Like cities built upon the hills, which spread their lights far and wide, these personalities reveal to us what we all can become if we are at one with ourselves and with all nature. Sometimes such personalities come to harmonious maturity by their own exertions. Sometimes, in a moment of crisis, a light seems suddenly to be shone and an individual becomes conscious that he has been guided along paths which were apparently not of his choosing, but which nevertheless shape his personality in fuller glory. Such was the experience of Saul of Tarsus, who in one moment of inner direction was changed into a master personality with full understanding, deep human sympathy, unshakable courage and inner spiritual harmony, at one with the deepest and highest forces of nature and the universe.

It is through these personalities from all our centuries of recorded human history that we can begin to know what the ideal personality will be if and when we reach our full maturity as human beings.

Smuts here described his version of this ideal personality:

"The ideal personality is he in whom this inner control is sufficiently powerful, whether exercised by conscious will or some unconscious activity, to harmonize all the discordant elements and tendencies of the personal character into one harmonious whole, and to restrain all wayward, random activities which are in conflict with that harmony."[11]

But he admits that this ideal is far from being realized. Yet personality in individuals is growing. It may be that a series of great personalities is followed by generations of the undistinguished or the confused.

It is also true that at present we cannot formulate a law of sequence for personality in the generations following one another. There is also uncertainty about individual personalities, and as we have not made a systematic study of the emergence of personality we cannot formulate a law of averages. We are still on the threshold of this vast and interesting subject.

Smuts in his first attempt at inquiring into personality, has shown it to be not a mere caprice in nature, without roots or functions. He has shown it to be in line with the whole trend of evolution. If today it is still vastly variable and fluctuating, it is so because it is still in the youth of human experience. It has not yet had time, except in the case of rare exceptions, to show its possibilities for human development. It is still a whole in the making, rather than a whole completely achieved. But its youthfulness does not detract either from its merits or its claims. In the course of human development it is destined, by the very nature of evolution, to reach pinnacles of maturity which only a few rare personalities among us can conceive of. It holds precious secrets for those who will seriously devote themselves to its study through the new science or discipline of Personology, remembering that a pure, free homogeneous spirit is the ideal of personality.

Holism, in the view of its creator, is directed and dedicated to this. The inner call of Holism is to its own victory in the personal life; to unity, freedom and free psychic power for the personality; to active moral efficiency and the suppression of harmful elements in the personal life; in a word, to the wholeness and perfection of the personality.

"The response to that call in the personal life constitutes the great inner drama, the warfare of the soul, which issues either in the attainment of Wholeness and Freedom and membership in the immortal Order of the Whole, or otherwise in defeat, enslavement and death.

"Personality is a spiritual gymnast, whose object is the freedom and harmony of the inner life through the refinement and sublimation of the cruder features in the Personality. If this object is secured by the Personality, all the rest will be added unto it: peace, joy, blessedness, goodness and all the great prizes of life."[12]

Wholeness as free and harmonious self-realization thus sums up the *summum bonum* of Holism, is his conclusion.

PART THREE

Statecraft

CHAPTER THIRTEEN

The Union of South Africa

A key to the work of a great leader is often found in an intense personal experience in his earlier years. More and more as the leaders of the modern world write their autobiographies it is clear that the motive for their public activities can be traced back and related to an intensely felt personal humiliation or inspiration. Clemenceau saw Paris in flames in 1871 and never forgot it. It was at the root of his deep and implacable hatred of the Germans which, through him, helped to win the war of 1914, but lost the peace of 1919. Hitler recorded in *Mein Kampf* the profound humiliation he suffered in Vienna as a struggling artist and again as a lowly corporal in the trenches. Out of that personal experience grew his fanatical determination for self-realization and revenge on all those who, in his opinion, were responsible for his youthful humiliations. And the entire world suffered for that in the catastrophe of the Second World War.

In the case of Jan Christiaan Smuts it was the opposite to humiliation and an inferiority complex which conditioned his life's work. It was an act of faith born of mercy and trust.

That this was so is remarkable. Smuts and his family suffered deeply during and after the Anglo-Boer War, and he felt the humiliation of defeat and the harsh peace agreement intensely. His suffering and his humiliation were infinitely greater and yet he was able to rise above them, to mould them eventually into the richness and beauty of his personality instead of being bound by them.

The Liberal British Prime Minister, Campbell-Bannerman, in January 1906 agreed to self-government for the defeated Boers of the Transvaal and Free State republics. Smuts's own conversion from an Afrikaner leader to a South African became the basis of his personality. Similarly this act of faith and mercy on the part of the British people, in tune with his own deep religious outlook, became the basis of his statecraft.

In many ways it formed the foundation of the great edifices – the Union of South Africa, the Commonwealth and even the League of Nations and the United Nations – which he helped to bring about.

Most great movements in life have small beginnings and so it was also with this. During the peace negotiations after the Anglo-Boer War, Smuts came up against two different personalities and two different views on the peace terms. One was Milner, inhuman as he was harsh, the business-like administrator who demanded unconditional surrender on the part of the Boers. The other was Kitchener, the soldier who brought the war to a close with stern, sometimes cruel military measures but who, having won the war, felt a measure of mercy and compassion for his brave adversaries. Kitchener with his soldierly instincts appreciated the feelings of a vanquished foe. He was in favour of a treaty of moderation and mercy.

When the Boer leaders met those two representatives of His Majesty's Government, Milner as the stronger of the two dominated. He was adamant in his demand for a crushing peace agreement. As the Boer leaders argued and negotiated one night in May 1902 in Pretoria, Smuts as the principal speaker for the defeated Boers, pleaded for mercy, for a compromise. Milner remained hard-hearted, but towards morning Kitchener gently touched Smuts on the shoulder and they went outside. There as they walked up and down Kitchener opened a door of hope to Smuts and the Boer cause.

"I can only give it to you as my opinion, but my opinion is that in two years' time a Liberal Government will be in power, and if a Liberal Government comes into power, it will grant you a constitution for South Africa," Kitchener told Smuts.[1]

With that ray of hope for the future, Smuts persuaded the Boer leaders to accept the peace agreement.

But it took four long and bitter years before that hope was fulfilled, years of despair and soul-searching, before Smuts persuaded Campbell-Bannerman in January 1906 to follow the path of mercy and magnanimity towards the defeated Boers and to grant them responsible government.

Smuts has often stated that he regarded this achievement of obtaining self-government from Britain four years after the end of the war, as one of the greatest of his life. The reason for that is clear. It was the deed from which all his other great acts of statesmanship flowed. It was an act of mercy, a miracle of trust and magnanimity, as he called it, which in its goodness and wisdom became the foundation of what he ever after regarded as true statesmanship. To him it seemed that nothing like it had ever happened in the history of mankind. He called it "one of the wisest political settlements ever made in the history of the English nation", adding later that "only the English could do it. They make mistakes but they are a big people."[2]

It is important to understand the deep impression which this magnanimity towards a beaten foe made on Smuts. It became the dominant political influence in his life and as it was fully in accordance with his religion, with the qualities of mercy and gentleness in Christianity, it became the star, which ever after guided him through the mists and the confusions of national and international affairs. To him it was expressed in the one word TRUST.

In studying his statecraft during the 44 years after this trust had been placed in him personally, I have become convinced that "trust" is the golden thread which runs through all his actions. Smuts was trusted by the British and ever after he trusted others to do the right thing, even though he was let down time and again. He trusted his own Boers and, in spite of everything he accomplished for them, many of them hated and reviled him most of his life. In international affairs he trusted peoples and governments to realize their best interests and to act accordingly. In spite of their having been the aggressors in two world wars, he continued to trust the Germans as a people. In the end, he felt, they would reveal their essential goodness and help mankind on the path of progress towards a better world. It is probably no accident that his last great speech, on his 80th birthday, was devoted to a plea to accept the Germans as equals in the shaping of the modern world. That was in May 1950, five years after the end of the Hitler war which caused so much suffering to so many. Did he in his hour of great pain, realizing that he had come to the end of his days, think back on that first act of mercy and trust shown to him and his people four years after the Anglo-Boer War?

Was this great trust in people and nations justified? Is it possible to build a lifetime of hard work on it?

Before we attempt to answer these questions, we must clear up one other important aspect of his statesmanship.

It is often said that Smuts's statecraft reveals or reflects his Holism. This is undoubtedly so when viewed from the perspective of the present, but we must not forget that though his holistic ideas simmered in his mind from his student days, he formulated them only when he was 56. In his case the German saying holds true: "*Im Anfang war die Tat.*" His statecraft started and was rooted in action. It was much later that Holism explained it and put it in the pattern of his greater ideas.

But this does not mean that his earlier activities in the spheres of politics and statesmanship conflicted with his holistic ideas. On the contrary, they were in harmony, for here again we must realize that with Smuts as with every individual, personality comes first and it is out of that that both our actions and our ideas are born. If our personalities are harmonious and truly one with our capabilities and our highest aspirations, it must necessarily follow that our actions and our ideas will also be harmonious. In fact there would be a unity between our actions and our ideas even though we are able only later to formulate our ideas properly. Action often comes first. We are living in an essentially and wholly active universe, as Smuts himself said in his Holism, and we as children of that universe reflect that action.

At the same time, we must bear in mind that Holism according to him referred essentially to organic wholes. A state or combination of groups or nations can never be called a holistic unity, for they remain mere aggregates of individuals. Unlike a holistic whole these individuals combine without losing their identity or individuality. Their association in a nation or a state is outward and mechanical. The state or the nation is never an organism. States and nations are never more than the sum of the individuals in them, nor are they above these individuals. In fact they are organizations, or as he called them, holoïds which have as their aim the true happiness and welfare of the individuals constituting them. Yet outwardly their pattern can be holistic as they combine into ever greater patterns without, however, losing their identity or becoming absorbed in the greater unity.[3]

In saying this I do not wish to convey the idea that Smuts had not reasoned out his actions before he acted or that he deviated from his holistic ideas. On the contrary, he knew what he wanted. Above all he wanted freedom. Freedom to him was always the highest ideal for both nations and individuals. And from the beginning he wanted unity – to build a united nation in South Africa. These two aspirations lay at the basis of his public work from his earliest years. Eventually they became the cornerstones of his Holism too. In fact his actions resulted from his principles as his ideas grew out of his actions. But the holistic pattern even though unexplained at first is plainly visible in his upward and ever greater groupings in his statecraft.

In studying his public life we see that these two trends which I have described, the one born of trust and based upon it, the other unifying and holistic with unity and freedom as its core, together shaped all he did.

At times we can see more clearly the working of the holistic pattern, at others, we discern more of his basic trust and his mercy born from that trust and his deeply felt religion.

In a third category of actions they combined and intermingled to create the new instruments of international governments with which he wished to shape the new world.

The pattern of his statecraft was always from a smaller to a larger to a still larger unity and it all began with the establishment of responsible government in the Transvaal in December 1906. Botha became Prime Minister and Smuts his Colonial Secretary and Minister of Education. With "colossal industry and persuasive tact" as *The Johannesburg Star* described his activities, he undertook the task of setting the house of the Transvaal in order. He gave it a new Education Act which still stands in principle to this day. He secured a loan of £5 million from England for the Transvaal in return for the presentation of the fabulous Cullinan diamond to the British Crown. He regulated the labour position which resulted in his first clash with organized labour and he came to grips with Gandhi who at the time was in the Transvaal on private business, but who took the lead in the struggle of the South African Indians against discrimination.

Without their knowing it, two giants who in many ways would make their mark on the international scene in years to come, were here pitted against one another. Gandhi, in spite of his small size, was a giant in moral courage and spiritual power.[4] Smuts with his massive brain was a greater intellectual, but as fearless in his approach to all problems. They met for the first time in 1907 in a jail in Pretoria, where they reached a compromise, although Gandhi accused Smuts of having betrayed him when it came to the application of their agreement.[5]

A larger unity loomed ahead in South Africa and Smuts with Botha took the lead to bring about the unification of the four provinces, the Cape, the Transvaal, Natal and the Orange Free State. Here we have ample opportunity to see both of his principles, the striving towards unity and his trust in the people and in the future, at work.

It is generally agreed that Smuts more than any other man was the architect of Union in South Africa, though he himself later said it was not "a man's work. It bears the imprint of a Higher Hand". What Alexander Hamilton did for the constitution of the United States, Smuts did for South Africa, only more so. What is additionally interesting is the remarkable similarity in many of their views about constitutions and government.

As a keen student and a prodigious worker Smuts studied the American constitution carefully and he undoubtedly was influenced by many of Hamilton's ideas.

As early as 1907 he started preparing the ground for Union in letters to a variety of leaders in the other provinces and in many speeches.[6]

In these he stressed especially the necessity of unity between the two white races in South Africa, the Afrikaners and the English, on a basis of equality.

"The Boer has fought for his independence, the Englishman for his Empire: all have fought for what they consider highest. Now the highest is Union . . . Let us have Union . . . not of top dog or under dog, but of brothers."

When the National Convention was convened, he prepared a draft constitution which he submitted to the various delegates. It was this draft which, after lengthy deliberations and many changes and additions, became the constitution of the Union of South Africa.

In his "Inner History of the South African Convention" Sir Edgar Walton, who was one of the delegates, gave a report of the many contributions made by the various delegates. His résumé of Smuts's opening address is especially important for our purpose. Here again we see trust and unity as the two paramount principles on which he wished the future to be built.

He put trust first and Sir Edgar Walton reports him as saying: "They (the delegates) must trust the people of South Africa, they must trust each other. Distrust and suspicion would be fatal. They must also trust future South Africans, trust their wisdom."[7]

With the idea of trust as the foundation of Union, he developed his argument further and told the delegates that they had no right to hamper future generations and bind them by any cast-iron system or constitution which only a revolution could amend.

His draft constitution was not rigid like that of the USA but flexible in the British tradition. He pointed out that the constitution in the United States had up till then only twice been altered, for the difficulties in the way of alteration were almost insuperable, and that the States were now working under a Constitution made in the eighteenth century when the conditions of the country were entirely different from what they are today. Machinery for alteration was devised, but it was found to be almost unworkable, and the experience of the States was an object lesson for South Africa.

Therefore he devised a constitution which would not tie the hands of future generations, but made it possible for them to alter the constitution.

This meant that there were no fundamental safeguards in South Africa's constitution as there are the fundamental declaration of rights in the American constitution. But in order to safeguard the language rights and the franchise rights of the non-European voters, the principle of a two-thirds majority was introduced to prevent a bare majority from endangering these rights.

This was the measure of Smuts's trust in the wisdom and integrity of future South Africans. Whether this trust was justified in the light of what has since happened we shall examine later. The fundamental fact to be borne in mind here is that trust was the one great rock on which the Union rested. The other was unity and not a loose federation. Here again Smuts's reasoning won the day. South Africa, he pointed out, could choose between a federation such as exists in Australia or a Union such as that of the United Kingdom, or they could follow a middle course with a strong central government and limited powers to the provincial governments.

He rejected the federal system for South Africa because it gives too much power to the provinces or states and makes them virtually independent of the central authority. Although it might be suitable in Australia and the USA, experience in these countries has already shown how difficult it is to work the federal system. However, the provinces in South Africa were not independent states but brothers.

Like Alexander Hamilton, he regarded the British system as the best in the world, a model which all free peoples could safely copy. It was therefore essential to adapt from the British constitution the system of a strong responsible government. As in Britain all power should be vested in the central parliament, which should be the whipping boy of the people. But to meet South Africa's special conditions, he agreed to a system of a central sovereign parliament together with provincial councils with delegated and defined powers and, of course, subject to the central parliament.

That was the system of unity in diversity which became the second rock on which the future of South Africa was built. Smuts thought that this middle course would give the least occasion for friction in the future, for it could accommodate itself to the needs of the people from time to time, and the powers of the local legislature could be extended or curtailed as occasion demanded.[8]

This was undoubtedly a system that was practical, and on the basis of this constitution the Union of South Africa came into being on May 31 1910. The system "worked" as Smuts predicted, but it "worked" for the most part because he made it work. As the tireless worker who carried the heaviest burdens of the new state, he became for South Africa and for General Botha, its first Prime Minister, what Alexander Hamilton had been for the USA and for George Washington. He, principally, shaped the new policy against the Boer rebels and in German South West Africa, East Africa and on the Western Front in Europe. Unlike Hamilton he had no aptitude for finance and his short period as Minister of Finance proved to be a mistake.

It is important to remember that Smuts in the course of the next 48 years, in four great crises, became the instrument of saving the Union from disruption. All four crises tested his powers to the full.

The first crisis came in 1912 with the breakaway of General Hertzog and a section of the Afrikaners. Botha and Smuts stood firm on the basis of union between the two white races.

The year after brought a new crisis when the mineworkers of the Rand imposed their will upon the Government. Because of the weakness of the new state, Botha and Smuts capitulated to the demands of the strikers and accepted their terms. He told Parliament shortly afterwards that the signing of the strikers' document was "one of the hardest things I have ever had to do".[9]

However, he swallowed his pride and bore the humiliation for the sake of the new union. But a year later when the strikers, drunk with power from their first success, again threatened to paralyse the state, he was ready, and with his Burgher Forces he taught them their first lessons as citizens. Nine strike leaders were deported without trial. Afterwards he had to rush through a Bill to indemnify the government for this illegality, which he justified by the argument that he had to save the Union. This action, as well as his merciless driving of himself and all who worked with him, strengthened the impression that he was an autocrat, and he was called "the ruthless philosopher".[10]

In the same year came the third and greatest of all tests for the new Union, the great war of 1914. When Germany invaded Belgium, General Botha said to the British Government: "We do not require your troops here, you may be able to use them better; we are in a position to look after ourselves." Under the leadership of Botha and Smuts the Union declared war on Germany. Almost at once a section of the Boers under General Christiaan de Wet and others rebelled and South Africa's future hung in the balance. It was one of the severest tests to which a young nation could be put, and for Smuts and Botha it was another supreme crisis in their lives. They had to make a most fateful decision, this time not against an outside enemy, but against their own comrades from the Anglo-Boer War, their own personal friends, their own flesh and blood.

What won the day for them and for the future of South Africa was born out of trust. When Great Britain gave the Union its freedom they felt morally bound to her as a friend. To them it became a question of honour and human dignity and when they had to choose between honour and trust, or revenge and selfish self-interest, they chose the former. This is nowhere better illustrated than in their personal conflict with one of their best friends, General Koos de la Rey. Smuts served under him in the Anglo-Boer War. He learnt his war strategy from this natural warrior of the veld. He and Botha were not only personal friends of De la Rey, but the latter always stayed with Smuts when in Pretoria. Smuts on a later occasion described him as "one of the whitest and noblest souls that ever lived".[11]

And now De la Rey, the greatest Boer fighter, saw an opportunity for the Boers to avenge the defeat and humiliation of the Anglo-Boer War. What is more, as a deeply religious man, he saw the Hand of God in this chance to release the Boer people from the bondage imposed on them at Vereeniging.

Smuts has feelingly described how Botha and he and a few other friends strove far into the night on the eve of the Rebellion, to convince General De la Rey that rebellion was not in the true interests of South Africa. The argument took a religious turn and Botha then uttered these historic words: "Oom Koos, it may be the will of God that this nation shall be free and independent. But nothing will ever convince me that it is the will of God that this shall be brought about through treachery and dishonour."[12]

In recalling these words many years later Smuts said that Botha's language at the time reminded him of one of the greatest passages in the Book of Job.

He himself acted according to his conviction that trust begets trust. Having been trusted, he felt it his duty to be worthy of that trust.

"The Dutch people of South Africa feel their honour is touched. They are determined to do their duty and wipe out this disgrace. Out of the late war (the Anglo-Boer War) the Boer people brought little except their good name. That is what they value as their greatest asset in the world. They are not going to allow anyone . . . to drag their good name in the mire."[13]

Botha and Smuts took their stand on the side of the Allied powers. They crushed the rebellion and South Africa played her part in bringing about the downfall of Germany in Africa and Europe. That decision undoubtedly saved the Union, for had they remained neutral or succumbed to the rebels, chaos and disunity would undoubtedly have resulted, to destroy the friendship of Boer and Briton and the unification of the provinces. Here they did for South Africa in agony of soul and through personal suffering and sacrifice, what Abraham Lincoln did for Union in the American Civil War.

As if one such test was not enough, a second came in 1939 with Hitler's War. Here again South Africa was at the crossroads and one wrong decision might have endangered the future of the Union. Again Smuts was faced with a great personal problem. Should he side with his fellow Afrikaners, men he had worked with and respected, or strike out boldly on a course which he thought right and honourable? Against him was pitted General Hertzog, the fiery Afrikaner leader under whom Smuts had served for six years and who as Smuts himself said, had rendered great service to the Union. Hertzog, in the crisis of September 1939, once again saw an opportunity to put into practice his ideal of nationalism based on complete isolation and independence from the Commonwealth and from the rest of the world. He proposed a policy of neutrality and secretly obtained an assurance of support, at first verbally, later in black and white, from Dr Malan and his "purified" National Party. Armed with this, General Hertzog confronted Smuts on the morning of Saturday, September 2 1939 with a demand that he support his policy of neutrality.

"Impossible," said Smuts and that one word again safeguarded Union.[14]

Instinctively Smuts saw that it was a question which went to the very roots of South Africa's national life and he had to make up his mind which road was best for Union. "I saw we had now reached a point where I would have to give away everything which I regarded as right for the people of South Africa when General Hertzog came to us with a ready-made plan of neutrality. We had reached down to bedrock". Again Smuts took his stand on the principles of trust and unity. In moving in Parliament that South Africa break its relations with Germany he urged South Africa to carry out her obligations and continue to co-operate with her friends and associates in the Commonwealth of Nations. South Africa he said, could not be a fairweather friend. She must stand by her friends. Again Britain's trust of 1906 bore fruit. Secondly he knew that unity was at stake. He himself was prepared to sacrifice his own interests, to give blood and sweat "to see that the young life of this nation is given a chance and for the people to have an opportunity to grow together".

The course of the war and the part South Africa played both in the field and on the industrial front as a new arsenal of the free countries, justified that policy of trust and unity to the full. In the general election of 1943 the people endorsed Smuts's stand by an overwhelming majority. Without conscription young Afrikaners flocked to the armed forces and English and Afrikaans South Africans fought side by side in East and North Africa and in Italy. South Africa emerged more united, much stronger and much more prosperous from the war. But like Churchill in England, Smuts was rejected by the voters in the first post-war election in May 1948.

The shock and the humiliation was a severe blow to him. But worse was to follow in the years to come and especially after his death. Under Dr Malan and his successor Mr Strijdom, the two-stream policy of dividing the Afrikaners from the English section became the official policy of the land. Separated in their schools, children grew up in antagonism and estrangement with the top-dog policy once again carrying the day.

In national affairs, the Strijdom government, taking a strong line, broke the white man's sacred promise to the million Cape Coloureds not to take away their political rights as voters on the common roll. In order to carry this policy through, Mr Strijdom interfered with the judiciary and circumvented the Constitution by creating an enlarged Senate to give him a two-thirds majority in a combined session of the Senate and the Legislative Assembly. It was a thoroughly ruthless and immoral policy, the opposite of that trust in the essential wisdom and good sense, the justice and righteousness which Smuts had hoped for the future.

Was this trust, in the light of his own betrayal by his people and of the events since then, justified or not? Is it still possible to believe in it and to build the future on it?

This question in its broader meaning has been debated in all ages and all over the world. It lies at the root of the beliefs and actions of all peoples. It is the basis of our religions and we find it as a creed in philosophy as in politics. Can people be trusted? Alexander Hamilton, the "Colossus of the Federalists" and the man who more than anyone else shaped George Washington's policies, was not inclined by temperament or experience to trust people too much. He would not bow to what he called "the majesty of the multitude" for he feared the fickleness of the people. Often portrayed as an enemy of the people, he was probably less afraid of the people than he was of the legislature. Yet he remained in American history the great believer in a strong central government. He wanted a government that could act. Not trust but action was his credo.

Although Smuts's views on trusting the people were far from those of Hamilton, like Hamilton he believed in a strong central government. And when he was in power he never hesitated to act. It was as a man both of action and of ideas that he saved the Union in the great crises.

With his clear mind, his stern sense of duty and his quick grasp of the essence of a situation, he was for South Africa and for General Botha, its first Prime Minister, what Hamilton was for George Washington and for the USA in its first formative difficult years.

Yet Smuts in his ideas and political outlook is much nearer to Jefferson's liberalism and Lincoln's trust in the ordinary people. With Lincoln he believed in the composite wisdom and moral rectitude of the common voters, although he never achieved Lincoln's supreme mastery in keeping the masses informed. Smuts was perhaps too much like Hamilton in this regard, preferring to do things himself and, in doing them and carrying a multitude of burdens, he seldom found time to explain the issues at stake adequately to the people.

If there is a flaw in his political ideas we can see it here in a further comparison with Lincoln. Lincoln loved and understood ordinary people and was happy with them and at one with them. Knowing the faults and the frailties of men and women, he understood them and he trusted them. He realized at the same time that the ideals of democracy might never be fully achieved, that they are goals to be approximated, but he was convinced that it was the best course, that men gain strength in striving for them.[15]

Smuts lacked Lincoln's great and abiding humanity. He himself said that he never had a love of human beings but a vast interest in them. He could appreciate their human qualities quite apart from their intellectual capacities, but he was inclined to compare them with himself, not realizing that others could not grasp what he grasped or do what he found it so easy to do. The result was that although he believed in people and trusted them, in his own manner of life he was more like Hamilton than Lincoln, and preferred to do things himself. It was this that gradually destroyed his own party after he fell away.

But of his genuine trust in people and his belief in the eventual triumph of the goodness of ordinary people there can be no doubt.

Like Lincoln he never despaired. Let down time and again, betrayed and humiliated by his own people, his buoyant optimism, his faith in the future and his trust in the goodness of people, came to the top again and again. He realized that all men make mistakes, that he himself made mistakes, but to him "a kind Providence has intervened and has woven all those mistakes and all those services into a strong and wonderful texture which we call the history of South Africa and of which we are proud. When we look at that wonderful history we are all cheered and encouraged to move forward in the hope that as our task has not been too difficult in the past, it may not prove entirely beyond us in the future."

He spoke those words in the bleak year of 1917 when the issue of the life and death struggle in Europe and in Africa still hung precariously in the balance, but it was in line with all his thinking, and even today can be applied to the present problems of South Africa.

It was wrong, he thought, to expect quick and easy solutions. He knew that patience was the essence of true statesmanship, not only in building one nation out of the Afrikaners and the English, but also in the solution of the great racial problems facing Southern Africa, as I will show. As early as 1895 he pleaded for "national unity" and in 1917 he was realistic enough to recognize that the political union of 1909 which brought about the Union of South Africa was not the same as national union. But in spite of setbacks all his life, he remained convinced that "South Africa, a nation, will follow from South Africa, a Union", as he said on Union Day, 1935. He knew that this would take time and perseverance, and in various speeches and private letters to friends he analysed the difficulties ahead before true national union would be experienced. When you have to deal with hard-headed races like the British and the Afrikaners – descendants from Dutch and French stock – you cannot expect results in one or two generations, was his explanation.

We have in South Africa, he said, people who prefer to stand aside from the great currents that are carrying South Africa to her new and greater destiny.

These are not merely Dutch or Afrikaners; many of them are English. We have English fellow-citizens who will always remain English, to whom even the sunshine and the wide open spaces of South Africa are not sufficient to bring about the great transformation of soul. There is also a large section of the Afrikaners who think the best policy is for them to stand aside and to remain in isolation. They think that in that way they will be better able to preserve their language, their traditions, and their national way of life, and not be swallowed up and submerged by new currents.

He understood these people and he understood their fears and their peculiar aspirations and prejudices. He regarded them all as in many ways so good and "to me so dear, that one is extremely anxious to build them up into a solid national block for the future of this subcontinent".

In the face of this diversity he felt all the more strongly that there must be national unity in South Africa, as the one sure basis of future stability and strength, and that national unity is entirely consistent with the preservation of the respective languages, traditions and cultures. Looking to the history of other countries he saw how all great nations have been built out of a mixture of various stocks. The British nation is one of the clearest proofs of that, and it completely routs the false idea of the so-called pure races, which the Germanized Englishman, Houston Chamberlain, expounded and which became the basis of Hitler's racial policy.

South Africa in his opinion has no pure race and no top dog and it was his policy to create "a blend out of the various nationalities, a new South African nation out of our allied stock". He felt convinced that if this could be done, "we shall achieve a new nationality embracing and harmonizing our various traits and blending them all into a richer national type than could otherwise have been achieved".

To achieve this ideal of national unity he asked his fellow South Africans to have faith in South Africa.

Summing up his credo for his own country he used these memorable words:

"Have faith in South Africa. After all we have come grandly out of the struggles of the past – through all that South Africa has gone, and it has been tested as no other young nation has been tested in history. In our generation she has been tested to the uttermost, and she has always come out with flying colours, and she is moving forward. There has been no fatal mistake by her people, but they have always been guided by sound sense – a nose, so to say, for the right; and I have the fullest faith that South Africa will continue like that. Do not fear. Look to the character of the people and see how they have struggled, and have had controversies which seemed to shake the country. They co-operated; they have done their duty on great particular occasions, and I say when we launch forward into the dark future, let us have some faith in the people of South Africa – in their innate sense of what is fair and right, and in their wisdom and their statesmanship. The past has taught us that in that faith we cannot go wrong."

In this faith he said he was prepared to persevere even though "one often finds that one's labour is that of Sisyphus – one step forward and two steps back". And yet he remained always an optimist. "Considering the history of South Africa can you wonder that I incline to optimism and faith in human nature?" he asked in 1935.

And this is the answer which he gave as a light on the way of all future generations:

"It is our experience which has given us faith in human nature and which makes us believe that whatever the future may bring we shall not utterly fail. History, sunshine, religion all combine to make South Africans optimists on the whole. Whatever our difficulties and our problems, there is nothing defeatist about the South African outlook. There is hopefulness, buoyancy and resilience everywhere. We are going to build something new. We are not going to stand still at the posts of our tradition. The people of South Africa are too virile for that.

"We stand not at a grave, but at the most important birth in the history of South Africa."[16]

In dealing with South Africa's second great issue, the colour problem, Smuts was likewise guided by trust and a policy of practical expediency. There are those who criticize him for not having solved this problem while he was Prime Minister. There are others who saw an inconsistency in his great international actions and his lack of action in improving the political and economic status of the African in his own country. Once again it was the old accusation: Others he can save, for his own country he can do nothing.

Both groups of critics ignore and forget the complexity of this great problem in South Africa, which is unique in many ways, as Smuts on many occasions pointed out. He himself knew that it was not a problem which could be cheaply and easily solved, and that in dealing with it no one theory or formula could explain all the facts. He saw it essentially as a human problem with its roots deep in the history of the past, and for the present and the future powerfully linked with the great issues of Christian Western civilization. But he warned equally against those who wished to perpetuate slavery in its newer and subtler forms and against the well-meaning but impractical sentimentalists who see the solution in a system of political equality. In 1895, shortly after he had returned from Cambridge he expressed his conviction: "You cannot safely apply to the barbarous and semi-barbarous natives the advanced political principles and practice of the foremost peoples of civilization."

Too often – he continued – we make the mistake of looking upon democracy as a deduction from abstract principles, instead of regarding it rather as the outcome of practical politics.

To him some form of separation between highly developed Europeans and primitive Africans living under tribal authority was imperative, not only in the interests of an African culture, and to prevent African traditions and institutions from being swamped by the more powerful organization of the Whites, but also for other important purposes such as public health, racial purity and public good order.[17]

It was for this reason that he was in favour of a form of parallel development where tribalized Africans remained in their own territories and retained their own form of life under a tribal system. But he realized at the same time that this was only half of the problem. The urbanized Africans living among the Whites constituted the real crux of the great issue facing South Africa, an issue which went far beyond the political sphere. These semi-civilized and detribalized Africans raised a problem for the whole principle of segregation, as they did not wish to be thrust back into the seclusion of their former tribal associations or forgo the new life amongst the Europeans.

"Were it not for this case of the urbanized or detribalized natives, the colour problem not only in South Africa, but elsewhere in Africa, would be shorn of most of its difficulties," he stated in his lectures on the Native Problem at Oxford in 1919.[18]

He saw no clear-cut answers to all the complications of life in a multi-racial society of this nature, but he formulated certain principles which he held to be essential.

The first of these was the safeguarding of the European civilization in Southern Africa. This he regarded as fundamental. In looking back on the history of Africa over many centuries he saw that at various times attempts have been made at civilization. He reminded his listeners in the Savoy Hotel in London in 1917 of the great Islamic civilization in Central Africa, and of the University of Timbuktu, to which centuries ago students came from other parts of the world. Similarly the huge Zimbabwe ruins in Rhodesia show signs of an unknown former civilization.

"Where are those civilizations now? They have all disappeared and barbarism once more rules over the land and makes the thoughtful man nervous about the White man's future in Southern Africa. There are many people in South Africa – and not very foolish people either – who do not feel certain that our White experiment will be a permanent success, or that we shall ever succeed in making a White man's land of Southern Africa, but at any rate, we mean to press on with the experiment. It has now been in progress for some 250 years (now 300) and perhaps the way we have set about it, may be the right way. Former civilizations in Africa have existed mostly for the purpose of exploiting the native populations, and in that way, and probably also through intermixture of blood, carried in them the seeds of decay."

In order to preserve this White civilization and avoid these mistakes of earlier unsuccessful attempts, he proposed two fundamental principles as the foundation of a practical policy.

The first – he called it the principal one – is "no intermixture of blood between Black and White". He hoped that the Whites in this way could avoid being rapidly submerged in the quicksands of the African flood.

The other axiom was that in "all our dealings with the natives we must build our practice on what I believe Lord Cromer has called the granite bedrock of the Christian moral code.[19] Honesty, fair-play, justice and the ordinary Christian virtues must be the basis of all our relations with the natives."

In the practical application of this policy in the political sphere he was against a system of segregation which would completely divide the Whites and Africans into separate sovereign states. He was in favour of parallel development, but under the one supreme parliament. He felt that all classes and colours should have representation in this central parliament. "There can be only one sovereign body in a country and that body should represent the weaker no less than the stronger. To that extent there should be agreement."

But whatever the final mode of representation or the way parallelism was to be applied, to his way of thinking the spirit in which these great human problems were tackled was all-important. He rejected fundamentally measures and an outlook based on fear. To him the future could only be built on trust. In 1937 he made this very clear in a speech, stating that it was essential for the welfare of South Africa that White and Black should co-operate and help one another. This, he felt, could only be done by maintaining the good feeling that has existed in the past between the races. But he saw new dangers on the horizon. The old spirit between the Europeans and the Africans was going. It was a development that could lead to most serious trouble.

He warned against the people who pretend to be friends of the African and who persuade him that he is an oppressed and downtrodden creature, that the White man is his enemy and exploiter and that his condition is little better than slavery. He was afraid that the African would eventually believe that the White man was his oppressor, and then enmity and hate would replace the spirit of goodwill and friendliness.

In outlining his policy against this background he stated: "There will be justice for both sides. The position of the European and his civilization will be protected, but with the goodwill and co-operation of the Native. The future of South Africa does not depend merely on the White man or the Black man, it depends jointly on both of us. I see only one future for South Africans, and that is one of co-operation. If the Natives are poor and oppressed, South Africa will be poor and oppressed. We can only be happy by raising the level of everybody, irrespective of race and colour."

Warning that it would be disastrous for South Africa if the Black man were treated with ill-feeling and injustice, he appealed to the European section to create a spirit of trust and goodwill towards the Natives.

He formulated this in simple direct words which Mrs Gillett remembered and recalled to me. It sums up his whole outlook on the human problems facing South Africa and the world as a whole.

"You must do the decent thing that you see you can do next, and whatever you do you must respect the dignity of the human being."[20]

However there were many South Africans who were also worried – to say the least – about this policy of racial inequality which Smuts seemed unable or unwilling to tackle and remove. One of them was Harry Oppenheimer who was elected to Parliament in 1948.

Oppenheimer recalls an early political conversation with Field-Marshal Smuts, on the subject. "I did once bravely say to Smuts – didn't he think the United Party should be clearer about racial policy in relations between Black and White? He said it would be impossible to do that until the prior question of creating unity between White South Africans had been achieved.

"I think that was his experience over many years and he was a man then of the age that I am now . . . and, of course, when you get to that sort of age, you are a little bit of a prisoner of your past experience. And while there was something in what he said, history didn't stand still – even for so great a man as Smuts."[21]

This was perhaps the greatest tragedy in his life that he could not solve the most important and most difficult problem of his own country and his own time, the racial division between Black and White. He himself during his lifetime experienced some measure of the deep-felt distaste and abhorrence in the eyes and minds of the rest of mankind about the policy of segregation between Black and White and even between Coloureds and Indians and Whites.

His inability to solve this problem in his own lifetime in his beloved South Africa and the legacy of neglect and insensitiveness to the pain and humiliation which this brought about, hit his country and his people like a tornado in the period after his death.

CHAPTER FOURTEEN

The United States of Southern Africa

The second step in the holistic pattern of Smuts's statecraft was some form of a United States of Southern Africa.

He regarded this as a logical step after Union in South Africa, but that the idea was in his mind even before Union is clear from speeches which he made before 1910.

"Let us make one big South Africa to start a Union here and to rule the country from Table Bay to the Congo and even beyond that. Let us be inventors of a great South Africa," was the appeal he made on the eve of the National Convention of 1909.

After the great and difficult task to establish Union as a practical state he found no time for his dream of a greater unity. But in 1923 his mind reverted to the subject and he took a practical step to bring the colony of Southern Rhodesia into the Union. It was at this time, (1923) that the contract of Cecil John Rhodes's famous Chartered Company in Southern Rhodesia came to an end and the inhabitants of the colony were given the choice between a form of self-government and unification with the Union of South Africa. Smuts saw the great opportunity to expand the Union and take a further step in his dream of a greater united state. He wanted to bridge the Limpopo with one state and one nation, and with this end in view he visited Southern Rhodesia. It must be remembered that he was Prime Minister at the time and he made it his official policy to work for amalgamation between Rhodesia and the Union of South Africa.

To make sure that this grand opportunity would not be missed he conducted the negotiations personally with both the British Government and the Chartered Company and he made his terms very accommodating and magnanimous. The British Government was convinced of the wisdom of the amalgamation and put pressure on the settlers to accept the offer by Smuts. There was much to be said in favour of this unity. Southern Rhodesia (now Zimbabwe) was a natural physical and geographical extension of the Union north of the Limpopo. As a land-locked territory with no harbours of its own it was also to a great extent dependent upon the Union for its economic growth. At the same time its inhabitants, both European settlers and Africans, were of the same stock as those in the Union.

The prospects for a greater Union therefore looked bright when the Smuts-Malcolm agreement was made. Upon its publication the shares of Rhodes's Chartered Company experienced a great boom.

Smuts at this time was in Rhodesia among the settlers – both English and Afrikaners, although the latter were in the minority – and it was natural that they came under the spell of his vision and his personality. Had he been able to stay until the final plebiscite the verdict of the settlers and the entire history of Southern Africa might have been different. But he was forced to leave, and in his absence the narrower view prevailed. The fears of the English-speaking settlers of Afrikaans domination gave the final blow to his scheme. Not trust and faith, but fear and prejudice won the day, and by a majority of 2 785 votes out of a total of 15 000 Rhodesia decided against amalgamation.[1]

Smuts's dream of a greater unity in Southern Africa received its greatest blow. The Union and Southern Rhodesia developed along different paths and in different directions. It also meant that the further implementing of this policy was stopped, for how could Smuts have hoped to extend his scheme to the other northern territories if Southern Rhodesia remained a stumbling block in his way?

A handful of people, in a moment of fear, had blocked a scheme which would have placed Southern Africa finally on the way to becoming a great united state. It was a tired and disillusioned Smuts who saw his dream shattered. This, combined with his difficulties in the Union itself, led him to an act almost of despair – one of the few in his long life. Without consulting his Cabinet or his Party caucus, he decided to resign and to appeal to the electorate, knowing, as he must have done, that his party was bound to be defeated by the Hertzog-Creswell combination in the Nationalist and Labour pact of April 23 1923.

His announcement came as a bombshell in the House of Parliament to both friend and foe. As was to be expected, Hertzog, father of the two-stream policy of parallel development of Afrikaners and English, won the election. Smuts was out and the ideal of a greater Union disappeared under the tide of nationalism which engulfed South Africa.

It was many years before Smuts came back to his dream of a "British confederation of African states – a great African Dominion stretching unbroken throughout Africa" as he had explained it to the voters at Ermelo in 1929, adding in his Rhodes lectures at Oxford the same year that such a confederal arrangement of British African territories should be "under White leadership".

He realized that it was useless to attempt any new scheme while the Afrikaner nationalism of Hertzog was rampant in the Union for, in his nationalistic policies, the Prime Minister of the Union was accentuating the very fears which had driven the Rhodesians into their own isolation. But in

1933, with the new pact of fusion between Hertzog and Smuts, the climate was once more favourable to ideas of a greater unity. Smuts, however, realized that he would have to be patient and long-suffering. He would have to sow the seeds of unity in barren earth hoping that somehow some seed would someday germinate and bear fruit.

1935 and 1936 seem to have been his most active years in this respect. Before that he had devoted his greatest attention to laying an enduring basis of peace in South Africa herself. After those years, the preparation for the new war he saw looming occupied most of his time.

In 1935 he began by addressing the Pan-African Postal Conference which was devoted to the improvement of postal communications in Africa. Smuts regarded this as a practical step in the right direction.

"I look upon communications as a great solvent of international troubles," he told the conference, "they draw us together in spite of idiosyncrasies."

He thought that this applied especially to the peoples of the African continent, where communications have a special significance. "I have been more and more impressed by my experience and travels by the unitary character of the continent. More than any other continent, Africa is one. It presents closely similar problems from one end to the other. Other continents present very diverse characteristics but not so the African continent."

Enumerating the common aspects of the continent he saw similarities in its native populations and in its physical features. Although the countries were politically divided and were different sovereignties, the peoples of Africa would work together in many amicable and useful ways.

"Our fauna are the same; our flora are the same in Africa from the Equator downwards. In these conditions of similarity, therefore there is a call on the governments in the southern part of the continent to work together as closely as possible."

He saw co-operation necessary to all Africans, White and Black, for their interests were all identical and their objectives much the same.

"We all stand for that great mother civilization inherited from Europe. We are here for the spreading of the light, for the bringing-up of the African continent according to the highest standards possible. We can all collaborate in the solutions of the problems before us," he told the delegates.

Less than a year later, in September 1936, he was to carry his ideas on co-operation in Africa further when he addressed the Southern African Transport Congress. It was an important occasion, the first time that the heads and leading members of Africa Governments or their representatives had met on African soil. Other similar international conferences on African affairs had been held before in Europe. What made the conference even more auspicious was that every country of Central and Southern Africa was represented, also the island of Madagascar. Besides Southern and Northern Rhodesia, Nyasaland, Tanganyika, Kenya and Uganda, the French and Portuguese colonies as well as the Belgian Congo took part. "What a rollcall of young nations in the making! What an unbroken and unbreakable girdle of strength and hope under the heart of Africa!" Smuts exclaimed in welcoming the delegates.

"The Union of South Africa which stands almost in the relation of a mother to some of these states, feels very proud of all of them. South African enterprise and brains and blood have gone into the making of them, and will continue to do so. Nothing that vitally concerns these countries could be alien to the Union. They are the far-flung outposts for which the inhabitants of the Union have laboured in the south. If the Union is interested in them it is not for selfish motives or points of view, but because she feels a deep pride in their achievements and a warm solicitude for the future. The people of the Union feel the pull of common ideals and the fear of common dangers."

Having explained the common bonds uniting them all, Smuts felt it necessary to reassure these countries. In doing so he laid down the pattern for unity and co-operation on the basis of freedom and faith.

"Judging from occasional stray utterances we are sometimes suspected of designs on these young communities to the north. Let me give you the assurance and set the minds of any doubters at rest on this point. I think I speak from the heart of South Africa when I say that never will the Union dream of approaching you or any of you except on your own invitation and your own overtures. So far as we are concerned, the initiative for your destiny is in your own hands. On the paths of Africa we have been strangely led, and we do not know what the world with all its gathering dangers has in store for us. But it is the determination of the Union to be to you not the grasping, but the helping hand. The good neighbourship of today, which is ever strengthening, must solve the problems of the future. There is no place for sterile suspicions in our relations, which are almost of a family character."

After this assurance he exhorted the representatives to practise the faith of the good neighbour to each other. He thought that while they scrupulously respected each other's rights, they could be helpful friends to each other, and he appealed to them to act in the spirit of a small League of Nations from which all fear, all suspicion was banished.

He pointed out that it was wrong to compare the position of Africa with that of the American continent in the early nineteenth century. With the expulsion of Spain from South America, the whole American continent was dissociated from Europe and the politics of the European powers. Canada was the only foothold of Europe on that continent, and it was Canning, the British Foreign Minister, who put up the notion to formulate the Monroe Doctrine.

But Africa was not free from Europe and European politics. It was still linked with the European colonial powers and a bone of contention between the Great Powers.

For South Africa to formulate a Monroe Doctrine in these circumstances he considered to be much beyond her influence and power. It might even look ridiculous.

But if a Monroe Doctrine were not possible for Africa, he looked for another formula which would prevent Africa becoming a pawn in the European game and a fresh field for sowing trouble. This he found in his idea of a League of Nations for Africa, which might attempt to keep the peace on the Continent. As he saw it, such a League might operate with the goodwill and co-operation of the European Powers who have possessions in Africa. In any case he felt that this idea was worth exploring.

How anxious he was for a great union in Southern Africa at this time and how far he was prepared to go to bring it about, is apparent from a letter he wrote in February 1937 to a Rhodesian friend. It was at a time when the inhabitants of the Rhodesias were again giving anxious thought to their future, not knowing whether to look south towards the Union of South Africa or northwards to their sister colonies in Northern Rhodesia and Nyasaland.

Smuts took the line that the Rhodesians must decide their own future. He still thought that they had missed a grand opportunity in 1923 when they voted against amalgamation with the Union. But South Africa had accepted the verdict and must leave any future initiatives in these matters to them. But he had not given up hope. "I am prepared to wait for the future to justify the line I took then, a line which, as is well known, was entirely in harmony with the great vision of the founder of Rhodesia."

Although he took the correct line of strict non-interference in the affairs of the neighbours to the north, he revealed how anxious he was to bring about the greater union and how far he was prepared to deviate from his previous policy. As the father of Union in South Africa he was naturally proud of his work. At the time when Union was formed he rejected a system of federal government in South Africa.

Looking back in 1937 on all that had happened since 1919, he considered that the Union Constitution had been an outstanding success.

But such was his anxiety for a greater union that he was prepared to introduce into the Union Constitution some form of federal element in order to incorporate other states in Southern Africa.

He did not explain his ideas in this regard in detail, but gave it as his personal opinion that union would not form the basis of a suitable arrangement with territories further north. For the purpose of close political co-operation with the northern states he felt a somewhat more elastic arrangement would have to be considered.

What form this "elastic arrangement" was to take he did not explain, merely stating that he had little doubt that in the events crowding in upon the African continent, some such basis of a federal character would be the more appropriate scheme to secure co-operation.

Unfortunately for the peoples of Southern Africa these ideas were not carried further, due to the vast preparations for war which then gripped the world. At the same time, it must be borne in mind that Smuts was not the Prime Minister of the Union at this stage. He was under the leadership of Hertzog and the latter seldom looked beyond the Limpopo. Greater African union never fitted into the narrower schemes of the father of Afrikaans nationalism. It was for this reason that Smuts expressed his views privately in a confidential letter to a Rhodesian friend. But with the outbreak of war in September 1939 and his split on the war issue with Hertzog, Smuts once again took over the leadership of South Africa.[2] His first task was to build a strong army to defend the Union and its northern approaches. To do this he linked the Union forces with those from the Rhodesias and he himself became the Supreme Commander of the combined armies of Southern Africa. Together, as brothers in arms, the Afrikaans and English troops of South Africa and the soldiers of the two Rhodesias helped to clear East and North Africa, and later Italy, of the foe. It was again a great demonstration of united action in the face of a common danger. It was followed by a series of acts in industry, trade, mining and transport in which South Africa and her northern neighbours co-operated to the fullest extent. In fact South Africa once again became the mother, taking the northern countries under her wing to shelter, protect, assist and nourish them.

In this climate of active co-operation and brotherly goodwill and friendliness Smuts once again saw an opportunity for the realization of his dream of a greater South Africa. But this time he decided to go about it more slowly, leaving the force of events in the modern world to bring these neighbouring countries together. He was prepared to wait for a closer political federation to grow naturally and spontaneously out of that. But meanwhile he was active behind the scenes and began to plan for the gradual extension of the Union.

His first step was to link up the Union and the mandated territory of South West Africa, the old German colony which he and General Botha conquered in the 1914-1918 war against strong opposition from Nationalists and even an armed protest on the part of General C. R. de Wet and his followers. After the war South Africa had taken charge of South West Africa as a "C" class Mandate under the control of the League of Nations.

This gave South Africa the right to administer the territory as an integral part of the Union but with no sovereignty to incorporate the territory legally. After the Second World War Smuts was determined to do just that, but with the approval of the international community. It is the considered opinion of his biographer Prof. W. K. Hancock that "not a dog would have barked during the Second World War" had he followed the Russian example and simply annexed the territory, but his old-fashioned respect for the legal fabric of the society of nations restrained him.[3]

When the United Nations was formed at the San Francisco Conference he was given notice that South Africa, like the other mandatory powers, would be invited to bring South West Africa into the proposed trusteeship system of the new world body. Smuts objected to this, but decided to postpone his legal arguments for incorporation to the new General Assembly.

Meanwhile he had tested the wishes of the inhabitants as to whether incorporation would be acceptable or not. The Whites in the territory decided by a unanimous vote of the Legislative Assembly to opt for incorporation. The wishes of the other inhabitants of the territory were established through the tribal system. Each tribal chief had a block vote equal to the number of tribesmen under him. In his subsequent statement to the General Assembly, Smuts was able to show that out of the total non-European vote of approximately 300 000 a majority of 208 850 against only 33 520 favoured incorporation. He frankly admitted that the Administration had not been able to consult 56 790 non-European voters for various reasons. Even the British Government of Mr Attlee declared itself satisfied with the procedure followed by Smuts to consult the inhabitants of South West Africa, but when the General Assembly met to discuss the Smuts motion for incorporation, the Indian delegates expressed themselves strongly against incorporation. This influenced most of the delegates and on December 14 1946 the General Assembly, by 37 votes to none, with nine abstentions, rejected incorporation and requested the South African Government to administer the territory in the spirit of the principles laid down in the mandate.[4]

It was a severe blow for Smuts not only as an international statesman, but also because the incorporation of South West Africa was to be a pillar of his attempt to form a Greater South Africa.

In a personal letter to Mrs Margaret Gillett written on January 14 1947, he refers to all his troubles resulting from the setback over South West Africa. "My failure with UNO has been a bitter experience, even where I know, or perhaps more *because* I know, that essentially it is South Africa's as much as mine. The world does not know or understand us, and we feel this deeply, even when we are conscious that we are much to blame in it all."[5]

In spite of his setback in South West Africa he continued his secret negotiations with the British and Rhodesian Governments for a merger on terms very favourable for the Rhodesias. The discussions took place against the background of the enforced active co-operation of the countries during and after the war. The atmosphere was favourable but he did not want to rush the issues involved. He was looking forward to his new term of office after the election of May 1948 to complete his schemes, both in regard to South West and the Rhodesias. No doubt he visualized the linking up with these countries and the formation of a greater Federation of Southern Africa as his last great contribution to the development of his native continent.

Smuts was fairly sure of his re-election. A week before the election he held a confidential press conference in his office in Cape Town. "On what platform are you fighting this election?" asked Mr Victor Norton, editor of the *Cape Times*. "On my record. My platform is well known to the public," replied a piqued Smuts. He was cocksure of victory and he was planning a great future for a greater South Africa.[6]

In that election of May 1948 the future of the entire Southern Africa once more hung in the balance. The issue at stake was whether Southern Africa was going to proceed, on the analogy of the United States of America, toward a greater unity and co-operation which would lay the basis of its future wealth and might, or whether the various countries would each one stay in its own orbit and build up forces against one another.

In rejecting Smuts and electing Dr Malan and his National Party, South Africa once again turned her back on the idea of a greater unity. For although Dr Malan with courage and determination incorporated South West into the Union, his policies in South Africa inevitably drove South Africa and the Rhodesias apart. As a result Southern Rhodesia turned her face to the north and started the scheme which eventually led to the Federation with Northern Rhodesia and Nyasaland. At the same time she took active steps to ensure her free outlet to the sea with railway connections through the Portuguese territories. The dream of a United States of Southern Africa had for the time being come to nothing.

This meant also the end of another great ideal of Smuts. He saw unity in Southern Africa as more than just a political federation. He conceived a deeper unity in the spheres of nature and the human spirit.

"I have had a vision of a great National Park stretching with few interruptions through Africa from the north of Kenya to join up with the Kruger National Park in the South," he explained in 1936. He saw this as a great corridor of Africa, through which its game would move more freely up and down, subject only to the necessary breaks and safeguards against the spread of disease and disease carriers and where game could be viewed by naturalists and tourists from all over the world.

He felt that this was necessary, not only to retain these priceless assets of Africa for all time, but also because of the unique spirit of Africa. On many occasions he pointed out the dangers of the congestion of modern life in almost every country. Pressure of people upon one another coupled with the industrial and mechanical processes of modern life destroyed the close contact of man with nature. Because of it, modern man was robbed of that deep peace which comes from being one with nature. Here, he felt, Africa with its vast open spaces, its game, its flora, could be a great asset to mankind, and he wanted the rulers of Africa to combine and preserve this quality.

The future development of African resources must have definite regard, he stated, to the peculiar character and characteristics, the peace and restfulness, the unique treasures and spirit of Africa, and the hand of the killer and the vandal, the enemy of its fauna and flora, should be stayed and controlled. The value of Africa to the world consists largely of its uniqueness, which should be preserved inviolate at all costs. Specially controlled parks stretching from south to north across the boundaries of the existing states, he considered, would be one way of doing that.

To show what he believed Africa could mean to the weary crowd-oppressed traveller from other continents, I shall quote this passage from one of his many orations on the spirit of Africa.

"The peace and refreshment of mind and body which a journey through Africa brings, no words can describe. With some congenial friends and a few light cars you can have the most glorious holiday. Everything is unusual, so different from one's daily experience in the busy world of civilization. There is a brooding quiet in the bush which produces an eerie feeling, time seems to stand still, and only space remains and stretches on and on endlessly. And you move from day to day to new sights, new and strange adventures, the world forgetting, by the world forgot.

"Life itself becomes an adventure in the wilds. Could any holiday more welcome be conceived in these days of hectic living and frayed nerves? It may yet be the lot of Africa to play a great part in the drama of civilization. What the Kruger National Park in the Union of South Africa has become to its active population, Africa may become to the rest of the world. Governments may plan repartitions and Geneva may scratch her head over Mandates, but Africa remains serene, imperturbable, aloof, unaffected by the wild noise and propaganda on the European stage. She keeps her secrets, she remains the mystery. The Sphinx is her symbol."

Concluding, he stated that Africa is the future paradise for the tourist and the holiday-maker in search of the pure delights of nature. To Africa they will come for refreshment and delight in ever-increasing numbers. "And those who can enter into the mysterious spirit of Africa will receive a message which will remain with them all their lives. The African tour will have been for them an initiation, an act of worship, which will give fresh courage for the struggle for life elsewhere."

High-minded and splendid as these visions were, his dream of a greater United States of Africa was never realized in his own lifetime and since his death in 1950 antagonisms and confrontation have taken the place of goodwill and co-operation.

CHAPTER FIFTEEN

The Commonwealth

Southern Africa and especially South Africa is in some respects a microcosm of the world at large. With its many races, nationalities, tribes, groups and sections with different religions, cultures, languages, customs and traditions it forms a fertile field for the study of human, racial and cultural relationships and interrelationships. As such it is in many ways a testing ground for experiments in interrelated co-operative ventures in the field of statecraft and economic interdependence.

If this applies to some extent to the world at large, it applies even more to the former British Empire which has since emerged as the Commonwealth of Nations.

What is significant in this development from an Empire into a Commonwealth was that Smuts played an important part in establishing the basic principles on which the Commonwealth was brought into being, and it was possibly the effect of his South African experience among a welter of races, nationalities and cultures which helped him to become an outstanding leader in the formation of the Commonwealth.

Smuts first used the word Commonwealth in a long political tract which he wrote during the Anglo-Boer War in January 1902, and addressed as an open letter to W. T. Stead with the intention, as he told Abraham Fisher, the Free State leader, to appeal to the conscience of the British people. He pleaded for an agreed peace which could open the door to a free and fraternal association of the Boers and British in a "stable Commonwealth in South Africa" as he called it.

"Let it clearly be understood that England shall meddle as little as possible with the internal concerns of this Commonwealth as with those of Canada or Australasia, and the best solution of the South African problem under existing circumstances will have been made, and a new Commonwealth of untold possibilities will have been launched on a joyous and prosperous career."

Turning to his religion he warned at the same time that if England "hardens her heart" then the ghost of the murdered Boer people will haunt the British Empire to its grave, then across the centuries the terrible curse of Isaiah will blast the British Empire: "Woe to thee that spoilest-" he spelled out Isaiah's curse.[1]

This plea fell on deaf ears in Britain, but as early as 1904, two years after the end of the Anglo-Boer War, when he was exchanging views on the future of South Africa with the Cape Liberal leader John X. Merriman, the word Commonwealth again cropped up in a letter Merriman wrote to him on June 4. Smuts had written on May 30 suggesting a policy of Federation and objecting to the stationing of "foreign" (British) troops in South Africa. Merriman corrected him and wrote this prophetic sentence:

"We must look forward to the time when British troops will be the troops of the British Commonwealth of which South Africa as well as Australia, New Zealand and Canada will form an integral part with all the rights of a free self-governing community."[2]

This was in line with Smuts's thinking as expressed in 1902 and must have invoked an immediate response, but there are no indications that he was then already thinking of a larger unity, as he was concentrating on obtaining self-government for the defeated Republics. When he and Botha met Merriman in Pretoria in November 1905, Merriman was so impressed with the two Boer leaders that he described them as the reincarnation of Washington and Hamilton.[3]

Thereafter it was Smuts who in many respects was to take the lead in the development of the concept of the Commonwealth. Hancock in his biography of Smuts rejected the idea that Smuts in his practical politics and wider statecraft purposely sought to apply the principle of Holism as the basis of his philosophic outlook. This I cannot accept. Although his book *Holism and Evolution* only appeared in 1926, there are many references to the holistic principle in his speeches, and especially in his private letters, long before 1926. In fact, when he took a leading part in the vital discussions on both the future of the British Empire and the wider international settlement following the First World War, the word Holism and more especially the word "whole" were often used by him. What must be remembered is that the concept of the "whole" and the later use of the word Holism formed an integral part of his unpublished manuscript *The Inquiry into the Whole* which was so cruelly rejected by his friend H. J. Wolstenholme, and which never saw the light of day.

Prof. Hancock in dealing with this matter gives full credence to the influence of religion on the ideas and actions of Smuts, but he denies the express purposeful application of the holistic principle on his politics and statecraft.

"His philosophy contained both the timescale of modern science which he had discovered in evolutionary theory, and the doctrine of the sovereignty of God, which his uncle Boudewyn had preached in the little church at Riebeek West."

However, Hancock denies that Smuts had applied his holistic concept of ever larger wholes being formed on to the practical level of his statecraft. "It is only in retrospect and by superficial analogy that some people (his enemies as well as his friends) have pretended to discover a precise translation of his philosophical tenets into his political loyalties: the Union of South Africa, the British Commonwealth, the League of Nations, each in turn a bigger and better whole – or a bigger and worse one, from the point of view of narrow nationalism. As if he had ever conceived the holistic process in terms of expanding size."[4]

Against this outright rejection of the acceptance and application of the holistic principle in Smuts's statecraft by Hancock, there is the irrefutable proof of Smuts's use of the concept of the "whole" in his famous address of May 15 1917 at the banquet given in his honour by both Houses of Parliament in London, an address which became a landmark in the eventual formation of the Commonwealth.

Here it was that his ideas of the importance of the "whole" in the political outlook as well as his idea of a larger Commonwealth, for the first time merged and emerged into the limelight. Smuts was to point the way to the future Commonwealth in one of his most brilliant dissertations.

"I would ask you not to forget in these times the British Commonwealth of Nations. Do not forget that larger world which is made up of all the nations that belong to the Empire . . . Your Empire is spread all over the world and you have to keep the whole before you in order to judge fairly and sanely of the factors which affect the whole," he told the assembled British leaders.[5]

There was much thinking and lively discussion at the time about the future of the Empire. Some British leaders thought in terms of an Imperial Parliament as the supreme body to govern the widespread Empire. This view was propagated by the quarterly journal called *The Round Table*, founded in November 1910 by a group which favoured Imperial federation with an Imperial Parliament to govern it.

Smuts was totally in opposition to this idea, but in his speech he never referred to it, preferring to ignore such an imperial superstructure. Already in a speech at Edinburgh on April 11 1917 when he received the Freedom of the City, he outlined his guiding principle of liberty as the future basis of the British world. "The cause I fought for fifteen years ago (in the Anglo-Boer War) is the cause for which I am fighting today (in the First World War). I fought for freedom and for liberty then, and I am fighting for them today. You are a largehearted people, and I am sure you will forgive me if I express my view that fifteen years ago, you were wrong. For a brief moment in your long national history you got off the track and you came to grips with a very small people, and in that struggle I did my best. I fought with whatever strength I had in me, just as my little people did, in order to conserve our self-existence and our liberty. I am sometimes proud to think that, according to the old

Apostolic injunction, we have heaped coals of fire upon your heads. The Boer people, perhaps in the wisdom of Providence, have been an instrument in bringing you back to the right track, to your old traditions of liberty – back to the old ideal of standing by small peoples."

Turning to the future of the British Empire, Smuts stated his conviction "that it is only on the basis of freedom and the completest autonomy that the British Empire will continue to exist and become stronger in the future."[6]

It was on this foundation of liberty and autonomy that he thereafter on May 15 1917 gave his concept of the future Commonwealth to the British parliamentarians. Rejecting the federal solution which means subordinate governments for the subordinate parts under one national Federal Parliament, he reminded his listeners that "in all the empires of the past, and even in the United States of America – the effort has been towards forming one nation . . . on the idea of assimilation, of trying to force different human material through one mould so as to form one nation".

Against this attempt at standardization he presented the ideal of the development of nations according to the tenets of self-government and freedom and liberty as the basis for fruitful association and co-operation.

"I think that this is the fundamental fact which we have to bear in mind – that the British Empire, or this British Commonwealth of Nations, does not stand for unity, standardization, or assimilation, or denationalization, but it stands for a fuller, a richer, and more varied life among all the nations that compose it. And even nations who have fought against you, like my own, must feel that they and their interests, their language, their religions, and their cultural interests are as safe and as secure under the British flag as those of the children of your household and your own blood."

It was on this basis that he exhorted the British leaders not "to force common governments, federal or otherwise, but to extend liberty, freedom and nationhood more and more in every part of the Empire".

Turning to the practical problems of how this was to be achieved, Smuts outlined two main instruments which he regarded as supreme in the formation of a free and autonomous Commonwealth. The first was his idea of the importance of "your hereditary kingship" as one of two "potent factors to keep this free world with all this enormous development toward a more varied and richer life amongst all the parts, together".

Smuts throughout his life maintained a very high regard for the value and importance of the monarchy, or royalty, as he often called it, toward ensuring order, stability and continuity in government. This was one of the reasons he later in some way prejudiced his own reputation and his friendship with Winston Churchill when, during the Second World War, he laboured to return the Greek royalty to the Greek throne. He regarded the re-establishment of monarchy in Greece after the Second World War as essential to stability and to countering the influence of the Communists in the Mediterranean region. He placed an even higher value on the retention of the monarchy in Great Britain, and especially as a binding factor in the Empire and the Commonwealth which he envisaged. It was for this reason that he rejected republicanism even though in his early years in the Transvaal Republic he was a staunch Republican and fought for the freedom of the Boer Republics.

In his speech in 1917 he stated his views on the monarchy versus republicanism in very clear language. Regarding the hereditary kingship as the first potent factor in British statecraft, he rejected categorically the idea of a republic in Britain or in the Empire and Commonwealth.

"You cannot make a republic in this country. You cannot make a republic of the British Commonwealth of Nations, because if you elect a President not only in these islands, but all over the British Empire, who will be the ruler and representative of all these peoples, you are facing an absolutely insoluble problem."[7]

Pointing out that in the theory of the British Constitution the King is not merely a King of the British Isles, but a King of all parts of the Empire, he stated: "He, the King, represents every part of the whole Commonwealth of Nations. If his place is to be taken by somebody else, then that somebody will have to be elected by a process which I think, will pass the wit of man to devise. Therefore let us be thankful for the mercies we have. We have a kingship here which is really not very different from a hereditary republic, and I am sure that more and more in the future the trend will be in that direction, and I shall not be surprised to see the time when our royal princes, instead of getting their consorts among the princelings of Central Europe, will go to the Dominions and the outlying portions of the Empire."

Smuts was convinced that it was impossible to attach too much importance to the monarchical institution. He thought that it could be developed to the greatest uses possible for its future preservation and development, and he envisaged that it would be necessary to go even further. "It is not only the symbol of unity which you have in the royal ruler, but you will have to develop further common institutions."

To achieve this he proposed the creation of better machinery for common consultation than the then existing Imperial Conferences which met every four years. In this regard he envisaged the calling together of an annual conference of the most important statesmen in the Empire to discuss matters which concern all parts of the Empire in common, and in order that causes of friction might be removed. He also proposed that a common policy should be laid down to determine the true orientation of "our Imperial policy".[8]

In discussing these matters as a former foe of the British Empire he was filled with gratitude for the reception he had received. He also spoke of his "gratitude to Time, the great and merciful judge, which has healed many wounds, and gratitude to that Divinity which shapes our ends, rough-hew them how we will".

This was the basis on which and in the spirit of which Smuts in his historic speech laid the foundation for the establishment of the Commonwealth. In the subsequent development of this institution many of his ideas were followed and he played his part, both as a public speaker and when he was Prime Minister of the Union of South Africa, to assist in its development and functioning.

But in the cardinal issue of the retention of the monarchy as the central pivot of the Commonwealth he lost the battle.

He was upset when Ireland on December 29 1937 after a plebiscite, declared herself a republic, and left the Commonwealth.

But the crucial test for the future of the Commonwealth came after the war and more especially in 1949 when the newly independent India opted for a republican status. Smuts was no longer Prime Minister of South Africa and this debarred him from attending the Commonwealth Conference of April 1949. Instead, his longstanding political opponent Dr D. F. Malan, who defeated him in the election of May 1948, was to attend. As was well known, Dr Malan and his purified National Party were in favour of an independent republic outside the Commonwealth. However, it was also known that Havenga of the Afrikaner Party, who had made an election pact with Malan, was against any policy to break the link with Britain and to leave the Commonwealth. He wanted to go no further than the admission of freedom to make republican propaganda.

The duality in the official policy of the Nationalist Government led to various interpretations. Some Government supporters regarded republicanism and secession from the British Crown as one and the same thing. Others opted for a republic inside the Commonwealth. The latter was also the line adopted by the Indian leaders.

Smuts was so worried about the future of the Commonwealth that he published a warning on the eve of the Prime Ministers' Conference of April 1949. The gist of his warning was that the weak toleration of republicanism inside the Commonwealth, which would inevitably cut the link to the monarchy, would drain away both the substance and the significance of the Commonwealth as he envisaged it in his first famous speech, and as it had developed until then.

"My personal view is that there is no middle course between the Crown and the Republic, between in and out of the Commonwealth. You are either in, or out of it, and if you choose to be out of it, you are out of it entirely and not on terms which can be devised. It is a case of the excluded middle. If in some nebulous or muddled way you can be both in and out of it, the whole concept of the Commonwealth goes, and what remains is a mere name without substance, the grin without the cat of *Alice in Wonderland.*"[9]

In spite of his warning and his objections the Prime Ministers at the

Conference agreed to allow republics to remain in and to become members of the Commonwealth. Smuts was upset and saw the new Commonwealth as a repetition of the former Holy Roman Empire, which was neither Holy nor Roman nor an Empire. He wrote privately to Churchill. Although recognizing the practical reasons why the British leaders made a compromise with India, he nevertheless feared that the Commonwealth would become a fictional entity. If that happened humanity would be the poorer. He also felt that the Nationalist Government in South Africa would regard the decision to include republics as "a tarred road to the republic" which they had always wanted.[10]

The subsequent growth and development of the Commonwealth has proved Smuts wrong. Although he was right in his prophecy that the Nationalist Government in South Africa would establish a republic and leave the Commonwealth, the body has continued to survive and to grow as more and more former British colonies after independence became members. Far from losing prestige and influence as he predicted, the Commonwealth has continued to play an important role as a middle force between the great powers.

Smuts's fears that the admission of republics in the Commonwealth would act to the detriment of the monarchy has also proved wrong. The British monarchy has retained its prestige and standing in spite of the fact that the majority of members of the Commonwealth are republics.

CHAPTER SIXTEEN

International organizations

The League of Nations; The United Nations

Smuts's deeply held religious convictions can be traced more clearly in his views as reflected in his writings, speeches and actions relating to international affairs. His experience during and after the Anglo-Boer War, when he learned the value of mercy and trust towards a defeated foe, as well as the spiritual influence of the Quakers on his thinking, steered his outlook and pronunciations on international issues in a decidedly religious direction.

This was especially noticeable during the First World War when as a member of the British War Cabinet he made his first appearance on the wider world arena.

On assuming command of the Union German East African Contingents to drive the German army from Africa, he privately expressed his fears to Mrs Margaret Gillett and asked her to "pray for your old friend who in these times is forced to do soldiering against his will . . . Do not as Friends (The Society of Friends, which is pacifist) think worse of me because of the work I am doing."[1]

To this plea Mrs Gillett replied on March 14 1916 expressing her views that "civilization would not be saved by fighting". She, however, expressed "my great hope that your present work may soon be done and that, with the status of that, you may come to Europe and help poor Europe to see a way, for I believe you could reconcile difficulties, and someone will have to emerge to do this".[2]

Smuts responded to this in a letter written in pouring rain from his headquarters in Noschi, German East Africa, on May 2 1916. Pointing out "how the whole world in which we grew up has been shattered in fragments", he expressed his belief that there was not a man living who would piece those fragments together again.

"The regeneration must come from within, from the soul; mankind must feel the pulsation of a new spiritual life before the wounds will heal and the new order will arise . . . Remember how the Boers went under but saved their souls as a people. My hope is that Europe will save her soul in this vast struggle and that the ground will be cleared for a slow, gradual, fresh start in the years to come. I am not much troubled over schemes of vengeance such as seem to delight the newspaper writers. When this war is over and we have counted the dead and our losses there will be little spirit left in any people to continue the hatreds and bitterness of the war. So at least I fervently hope and pray."[3]

In a later letter written on October 24 1916 from Morogoro in East Africa, he predicted "a great revival of Quaker religion" if a threatened commercial war was to follow on the conclusion of hostilities.

"In fact, I would myself join those who believe in the Inner light and forswear the Satan of bloodshed."[4]

It was in this spirit and equipped with deep spiritual visions that he travelled to England as the first conquering hero of the war on the Allied side. In London he was welcomed by all except his old friend Emily Hobhouse, who wrote to him on March 7 1917:

"Years ago I prophesied to you that the day would come when your name would be seen in big print in *The Times*, that mighty organ that emulates Divinity for 'it pulleth down one and setteth up another' and I further said I should live to see you Earl of Irene and Lord of Doornkloof and lo! are not these words fulfilling themselves – in the essence if not the letter? For I know from of old that honours come showering down upon those who tread the 'Imperialist' paths. Still I hope something of the old 'Oom Jannie' yet remains, enough to enjoy association with the Pacifist and Anti-Imperialist I am prouder than ever to be."[5]

Miss Hobhouse need have had few misgivings on Smuts's plans and intentions. Shortly after his arrival in London he turned his mind to a scheme to establish a League of Nations after the war. D. Lloyd George in his *War Memoirs* (Vol. IX, p. 1798) outlined the earliest formulation of Smuts's conception of a League of Nations. It took the form of a draft resolution which Smuts wrote on April 21 1917 in his own handwriting, and which was submitted to the Imperial War Cabinet five days later.

The original draft of this historic letter, which marks his entry to the arena of international affairs, is in the *Smuts Collection*. Under the title of League of Nations he proposed that the Imperial War Cabinet "affirm in principle that some form of conference or conciliation among the Powers should be established to deal with international disputes not susceptible to arbitration or judicial procedure, and that the details of the scheme should be discussed with our allies and especially the USA before the conclusion of the war. In their opinion such a scheme to promote future peace should, if possible, be embodied in the peace treaty itself."[6]

It was a bold move on the part of Smuts at a time when the war was raging with no end in sight, and when he as a former enemy of the British Empire was still suspect in some quarters. However, having been accepted by Lloyd George, he struck out boldly and established his reputation as a leader with a vision for the future. As this move on his part remained hidden in the confidential minutes of the Imperial War Cabinet, his friends and the outside world were unaware of the great contributions Smuts had made for international conciliation and co-operation. On the same day that he drafted the resolution, he wrote to Mrs Gillett: "Miss Hobhouse has now moved into town in order to more effectively labour for the salvation of my soul."[7]

Having established his belief in a League of Nations to be written into any subsequent peace treaty and to be established after the war, Smuts threw himself into the task of winning the war. He was active on many fronts and used by Lloyd George and the War Cabinet in a variety of ways. However, the idea of a League of Nations simmered in his mind, and on December 17 1918 he wrote to his wife that he had resigned as a member of the War Cabinet.

"In the last few days I have written a pamphlet about the League of Nations, which will appear early in January. I am very much interested in the idea, as perhaps a way out of the pitiable condition in which the old world finds itself."[8]

There is no doubt that his Quaker friends and especially the Clark and Gillett families had a profound influence on some of his ideas on a League of Nations to solve the international problems and safeguard the future peace. It was shortly after the Armistice, while he was suffering from influenza and convalescing in the bedroom of 102 Banbury Road in Oxford, the home of Arthur and Margaret Gillett, that he wrote the final version of his famous pamphlet *The League of Nations: A Practical Suggestion.*

Already on January 15 1919, he was able to write from Paris how well his pamphlet was received. To his Quaker friend Alice Clark, a sister of Mrs Gillett, he wrote:

"The League of Nations is making headway quite well. Wilson has read my pamphlet carefully, and the Prime Minister (Lloyd George) says he is now beginning to talk enthusiastically of this scheme and will probably end by giving it to the world as his own.

"Well, as long as the Lord gives the vital growth I don't care whether it is Paul who plants or Apollos who waters."[9]

He told her that the French translation of the pamphlet had gone all wrong. From London it was sent to Switzerland for the purpose of translation and printing. However, it disappeared on the way.

"I suppose some censor looked upon it as Bolshevist propaganda and confiscated the lot. Such is the way of the world."[10]

He was able to inform his wife by letter on the same day "the League of Nations is progressing well; my pamphlet has made a great impression in high circles, and not the least on President Wilson".

The American President, in a private letter to Smuts, accepted the "larger features of the plan" but drafted his own version of it. He sent this to Smuts and asked for his help, but Smuts was not enamoured of Wilson's draft.

He wrote to Mrs Gillett:

"He (Wilson) has drafted a scheme which is practically my twenty-one paragraphs with some alterations, which are unfortunately not improvements, but much the reverse. But I feel that I am perhaps too keen and impatient on this matter."

He then quotes from Walt Whitman's poem entitled "Faces" from the book *Leaves of Grass.*

"The Lord advances and ever advances – but oh! how slow, with what dark shadows and meanderings and retracings."[11]

On January 20 1919, Smuts was able to report privately to Mrs M. C. Gillett that he, Wilson and Lord Robert Cecil had spent the previous night until 11.30 discussing the League of Nations.

"His ideas (may I confess?) seem mostly taken from my pamphlet. Even my mistakes are appropriated. This seriously alarms me, as the paper was hurriedly written as you know, and many things I would rather now put differently. Not so, Wilson; for him the first rapture is enough. I am sorry, but fail to carry amendments on which I am now set! The idea is to work out the Convention or "Covenant" as he calls it in remembrance of his Covenanter descent, in full and then get the Conference to pass it formally. He is entirely opposed to our annexing a little German colony here and there, which pains me deeply and will move Billy Hughes (of Australia) to great explosions of righteous wrath."[12]

In spite of setbacks, changes and frustrations, the final draft of the League was published in February 1919. Smuts wrote to Alice Clark that it was almost entirely his original conception and although he was naturally pleased at the acceptance of his ideas, he kept well in the background so that "others might have the credit for the League, as in that way their co-operation could be secured."[13]

Although Smuts was successful in launching his ideas on the League of Nations, he was unable to steer the resulting Peace Conference with which the League was to be associated, in the direction he preferred. His active participation in the peace negotiations after the First World War again revealed his basic religious Christian approach. He was against revenge as the basis of a peace treaty and proposed a treaty based on mercy and reconciliation. Already on March 26 1919, he warned Lloyd George in a private letter that "the peace to which we are working is an impossible peace, conceived on a wrong basis; that it will not be accepted by Germany, and even if accepted, that it will prove utterly unstable, and only serve to promote the anarchy which is rapidly overtaking Europe".[14]

In a private letter to Mrs M. C. Gillett the next day (March 27 1919), he spells it out even more clearly. Stating that Lloyd George leaned on him more than he thought he was doing and that the "still, small voice is always there", he wrote:

"Well, let us do our duty and leave the rest to God. You know that is my religion, and it produces great serenity of mind."[15]

Later the same day he wrote Mrs Gillett a second letter in which he stated that the position of the world was most critical.

"Only a miracle could now save Europe. But of course miracles do happen; I have seen several in my short life."[16]

Smuts and Botha at this juncture of the peace negotiations were fighting all the time for a just peace. They protested strenuously against the so-called "punishment clauses" which the Allied leaders wanted to include in the final documents. Smuts's Quaker friends and especially Mrs Gillett and her sister Alice supported him to the hilt.

Alice had written to him on April 25 1919 suggesting that he apply the term "mortal mind" to the "small and trivial intellects which are so busy talking around you and patching together treaties and ideas which have no roots in the divine Universal mind, which creates all things that exist".

Smuts in a letter to Mrs Gillett referred to this letter of Alice's, "pitched in a higher key" as "pure Holism which she chooses to call Christian Science"!

"You again call it a 'Message for Seekers' but it is pure Holism all the time. And it does you good. And me too. To feel that you are not merely individual or thrown on your own individual resources, but so to say an outpost, if not a real centre, of the Divine, the all-vital and all-essential in the universe, or that your little efforts are reinforced by the great movements and currents of the spiritual world – is a great consolation. And it is as true as it is consolatory."[17]

Although he and Botha were able to remove some of the "punishment clauses" from the final revised Covenant of the League of Nations and from the Labour Convention dealing with the international regulation of Labour, they had to accept the final harsh peace treaty of Versailles.

Smuts was uneasy and unhappy over the terms of peace.

"I think they are wrong . . . They will outrage the sense of fairness of decent people and in the end will prove the undoing of whatever stable government still exists in the world . . . What shall I do? What could one do? I am much troubled and puzzled."[18]

Smuts turned to his religion and his Holism and in a letter to Alice he wrote:

"Yes, your Holism is very attractive and very true. Life is creative, beneficent, holistic, and our prayer should be to 'love life and love it more abundantly' (St John 10:10). While the material (like water) always tends to run down to the lowest level, life always tends to rise above itself in ever higher ideals . . . Life is creative through the union of the partial into the whole."[19]

In this mood he took the bull by the horns and wrote a strongly worded memorandum to Lloyd George, criticizing the Peace Treaty.[20] This caused anger among the Allied leaders and on May 19, Smuts reported to Mrs Gillett:

"I understand the Prime Minister is very angry with me. Wilson is also failing me. He is not really a great man and Clemenceau has proved too strong both for him and our mercurial tricky Prime Minister. But I don't mean to give in so easily, and have fired off some shots which I hope will hit somebody hard."

When, in spite of his objections, the harsh peace treaty was eventually published, his first inclination was not to become a signatory to it unless important alterations were made to it. He even thought of resigning as a Minister of the Union and starting a campaign against it. He outlined these alterations in a memorandum to Lloyd George on May 22 1919 and referred to them in a private letter to Woodrow Wilson four days later. However, under pressure from Botha, on June 24 he was able to tell Mrs Gillett that he had decided to sign the Treaty after all.

"Any other course would make the position of General Botha (who *must* sign) indefensible and impossible. People in South Africa will say either he is right or I am right, and in the end irreparable mischief will be done . . . And I adopt your formula in your dear, great, last letter . . . Not in criticism but in faith."[21]

In signing the Treaty, Smuts thought it advisable to issue a statement on the afternoon of June 28 1919 in which he set out his hope for the future. Regarding the Treaty as simply the liquidation of the war situation, he made it clear that the victory of the great human ideals and the fulfilment of the aspirations towards a new international order and a fairer better world were not written in the Treaty and would not be written in treaties. Then turning to his religion he added:

"Not in this mountain, nor in Jerusalem, but in the spirit and in truth as the Great Master said, must the foundations of the new order be laid. A new heart must be given not only to our enemies, but also to us; a contrite spirit for the woes which have overwhelmed the world; a spirit of pity, mercy and forgiveness for the sins and wrongs we have suffered."[22]

Having taken the lead in laying the foundations of the League of Nations, but having failed to obtain a just and merciful peace, Smuts after the sudden death of Botha became Prime Minister of South Africa. His main attention thereafter was concentrated on South Africa, and apart from occasional speeches and statements he took no active part in international affairs. He could see, however, the fulfilment of his prophecies that Europe would fall into instability and even chaos which resulted in the rise of dictators in several countries. Smuts with his experience and keen perception saw another world conflict approaching and from 1931 onwards he again began to sound warnings. He regarded the rise of Hitler and his National-Socialist Party in Germany as especially ominous.

"It was always said that the Germans were too highly cultured to imitate the Bolshevists. But Nazi Germany seems to me even more repulsive in her methods than Russia ever was or than Fascist Italy was. I am deeply puzzled by this as it fills me with doubt and misgiving for the future," he wrote privately in July 1934.[23]

In public at St Andrews on October 17 1934, he warned the students that the "cult of force . . . has for the moment triumphed over large parts of Europe.

Intellectual freedom is disappearing with political freedom . . . Even freedom of religion is no longer safe."[24]

Again Smuts warned that Europe and the world were moving towards war, and when war broke out on September 1 1939, he took the lead to involve South Africa. He took his stand on the principle that South Africa should support the Commonwealth and declare war on Germany. When Smuts's amendment on the basis of this stand carried the day in the South African Parliament, he took over the Government and became Prime Minister. Thereafter Smuts again became one of the leaders on the international arena, first to defeat the enemy and thereafter to revive a form of international organization to safeguard the peace. At first his energies were concentrated on winning the war, especially in East and North Africa, but after the Allied armies had cleared Africa of the enemy and the USA had made her power felt in Europe and the Far East, he again started to give continuous thought to ways and means of achieving a free and stable world after the war was over.

When he was asked to address the Empire Parliamentary Association in London on November 25 1943, he submitted some "thoughts on the new world" to the assembled members of the Lords and Commons. Stating that world peace was his objective, he suggested that the League of Nations had failed because the men who made it – himself included – had shut their eyes to the realities of power. In the new organization he envisaged, leadership and power must, he said, go together. On the basis of this principle, he deduced the need for a new world organization with effective peace-keeping authority vested primarily in the Great Powers. He adopted the name United Nations which Roosevelt had previously used and stated that the three great powers, Great Britain, the USA and Russia form the trinity of the United Nations fighting the cause of humanity.

"We shall have to see to it that in the new international organization the leadership remains in the hands of this great trinity of powers."[25]

Here Smuts again became the prophet of the new international organization, this time the United Nations. His concept of power confined to the Great Powers was subsequently adopted as the basis for the Security Council with the veto in the hands of the superpowers as the final instrument of their dominant role in world affairs.

But when he saw "the footsteps of the Russian giant" moving to Central Europe he became alarmed at the prospect of Russian domination of the continent. To Mrs M. C. Gillett he wrote on March 4 1945:

"I know how dangerous the predominance of any one power can be, and how liable such dominant power is to abuse. I remember British jingoism and the Boer War, and I know Russia has even less experience and human wisdom than the British. And so my faith in man does not extend to faith in Russia, with no check on her in Europe and Asia, and mistress of the continent of Europe."[26]

Again he reverted to his religion and on February 10 1945, shortly after the fateful Yalta conference between Roosevelt, Churchill and Stalin, he expressed his fears for the future of mankind to Mrs Gillett:

"One's mind keeps moving in the world where Destiny is weaving our future. God gives wisdom and foresightedness to our leaders and especially to the three leaders who are now at this moment deciding the pattern of the future so far as that is humanly possible."

Smuts at this time of sorrow and tragedy for so many millions of human beings in the war-torn world felt the need for religion even more than before. His letters to his many friends and especially to his Quaker friends reveal how he looked upon religion to pave the way to solving the world's problems. He was thinking how Jesus would have solved the great issues confronting mankind. "What would *He* have done if in Caesar's place," he had asked in a letter to Mrs Gillett in 1941 and in 1945 he himself gave an answer to his own question. Pointing out that the Jews at the time of Jesus' teaching were looking forward to a worldly kingdom for their resurrection and rise from thraldom, he wrote:

"And Jesus spread the message that not along those lines would Salvation come. The soul, Man's relation to God, the inner purification and the practice of the gentler virtues would herald . . . the Kingdom of Heaven. Is this thought not basic in the truest sense? Has mankind not first to find its Soul before it finds the new kingdom?" The situation, he wrote further, is "at bottom a religious problem".[27]

Although "only a distant spectator" when the first shape of the new world organization was hammered out at Dumbarton Oaks in September 1944, Smuts played a significant role in persuading both Churchill and Roosevelt to accept the Russian insistence on the right of a Great Power to veto decisions of the Security Council.

He advised Churchill on September 20 1944 to accept the Russian demand on grounds of political necessity. Churchill was sceptical, but showed Smuts's letter to Roosevelt, and "no doubt it played some part in promoting the reappraisals and compromises of Yalta, and consequently in bringing UNO to birth".

Smuts made a second contribution to the new international body. During the meeting of the Commonwealth Prime Ministers in London on the eve of the San Francisco conference, he wrote a Preamble to the Charter and suggested that it be proposed by the Commonwealth leaders, as an eloquent declaration of humanity's hopes and faith, as part of the new Charter. This draft of Smuts's was somewhat changed by incorporating parts of a draft by Sir Charles Webster, and later by the acceptance of the opening words of Mrs Dean Gildersleeve: "We, the people of the United Nations," but the final version which is now the noble Preamble to the Charter of the United Nations, retains his vision and his wording. His draft introduced "fundamental human rights" into the Charter of the United Nations and although his enemies, both at home and on the international arena, used his own words and his vision as a stick to beat him in his declining years, the Preamble expressed in noble language all that is best in his character and his service in the cause of humanity.

What vision did Smuts have for the future of mankind? At the beginning of the Second World War, Mrs Gillett asked him what he thought of a future settlement after the war. Smuts's letter of January 24 1940 is perhaps one of the most revealing documents of how Jesus influenced his thinking on international affairs.[28]

"Can there be any institutional change where there is no change of the spirit? Can we build effectively except from the depths of the human spirit? Is Jesus not right, and is it at bottom not a spiritual issue, just as it is a spiritual disease from which we suffer?" he asked in replying to her query.

Saying that some constitutional form or mechanism must accompany the inner change of spirit, he continued:

"My recent studies of the times of Jesus have shown me how dangerous it is to cherish vain hopes and illusions as an escape from great disasters and sufferings. The Messianic idea which emerged from the Dispersion and the Maccabean success proved the undoing of Israel in the end. They were always looking for the Messiah, missed the real one, and followed false ones until they were finally crushed and finished. It is a curious story, in which Jesus forms a link and was by his own people mistaken for one of the false ones. Some false Messianic hope may emerge from the present world despair, which may once more prove a snare and a delusion," was his prophetic declaration.

Judging by the sorry state of the world and the violence which has once again taken hold of mankind, who would say that Smuts was wrong in his diagnosis and his prophecy?

He was especially sceptical of the future of the United Nations. As early as March 31 1947 he wrote to his American friend, F. Lamont that the United Nations had been a grave disappointment to him, "not only personally, but from the larger viewpoint which we have at heart.

"Our primary intention was to provide for world security against War. But look at the Security Council and its sorry antics! Even our old League did better. It managed world affairs with a decency and fair success for ten years and thereafter was struck by the Hitler blitz, which proved too much for it. The UNO in its security arrangements is moving all wrong from the very start, and the international situation is more clouded and uncertain than ever before.

"Then again the UNO has prematurely started on an enterprise which looks very much like world government and world reform in all directions – a task for which it is hopelessly unfitted. It is interfering with domestic affairs of other countries, which must make the already difficult task of government in an unsettled world more difficult than ever. I can only judge from its influence on government in South Africa. After all, we have a well-ordered, well-governed state, but the influence of UNO policies has been profoundly disturbing and upsetting. Countries who cannot govern themselves now sit in judgement on others who have done their job fairly well in spite of all sorts of difficulties."

Smuts added that all these things caused him grave anxiety, but with his usual optimism he thought that mankind would somehow pull through the dangerous times, "but I wonder whether the present set-up of UNO is such as to fit it for its task. Democracy without leadership is a sham, and the UNO seems to me a democracy without leadership."

Smuts thought that mankind would have to bring about a thorough revision and establish an international organization more modest "but more real and effective than this general Areopagus or talking shop in which incompetents and misfits rule by counting of heads".[29]

PART FOUR

Evaluation

CHAPTER SEVENTEEN

The flaws

There is an apparent duality in the character of Smuts. In spite of his holistic personality as set out in Chapter 8, there are not only contradictions in his actions, but also inconsistencies in his private views and intimate thoughts as revealed in letters he wrote to various friends. In this he was only human and he himself was the first to admit that: "I prefer to be what I am – a poor errant soul forever seeking and seldom finding – a pilgrim of the world and of life," as I have already quoted in Chapter 4.

And yet there are indications that Smuts in some periods of his long life saw himself on a higher plane of being, where because of his great intellect and remarkable gifts and talents he aspired to an almost divine make-up. This was especially the case toward the end of his days when the figure and personality of Jesus were constantly before him and in his thoughts.

Smuts regarded the human personality as capable of growth and upward movement, not only in individual cases, but also in the larger cosmological time-scale of science. From its modest beginnings in the evolutionary scale the personality could develop to the divine level. Whether he consciously thought that his own personality had approached or achieved that level is not confirmed in his writings, but there are some instances in his utterances, writings and behaviour where he undoubtedly assumed a pretence of almost divine qualities. It was almost as if he wished to identify himself with the divine personality of the Christ.

When Lloyd George in May 1917 offered Smuts the Palestine Command in the Middle East, he declined it and wrote to Mrs M. C. Gillett:

"I have today declined the Palestine Command. I was taken on a high hill and shown the kingdoms of the world. And I have renounced them."[1]

Did Smuts see himself here as a second Christ who was taken up unto an exceeding high mountain by the devil as recorded in St Matthew 4:8?

There is also his reaction when he was defeated in the general election of May 1948. In the privacy of his book-lined study on his farm Doornkloof at Irene, he exclaimed to Sen. A. M. Conroy:

"They have crucified me, they have crucified me."[2]

On a lower level he became very vain and resented any form of criticism from even his former trusted advisers and personal friends. Vanity, especially through his contact with royalty and members of the aristocracy, became a characteristic of the last years of his life. There is the recorded instance of his visit to Southampton shortly after the end of the Second World War, when he criticized the arrangements made for his reception. The mayor of Southampton afterwards said that he had never met a more vain man; "he even surpassed royalty", was his private comment.

In her private diary Lady Moore in 1943 recorded some instances of how Smuts, the Boer leader, became enamoured of royalty. On one occasion he expressed anger that the members of his family did not rise when the young Greek princess Frederica entered the room. Lady Moore wrote:

"Smuts is losing touch with the feeling of the country and there is much criticism of him and much comment that he is always with the Greeks and does not mix with his own people."[3]

The diary also reveals that Smuts on looking back on his life, thought that he had made a mistake when he refused an offer from the King in 1919 to become Prime Minister of Great Britain. He also mentioned this to Princess Frederica on one of his walks with her over the Cape mountains. In her autobiography she recorded:

"On one of these walks across the highland above Muizenberg, Cape Town, the idea of the United Nations was born. It was long before the end of the war (the Second World War). I had asked him: "Why did things go wrong? Why did our generation, who had already fought one war, not prevent the outbreak of another?'

"'I will tell you why it went wrong. There are three reasons: One is that we Allies believed in France, the second is that America let us down, and the third reason is that I ran away. I was in England during and at the end of the war (the First World War) and a member of the War Cabinet. The King had privately asked me to stay on and become Prime Minister. I felt my own country needed me, as General Botha had just died. I refused, although this would have been a unique situation and opportunity. You see, I ran away, so do not rub it in. I know my responsibilities.'"[4]

That Smuts was highly thought of at the time is well known. I have already referred to it, but his idea that he could have become Prime Minister of Great Britain after the war, and in that position could have changed the course of modern history, reveals an exaggerated opinion of his own value and capabilities. Even more so was his suggestion, made in a personal letter to Lloyd George, that he be appointed to lead the American Expeditionary Forces as a "veg-generaal" (combat general) in an offensive campaign on the Western front.

"I am naturally most reluctant to bring forward my own name as you can well understand. But I have unusual experience and qualifications to lead a force such as the American Army will be in an offensive campaign. I think that if American *amour propre* could be satisfied, I could in that capacity render very great service to our Cause."[5]

Was this strange proposal arrogance on the part of Smuts or was it the result of his romantic vision of himself as a latter-day Crusader in the cause of justice and Christianity? Lloyd George fortunately at the time protected the reputation of Smuts by not letting the suggestion go beyond himself. Even in his *War Memoirs* later he still omitted any reference to it and it was only in 1954 that it first became known in the book *Tempestuous Journey* by Frank Owen.[6]

Another instance of his vanity occurred in 1946 when he visited the United States and let it be known that he would like to address a joint sitting of the American Senate and the House of Representatives. He waited for some time, exploring the scenic beauties of California, for the invitation from Washington. That it never came was one of the great disappointments of his life. Whether he made such a suggestion to President Harry S. Truman is not known. He had met Truman at the time and wrote favourably about him to Lady Moore who was then in Ceylon (Sri Lanka).

The duality in the character and personality of Smuts is revealed even more strikingly in his private correspondence with Lady Moore. Whereas the popular idea was that he was a severe uncompromising leader, sure of himself and even ruthless and tyrannical, Lady Moore describes him as "painfully sensitive" and a man of charm and sensitivity. On the same level Queen Frederica referred to him "as a giver rather than a taker". Smuts in one of his letters to Lady Moore referred to the friendship between them and his appreciation of her qualities:

"I had understood the intellectual and critical side of you well before; now I began to sense the deeper emotional layers, and I was glad to do so. After all, intellect, brilliant as it may be, is more an aspect of the surface – the emotional nature constitutes the very soul and core and so you laid yourself bare and open to the friendship which surely is the greatest thing in the world – 'Life's great meaning, dear my Lord.' I thank you for this friendship, this richesse of the spirit, this revelation of the deeper self. Perhaps you saw beneath my intellectual skin too, and so we have become clear to each other in life's deeper meaning. Is this in the end not all we get out of this life of ours? What else is there in it? A poor thing at best, but the key which unlocks the door of this universe, and links the human with the divine."[7]

To this analysis of their friendship and their personalities by the great statesman, Lady Moore replied in a long letter on April 4 1947.

"So you thought me intellectual and critical. The latter is true, but I have no intellect, alas, only a sort of cleverness – a flashy kind of quality. All artists, however successful, are primarily emotional but, if transplanted out of their natural environment, are driven to conceal the guilty secret under one disguise or another, sometimes in self-defence or aggressiveness.

"Being principally sensitive yourself you can understand not only the intensity of feeling necessary for creative work of any sort but also the agony of pain and humiliation possible to the possessor of super-sensitive make-up. The consolation, of course, lies in the capacity to feel exaltation as well as pain."[8]

It was at this time in his life that Smuts came under criticism for his friendship, if not infatuation, with the young Greek princess Frederica, the granddaughter of the German Kaiser Wilhelm II. The feeling in his own party and family circle was that he spent too much time with the members of the Greek Royal family, and that he was indiscreet in his attentions to the Princess.

There are various indications in the letters of Lady Moore that she was not happy about his intense friendship with the Greek princess. As early as 1943 she gave vent to her feelings on what she called the "Greek situation".

"Surely it is not right that the Prince (Prince Paul) and the Princess should at this juncture in Greece's history be spending their time lazing on the beach all morning, sleeping in the afternoon and going to parties in the evening? I assure you that except for endless discussions of their affairs, that is all they are doing, and I do not think it can do their cause any good. They move in wealthy and luxury-loving circles in Alex (Alexandria in Egypt) but even their hostess, Madame Benachi, said to me that she wished the Princess would go around more to visit canteens and hospitals and Greek welfare organizations. They were most venomously criticized in the Union (of South Africa) for the life they led there and I fear there is much talk in Egypt of the same kind.

"More than once I tried to persuade the Princess of the folly of her ways, but though she professes to respect my advice she merely said that she was not interested in local things and without being brutally frank I could not prevail . . . She is such a darling but her burning zeal is combined with a dangerous degree of intolerance and impatience – all due to youth, I know."[9]

There is no letter from Smuts in reply to this blunt epistle from Lady Moore in the *Smuts Papers*. But she did not give up and returned to the subject which she knew was dear to his heart. In one letter she described a lunch she had in Cairo with the then Greek King and Princess Frederica. She did not think much of the King of Greece, as he displayed weakness of character and a general attitude of *laisser-aller*. What struck her was that the King did not talk politics with Princess Frederica. It was obvious that the King did not like her. He even tried to prevent her return to Egypt. She had heard confidentially that the King was nervous of the Princess taking an active part in affairs because (a) she was German and (b) he regarded her as impulsive, impetuous and therefore unwise. She felt that Freddie (as the Princess was known to Smuts) should be allowed to work in the Greek Relief Fund because she wanted work "but my private opinion is that she has no idea what the word means".

Again there is no evidence that Smuts took kindly to this advice from Lady

Moore, but he did not allow it to influence their friendship or interrupt their letter-writing. Then in April 1947, the Greek King died and Crown Prince Paul, Princess Frederica's husband, became King of Greece. Lady Moore was thrilled for her and for Smuts, her mentor.

"My dear Oom Jannie," she wrote on April 2 1947, "So Freddie is Queen! I am thinking a lot about her – having achieved her ambition . . . Like you I believe in her destiny and that she will make history, but I wish I was sure that tragedy will not dog her footsteps and that her path will not be strewn with troubles and with blood.

"I am thinking also about you, who love her and have helped her to be ready for this new task. Your feelings must be mixed up, for a barrier has been set up and however unchanged your friendship – you must be sad to know that she will never climb the Mountain with you again or come to South Africa for care-free days in the sun and the wind. 'Look your last on all things lovely' – you remember?"[10]

Three weeks later Lady Moore wrote to Smuts again about Queen Frederica. It was on April 26 1947.

"Oddly enough the day after I had asked you to give me news of Freddie (Queen Frederica) I got a letter from her and now your letter gives me further news and comments. She was very pleased with Ouma's (Mrs Isie Smuts, the wife of Smuts) letter and it was indeed nice of her to write. You have never realized how deeply Ouma feels on the subject and when I tried to tell you a long time ago you thought I was trying to bar you from Freddie!!!

"No, you never realized and I was hurt that you had so misunderstood my motives. Did you think it was jealousy? Freddie writes of your 'very sweet letter' after your official cable and says: 'I am glad more than ever of this great friendship that came to me in my life. It made me ready to face life with all its responsibilities and has given me strength . . . I am afraid there are only two kinds of people in the world, those who give and those who take. He (Smuts) and Palo (her husband, King Paul) belong to the first and I to the second.'"

And then Lady Moore's comment:

"How fortunate that she is so devoted to Palo: I hope that it will always continue even after she fully realizes her superior power."[11]

Although the public regarded Smuts foremost as a realist, he saw himself as a romanticist and he made no bones about it that he preferred the friendship and company of women to that of men.[12]

Hancock in referring to the romantic streak in Smuts, thought that his "realism played a larger part than his romanticism in bringing him to a decision".[13]

There is, however, an even larger and more real duality if not an outright contradiction in the make-up, beliefs and actions or omissions of Smuts as a thinker and a leader. This has to do with his position as a South African leader in the context of the modern emphasis on racial equality and the safeguarding of human rights for all. Smuts was a powerful leader who during the last 40 years of his life was Prime Minister for 14 years and a member of the governments of Botha and Hertzog for another 14 years. There is no evidence that he can be regarded as a racialist, as I will show. Yet Smuts was not only against equal rights, but in all his time in government, he neglected to bring about changes to remove racialism and discrimination in South African affairs.

Professor Hancock, in discussing this glaring discrepancy between his holistic philosophy with the emphasis on the supreme worth of the human personality and the jarring racial discords which he failed to eliminate in South Africa, saw this as "a problem of central importance" for his biography of Smuts.

"The biographer, however, cannot find any short cut to its solution; in particular, he cannot identify any particular scheme of race relations as the proper counterpart of the Inquiry into the Whole. As a philosopher Smuts employed the cosmological time-scale; as a politician, he had to reckon time from one election to the next and sometimes from one day to the next.

"His cosmological outlook, reinforced in later life by studies of palaeontology and pre-history, excluded the crude doctrine of the inequality of races, but it contained no quick cure for the racial prejudices of his constituents, still less for those stubborn, factual inequalities that were rooted so deeply in the history of his country. It pleased him, twenty years later, to place European Man and the South African Bushman upon the same branch of humanity's family tree; to be sure, the European had developed his latent powers while the Bushman had remained isolated and static, but this was the luck of the evolutionary game."[14]

Smuts, for all his high ideals, his great intellect and the supreme value he placed on the human personality, was bound by his environment and the limitations, indeed restrictions, of his background as a South African.

It must be remembered that Smuts, born on Queen Victoria's birthday halfway through her reign, was influenced not only by his environment in South Africa where the master/servant relationship existed, but also by the nineteenth-century outlook of the Black man as the White man's burden. This meant in effect that the White man, regarding himself as the superior in intellect, achievements and civilization, took a paternalistic attitude towards the Brown and Black man. The idea and the ideal was to educate and civilize the non-Whites, but on the basis of the "inevitability of gradualness".

Smuts, brought up on a Cape farm where the master/servant relationship was a fact of existence, was influenced by this fact throughout his life. Already in January 1902 he gave an indication of his view that the "native question" as he called it would "never pass away; it will become more difficult as time goes on". This was in his famous letter to the British writer W. T. Stead, when he pleaded for a just and merciful peace between Boer and Briton.

It is significant that when Smuts at this time of his life used the word racialism he meant it to refer to the attitude between the Boers and the British and not to the relationship between White and Black.

It is clear from his memorandum of January 1906 in which he discussed the voting arrangements in the Transvaal that he gave no consideration to a vote for non-Whites. For this omission he was criticized by the Cape leader, John Merriman, and this led to a lively correspondence between them. It must be remembered that in the Cape at that time the policy was to give the vote to all persons, irrespective of race or colour, who achieved the educational and economic standards established by the franchise laws. In the three other provinces of the Transvaal, the Orange Free State and Natal, this vote was exclusively in the hands of the Whites and denied to the other races, Brown or Black.[15]

Merriman defended the Cape franchise for all as "a safety valve and though it makes some noise and a nasty smell it is the most reasonable guarantee against an explosion". His cynical solution was to give every man who qualifies a vote, but to set the qualifications reasonably high so that only very few Blacks would obtain the vote.

Smuts in replying to Merriman expressed his profound sympathy with the Black races of South Africa and he felt it should be the policy of all parties to do justice to the Blacks and to take all wise and prudent measures for their civilization and improvement.

"But I don't believe in politics for them. Perhaps at bottom I do not believe in politics at all as a means for the attainment of the highest ends, but certainly so far as the natives are concerned politics will to my mind only have an unsettling influence. I would therefore not give them the franchise, which in any case would not affect more than a negligible number at present."

And then Smuts added these words which became characteristic of his outlook and his attitude and may explain his inaction even when he was Prime Minister:

"When I consider the political future of natives in South Africa I must say that I look into shadows and darkness, and then I feel inclined to shift the intolerable burden of solving that sphinx problem to the ampler shoulders and stronger brains of the future. Sufficient unto the day etc. My feeling is that strong forces are at work which will transform the Afrikaner attitudes to the natives."[16]

Smuts's look into the "shadows and darkness" characterized his actions or rather inaction as far as a solution of the so-called native problem in South Africa was concerned, but circumstances forced him to apply his mind and energies to the Indian problem in the Transvaal when the redoubtable Gandhi appeared on the scene to resist discrimination against the Indian community and to fight for their rights. Gandhi brought the spiritual forces of his newly founded Satyagraha movement into the battle, but Smuts in spite of his religious beliefs fought the Indian leader with purely legal weapons. What must be borne in mind is that Smuts at the time was concentrating his major efforts on bringing about the Union of South Africa and that he had not the time to devote his full energies to Gandhi. Yet in the end Smuts and Gandhi reached a settlement which removed some forms of discrimination and safeguarded the "vested rights" of the Indian community, but left a final solution in the air. When Gandhi, shortly after the Indian Relief Act was passed in July 1914, left South Africa to go to India where he was to inaugurate his campaign of civil disobedience against British discrimination, Smuts wrote:

"The saint has left our shores. I sincerely hope for ever."

Yet he kept up his ties with the Indian leader, who never imputed racial prejudice to Smuts.[17]

Smuts later wrote a revealing letter to Gandhi which goes a long way to explain his actions and inaction in trying to solve the so-called Indian problem in South Africa:

"When I was, about the same time as you, studying in England, I had no race prejudice or colour prejudice against your people. In fact if we had known each other we would have been friends. Why is it then that now we have become rivals we have conflicting interests? It is not colour prejudice or race prejudice, though some of our people do ignorantly talk in those terms, but then there is one thing which I want you to recognize. It is this. I may have no racial legislation, but how will you solve the difficulty about the fundamental difference of our cultures? Let alone the question of superiority, there is no doubt that your civilization is different from ours. Ours must not be overwhelmed by yours. That is why we have to go in for legislation which must in effect put disabilities on you."

Gandhi with his astute mind said that he understood what Smuts meant.

"If therefore we (as Indians) wanted to live in South Africa we must adopt their standard of life, so long as it was not against morality."[18]

When Gandhi celebrated his 70th birthday in 1939, Smuts wrote an essay on Gandhi's political method for a commemorative volume:

"It was my fate to be the antagonist of a man for whom even then I had the highest respect. I must frankly admit that his activities at that time were very trying to me. Together with other South African leaders I was then busily engaged on the task of welding the old colonies into a unified state . . . It was a colossal work which took every moment of my time. Suddenly in the midst of all those engrossing preoccupations Gandhi raised a most troublesome issue. We had a skeleton in our cupboard . . ."[19]

It was a skeleton not only for South Africa, but more especially for Smuts when in 1946 he went as Prime Minister of South Africa, to the first meeting of the newly created United Nations at Flushing Meadow outside New York. Smuts had meanwhile drafted the high-minded, idealistic Preamble for the United Nations. He had also played a very important part in helping to win the war against the dictators to ensure freedom and democracy. His one demand for all his good work was to incorporate South West Africa into the Union of South Africa.

However, at this first session, India took the lead not only in thwarting his scheme to incorporate the mandated territory, but also to attack South Africa for its discriminatory policies. Smuts's neglect to solve the Indian and native problems and remove inequality and discrimination became the weapon which destroyed his plans for the future and his standing and acceptance in the international community. He was bitterly frustrated and disappointed. Although in an official broadcast he laid stress upon the colour consciousness, the emotionalism, the demagogy and the intense lobbying which characterized the new United Nations, privately he expressed his disappointment to a friend:

"The world does not know or understand us and we feel this deeply, even when we are conscious that we are much to blame for it all. It is a good country and a good people, but the world sees its mistakes more clearly than its goodness and virtues. I do not despair of the future, but it will not be easy to keep South Africa steady in this avalanche of condemnation, which has so suddenly and unexpectedly overwhelmed it. People simply cannot understand it and are running over with resentment. It will be my part to keep them cool and if possible reflective, so that good may come out of this evil."

The problem was, however, how to do this. He had received a severe mauling at the United Nations, and in South Africa this had "a great effect in all directions", as he wrote in a private letter to Mrs Gillett.

"We even hear about them from our own domestic and farm natives who really have nothing to complain of, but are deeply stirred by all this talk of equality and non-discrimination. I am anxious to stay this rot and get a move on for better relations, but it is even more difficult now in view of these Native claims which have got the opposite effect upon the European mentality. Both extremes are gathering strength."[20]

Here Smuts, the man of action, the Christian and the philosopher, stood before his greatest problem. He simply did not know what to do, so he did nothing. It was the result of the extreme duality in his being. On the one hand he was the deep spiritual thinker and humanist who poured out his highest idealism in the Preamble to the Charter of the United Nations; on the other hand as a South African with the traditions and experiences of the White race, living and working with the Black races of Africa, proud of his heritage and determined to maintain it, he lacked the wisdom and the will to impose a solution which would inevitably antagonize the White electorate. This was especially difficult on the eve of the important general election scheduled for May 1948. In the agony of his soul he turned to Lady Moore. On March 2 1947 he wrote to her one of his most revealing letters:

"Colour in the world and in South Africa has become more intransigent because of the acclaim of human rights at UNO. How is the practical compromise to be found? That is the problem which confronts us in South Africa and me in particular. The world is reeling between the two poles of White and Colour. What is the future of our races going to be? And in South Africa the problem is coming to a head."

Lady Moore responded by telling him:

"I am sorry for you, for the conflict in your mind must exhaust you; even if you come to the conclusions that satisfy your own intellect and conscience, you may from force of circumstances have to compromise with yourself and say publicly not what you think, but what is best for people to hear."

At the same time she told him bluntly that there is "no possibility of compromise in the colour question; either the white race fights for its supremacy, confident of its superiority; or we admit that all men are alike under God and that Christianity and the other codes of ethics in which we believe make no distinction between a white skin and a brown, so why should we? The trouble is that the subject is one which it is difficult to be logical about because of the underlying fear, repulsion or whatever it is that the white man feels for the black and which to you in South Africa, with generations of colour-strife in your blood, is an essential element of your characters of which you are almost unaware.

"English people with their copy-book maxims and their smug humanitarian theories, cannot understand the instinct inherited from forebears who have had to fight black races for their very existence . . . How can you have a practical compromise?"[21]

For Smuts there was no compromise, no solution and no reprieve. He lost the general election of May 1948 on the colour issue. The one issue which he neglected all his life proved to be his Achilles heel and produced the blemish on his character and his international reputation. That he was conscious of this is revealed in his letter to Mrs Gillett on January 14 1947.

"Here is the author of the great Preamble of the Charter, exposed as a hypocrite and a double-faced time-server! They (the opposition) are of course right and so is dear South Africa. But look at this bad fellow who is responsible for it all."[22]

CHAPTER EIGHTEEN

His legacy

Mankind requires to be guided by some light, some vision, through the maze of life. This is especially true in modern times, which mark a transition period between the old and the new. It is one of the most daunting and at the same time one of the most interesting periods that any generation has had to pass through.

What mankind, in the view of Smuts, needs above all is some larger synthesis, some idea that will bring together the manifold details with which modern man has to deal. There has been an immense movement forward in thought, science, philosophy and most forms of human development. Mankind is running the risk of getting lost, becoming submerged in the details, and it is all-important to get some larger view of all this vast mass. What we need, in his view, is a synoptic vision of all the details.

Smuts denied that he had such a synoptic vision.

"I have only an idea which occurred to me and which may, to some small extent, help to guide us through the surrounding difficulties. Holism is an attempt at synthesis, an attempt at bringing together many currents of thought and development such as we have seen in our day. It is not a system of philosophy. I do not believe very much in systems. They are sometimes helpful, but it is most difficult, in matters so complex as life and thought, to take one concept that might embrace adequately the whole. Holism – the theory of the whole – tries to emphasize one aspect of thought that has been hitherto a neglected factor. I am trying to hammer out this neglected factor, which is, to my mind, all-important in getting the synoptic vision."[1]

One important aspect of Holism which is here made clear is that it is not a system trying to embrace everything in one grand formula. It is one aspect of reality. And it is not merely formal or abstract. It is a real factor, impressing itself in an inner arranging, organizing way on all parts, and thus with the parts and in its relation to them, it constitutes a whole. As such he regarded Holism as a true functioning, causal factor in reality.

As a real factor he saw it in the same light as Darwin's evolution and as Einstein's relativity – a key which will unlock new doors of knowledge and bring a reform of our outlook in science, ethics and religion.

It is in this sense that he himself, rightly or wrongly, saw Holism as a new concept which could have far-reaching effects on the history of ideas. He saw our modern situation as somewhat parallel to that described by Socrates in his own age. In his youth and early manhood, physical science and speculation had formed the dominant intellectual interest in the Greek world. The movement had spread from the Greek settlements in Asia Minor and had inaugurated what is generally recognized as one of the most brilliant golden ages in human thought.

Many of the scientific ideals of that time form the basis of our culture today. But much was of mere intellectual interest, barren of practical results and in the end leading nowhere. Socrates, like other thinkers of his time, entered with enthusiasm upon this scientific speculation. He studied physics; became versed in astronomy. Gradually in his search for truth he became convinced that the whole direction of Greek thought was fundamentally wrong and that neither physics nor abstract speculation, but practical human interests were the important things in life. And so he transferred his life-work from physics to the study of the human sciences. The result was that he re-established contact with reality and so brought philosophy from the heavens down to earth, but in the process he paid for his innovation with his life.

That new direction of Socrates, however, was passed on to his associates and to his successors, and the whole trend of Western thinking was transformed for ever after.

In the view of Smuts something similar is happening in our time. Materialistic scientific interests have dominated our culture. In that way we have all but established our mastery over the physical world.

But what of our social and spiritual interests? Smuts was convinced that mankind was reaching the stage in world development where human interests were beginning to transcend all others, and to call insistently for consideration. He felt that the belief was growing all over the world that the social and spiritual interests of man had been unduly neglected in this scientific preoccupation and should now receive closer attention.

What is remarkable is that Smuts with these views, expounded in the twenties and thirties of this century, predated by nearly half a century the recent emphasis on human rights as the basis of national and international affairs. He was to stress these ideas still further in the last years of his life when he pointed out that the two world wars and their tragic aftermath have intensified the sense of human tragedy and of the importance of the human aspect in experience. He also felt that the decay of religion in the West has reinforced the feeling of unrest and unsatisfied human needs.

These and other causes in his view are calling for a new direction in science, and for a broadening-out of our thought and research from the physical and biological to human needs in their social and spiritual aspects.

"Something similar to the Attic transformation which Socrates initiated is taking place in our intellectual life today. Everywhere there are indications of a far-reaching change-over from one atmosphere of thought to another. In some countries perhaps more happily situated than others, the change is still of a more or less academic character.

"But in others where suffering has bitten deeply into the social organism, the process has gone much further, and has reached the stage of social convulsion and revolution, and of a new ideological orientation."[2]

In his view all this calls for a new direction and for a new holistic vision. The gulf between matter and mind must be bridged in human beings. Science as the servant and not the master of mankind will have to make terms with human social and spiritual interests if it is to play its great part in our culture and supply guidance in the dark passages upon which our race is now entering. What we must realize above all is that in the end it is only human beings, men and women, who matter. In placing the human personality supreme, Holism strives not only to combine science, ethics and religion from whence spring our highest values, but also to bring nearer to fulfilment that greater ideal of the nobler and purer personality which is the highest end.

From this it is clear that Smuts saw Holism not as a mere abstract idea, but as an idea linked with reality, a great central truth which illuminates all other truths. He saw clearly the scientific and philosophic importance of the idea. He realized what a transforming power it is bound to exercise over most of the viewpoints in science and philosophy. And as one to whom faith was a reality and belief in God part of life, to whom Jesus Christ was the greatest and noblest personality to walk this earth, he was conscious of its deep significance in the domain of religion.

Will Holism as a central truth be accepted as Evolution or Relativity is accepted? It is too early to give a definite answer to the question. Although scientific Holism has been advanced in both systems and structuralist theories, and philosophers have concentrated on perspectivist approaches which can be regarded as holistic, to the masses at large it is still beyond easy understanding. It has still to be explained in terms of our daily life and its necessities, before it can be expected to penetrate to the ordinary man and woman. And as with all new ideas, that takes time. Smuts knew it and he was prepared for it. "I am content to be patient and wait for actual results," he wrote to Professor Meyer of Hamburg in November 1938. "New ideas take a long time to filter into the public mind, and Holism may not produce early results, but in the long run and in the end I have little doubt that it will secure its place in the development of human thought, and will help to lead public opinion away from the destructive atmosphere of the past to that saner and larger viewpoint, which will once more bridge the gaps and fill the fissures which the mechanistic science and philosophy have created for the human spirit."

To Dr Minkowski of Berlin he expressed at about the same time the hope that Holism would in the end prove fruitful not only in philosophy but in human affairs generally. "Our shattered world has to be re-united and reconstructed for the future good and peace of human kind, and I have the hope that Holism in its small way might make a contribution to this great end."

Unfortunately when *Holism and Evolution* first appeared the impression was created that Smuts denied the existence of God and that he deviated from accepted beliefs and religious philosophy. As I pointed out in Chapter 1 this was the conclusion drawn from his acceptance of the argument of Kant that from the facts of nature no inference of God is justified.

This has nowhere been more clearly shown than in a short criticism of the Holistic view by his friend, Dr F. C. Kolbe, who criticized Smuts's Holism from the point of view that he lost sight of the First or Absolute Cause in dealing with the material world.

This led to a lively correspondence between Smuts and Kolbe which unfortunately escaped the attention of his biographers. In my estimation this exchange of views between the two friends provides a clue not only to Smuts's religious views, but also to the concept he had in mind for a sequel to Holism as applied on the spiritual plane. As such, a short discussion of the arguments used is of crucial importance in evaluating Smuts's contribution to the borderline study between philosophy and religion.

Kolbe, who was an examiner of Smuts's first contribution to philosophy when he was still a student at Stellenbosch University, readily admitted that Smuts was a deep thinker who should be taken seriously. In discussing *Holism and Evolution* he realized that if one asked Smuts how matter got its creative power or what place the idea of the Creator had in his scheme of things, he would say that in Holism he was writing scientific philosophy and not metaphysics or natural theology.

Kolbe accepts this but still holds that Smuts in dealing with secondary causes should relate them to the First Cause. In discussing the finite material world he cannot understand it "wholly" without reference to the Infinite, was his contention.

It was in this connection that he levelled his main criticism against Smuts's acceptance of Kant's famous argument that from the facts of nature no inference of God is justified. Kolbe agrees that this does not mean that Smuts utterly rejects the idea of God. Referring to this, Smuts stated clearly in *Holism and Evolution* that belief in the Divine Being rests, and necessarily must rest, on quite different grounds.

But Kolbe feels that even this is not enough. His view is that if a person acquires a belief in the Divine Being it should have its place in his science as well as his religion. All that we know of God, however we acquire it, necessarily forms part of our concept of any of His work.

He points out that Smuts, being a Holist, should deal with whole concepts and that when discussing the finite material world it should be set in its relation or relativity to the Infinite.

Smuts in his reply to Kolbe realized and acknowledged this. He explained why he had not touched upon the profound significance of Holism in the domain of religion. He stated that he was trying to lay the foundations of the philosophy and to build the new structure from its foundations.

"The Religious Ideal, like the other great Ideals and Values of the spirit, is not yet reached in my treatment of Holism, although, to be sure, the understanding reader will find more in the book than is actually written there."

It was especially from this point of view that he welcomed Kolbe's criticism, for the latter felt called upon to state explicitly what is not directly set out in Holism.

"Within the limited scientific purview of the book I do not discuss God, as such a discussion would in my opinion have been out of place in such a context."

But at the same time he can understand why Kolbe, from the Catholic point of view, holds that not even a scientific statement of the universe is correct which does not make explicit reference to the First Cause which underlies and sustains all secondary or particular causes. It is to guard against the view that the infinite is an unnecessary surplusage in a scientific scheme.

"Not that he attributes such a view to me," Smuts continued, "but he wishes to prevent others from wrongly inferring such a view from my silence."

He explained that his silence on this point was due to the limited introductory scope of his book.

In his development of Holism he had yet to come to the consideration of such subjects as the infinite.

"And yet even so, the relation of the finite to the infinite is implicit in all that I say in regard to the whole. My treatment of Holism is destructive of the self-sufficiency of the particular or the finite."

How did he do this? By showing that the popular view of the finite particular of "thing" is a false abstraction. A "thing" does not stand by itself as an isolated entity. Everything has a "field". Nothing is therefore complete in itself or sufficient unto itself. The finite endures in the communion of the infinite.

Contending that Holism by its very nature denies reality to the particular by itself and in itself and apart from the context of its field, Smuts put forth the view that the religious aspect of this truth seems to be implied in this idea of Holism.

"Even though the material world is the creation of the Divine Power and therefore has its purpose in the Divine Being, we can and must study it by itself to seek there the laws which are also of the infinite."

It is in this sense that Smuts welcomed the criticism of his friend Kolbe. It showed that there are these wider and important implications and applications of Holism to philosophical and religious thought still to be made.

"But in my book all this is still more or less implicit and the task of explicit development has still to be undertaken."

I have quoted at length from this controversy between Kolbe and Smuts as it gives us a clue as to what he had in mind as a sequel to his *Holism and Evolution*.[3]

In the preface to this book he referred to the wider application of his holistic ideas to religion and allied subjects. He called his book an introductory sketch which was intended more to lay the foundations than to build the superstructure. The aspects and bearings of Holism in which he was mainly interested had not yet been reached in this study.

"But I hope in the years to come to find time to follow up the subject and to show how it affects the higher spiritual interests of mankind. The old concepts and formulas are no longer adequate to express our modern outlook. The old bottles will no longer hold the new wine. The spiritual temple of the future, while it will be built largely of the old well-proved materials, will require new and ampler foundations in the light of the immense extension of our intellectual horizons."[4]

And "this little book" as he called his immense study, indicates the lines along which his own mind had travelled in the search for new and more satisfactory concepts.

Already in September 1931, five years after the first appearance of *Holism and Evolution*, Smuts was contemplating writing his second book as a sequel dealing with the higher forms of life and more especially with the concept of value. In a letter to his American friend, Mrs Florence Lamont, he told her that they were both addicted to inquiry.

Children asked the most enormous questions in the most matter-of-fact way, and what were they but grown-up children.

"I want an answer," he continued his letter, "to the insistent question: how value becomes a reality?"[5]

He gave the answer in his presidential address to the British Association at its centenary celebrations in September 1931. Sketching the evolutionary process which led to the free creativeness of mind, he expressed the view that the highest reach of this creative process is seen in the realm of value.

It was in the pursuit of this enquiry into value that Smuts brooded for many years with the idea of writing his sequal to *Holism and Evolution*. He had thought of writing it before the Second World War, but when South Africa entered the war in September 1939 he half jokingly told his associates that he would not find the time to write his book.

"And so much profundity will be buried with me. But the world will be none the worse, although it may be much the worse if we lose the war – that is the difference between thinking and doing."[6]

Towards the end of the war he returned to the idea of writing his sequel to *Holism and Evolution*. Already on January 3 1945 he wrote to the Master of his old College at Cambridge, C. E. Raven, indicating the direction his thinking was following. Stating that science was the great revelation of the modern world, but not the only revelation, he thought that the time had come for trying to bridge the chasm which now separated the different revelations, and thus to restore unity in the higher life of mankind.

"Science so far has had far too much to do with the things of sense and of matter, and the things of the spirit have been by-passed. But can it be said that atoms are more real than souls? And souls we have left to the novelists, while atoms have been tackled by the highest brains which our century has produced. Did I say novelists? I should have said parsons – and mostly such parsons!"[7]

Shortly after the war, on November 9 1945, he wrote to Mrs Gillett that he longed for "time to write my second volume and let the first become antiquarian as it is practically antiquated". His thought took a decidedly religious direction. He stated clearly that the situation in which mankind found itself after the war with all its hatred and destruction, was "at bottom a religious problem" as he wrote to Mrs Gillett. Like Jesus he thought that the "Soul, Man's relation to God, the inner purification and the practice of the gentler virtues would herald . . . the Kingdom of Heaven. Is this thought not basic in the truest sense? Has mankind not first to find its soul again before it finds the new Kingdom?" he asked in his letter.

How he wanted to fit this into his continuation of the concept of Holism, he outlined in a letter to Mrs Gillett on September 8 1948.[8]

"I was discussing with two young Calvinist parsons the other day the concept of Holism, which they took as purely humanistic and a denial of the theistic concept. I explained to them that I did not agree with Calvin's legalistic conception of human alienation and depravity. With John's Gospel I believed in Incarnation – the Word become flesh – the divine immanent in the human, and in matter and its patterns as a revelation of the Divine. Holism is therefore the approach towards the theistic concept from the side of nature, and builds as it were a bridge between humanism and divinity."

This is what he had in mind for his second book, an inquiry into the source of value and the spiritual nature of man. He had previously drafted four studies for this second book. These are to be found amongst his papers. The four titles he had in mind, perhaps as chapters were (i) Sensation and Perception; (ii) From Substance to Pattern; (iii) The Nature of Holism; (iv) Holism and Psychology.

Unfortunately he never proceeded with the writing of these subjects, but he had visualized the book as a philosophical bridge between the material and the spiritual worlds.[9] In building the bridge he felt that feeling came before thought and he saw the arches of the bridge as faith, hope and love and not merely as systematic reasoning.

In a letter to Lady Moore on April 8 1948 he told how he had discussed

Holism with Prof. Camp of Berkeley University and his wife, who had visited him:

"Why is it that there is an upward trend in evolution, and higher and more advanced forms arise from lower, more primitive forms? Why is there a curiously pronounced progress towards the higher? Is there a direction, is there a trend, a bias in a certain direction? Is there design and Providence? This is of course the central problem in the great mystery of life. Matter runs down like water, life and mind rise up to ever higher levels. How and why is this? I tried to explain how my theory of Holism tries to account for this tendency, which is so apparent and yet so mysterious, on purely scientific lines of thought. I hope I did not confuse them. I told them I intended still to continue my work on Holism and deal with some of the deeper problems which I deliberately left alone in my earlier work. The question is just whether I can live and remain sane enough to do this."[10]

Then he added that the indications were that he would again win the election which was scheduled for May 1948 and "that I shall be compelled to carry on as prime minister. But how long, O Lord? Will there be no quiet afternoon for release and reflection?"

Smuts of course lost the election and he could have been released from politics to devote himself to the second Holism. Many of his friends and associates thought he would do so. Unfortunately he was persuaded to continue as Leader of the United Party, and from then on until his death he was again so occupied with politics that he never found the time to continue his inquiry.

In July 1948, after his defeat at the polls, Smuts wrote to Prof. Adolf Meyer-Abich of Hamburg who had written to him at length about Holism.

"At the present moment I can do nothing about Holism. My political responsibilities at my age are so heavy that I cannot find time for the revision of the old book, nor the writing of the new book which has been simmering in my mind for some years. When I look at the world unrest today and the confusion which prevails in science, in philosophy, in religion and in our whole human outlook and set-up, I feel drawn more and more to ultimate solutions.

"Something holistic is at the heart of things and in the nature of this universe, which is not a mere chance or random assemblement of items. The detailed things derive most of their meaning, significance and functioning from the whole, of which they are but parts. They are not mere parts but really members of wholes.

"Both as a metaphysical and as a scientific concept the whole is basic to an understanding of the world. And in sociology and religion this is more clearly the case. Relativity is only a halfway house to this more fundamental concept.

"This being my conviction, you will realise how much importance I attach to Holism, and how anxious I am to give the concept a further push forward. But at present I can do nothing about it. But I still hope against hope to return to Holism at the end . . ."[11]

Unfortunately for all of us this hope was never realized. The tragedy in the life of Smuts was that he never found time to complete his great task. That which he thought he had to give mankind remained with him, and when the end came two years later he carried his thoughts with him into death.

This is a great pity, and with his deep religious feelings, his abiding faith in God, his supreme estimation of the person and personality of Christ, the power of his intellect and his ability to express himself clearly, he could have produced a great book as a guide to modern man in his search for truth and direction. We can only surmise what Smuts had finally in mind.

Fortunately he has left an invaluable collection of documents, letters, memoranda and notes, from which we can deduce the direction his thoughts took in preparation for the sequel to his first book. *Holism and Evolution* itself provides valuable clues as to what he had in mind as a superstructure to be constructed on the original concept of wholes in the universe. He himself regarded *Holism* as "introductory" but containing some glimpse into his ideas of the nature of the holistic universe which is partly material and partly spiritual.

He points out that there are those who think that the only thing that matters in the universe is matter. They are the naturalists or materialists who represent the universe as a vast reservoir of energy subject to unchangeable laws where life and mind are nothing but shadows on the shores of this ocean of energy.

"Reality to them exists only in matter or its energy. Man himself is but an impotent spectator of this vast scene, wrapped up in his own illusions."

It is clear from the importance with which Smuts endows man as a free personality creating his own values, that he rejects this purely materialistic view of the universe. To him Materialism or Naturalism is inconsistent with the great fact of evolution.

"Creative evolution is the rock on which the materialist universe must founder. For how can the materialists explain the "more" which results from growth and development and which creates the atoms, the cells, life, mind and personality if only material forces operate in the universe?"

But at the other extreme Holism equally rejects those cosmic theories which try to explain the world as a result of purely spiritual forces. There are many thinkers who deny the material reality and place it in subjection to mysterious spiritual forces. Some call themselves Idealists, others like Leibnitz, Moralists, some Spiritual Pluralists or again Panpsychists like Prof. James Ward.[12]

Just as he rejects materialism because it conflicts with creative evolution, Smuts shows that this spiritual world outlook is a fantasy devoid of material foundations. He points out that the spirit and the spiritual properties which we encounter in life are of recent origin.

Although a real factor in life, mind and personality, it did not exist either explicitly or implicitly at the beginning. The basic fact in its evaluation as far as we mortals are concerned is that it has arisen creatively in the course of organic evolution.

Here we come upon a cornerstone of Smuts's holistic universe. He sees no contradiction between mind and matter, between the material world and the world of the spirit. They are one because they are fundamentally unified in their origins and their natures. The materialists who stare themselves blind on matter fail to realize that there is something "more" in matter than mere matter. There is a fundamentally synthesizing, ordering, organizing, regulating activity in the universe. There is, in other words, a pattern and a principle of wholeness which operates according to categories. These are essentially the same everywhere, but through the whole-making patterns they assume ever more closely unified and synthesized forms in the progressive course of their operations.

Thus the four great series in reality, matter, life, mind and personality, apparently so far removed from one another, are but steps in the progressive development of one and the same factor. Life, mind and personality are not illusions but as real as matter, yet above matter but always retaining their basic link with matter.

The pattern and principle which in his view binds the entire process together is Holism.

Holism thus leads evolution into the sphere of the spirit and the ideal values which arise from man's spiritual nature.

The first basic truth in our cosmic view is that there is no dualism between matter and mind. They are one in different manifestations. Each individual has both a material body and a spiritual nature, which through holistic evolution are one. There is no conflict between our bodies and our souls. And as we are a unity, so there is an underlying unity in all nature and the entire universe.

Far from being an arrogant thinker regarding man as a god in his own right, Smuts here reveals his basic humility. Without detracting from the importance of the person and his spiritual values, he constantly reminds us that we are not children of an alien spiritual world, but that we have our roots in the material world, and that we are akin to the lowest forms of life and matter. This is the great lesson of humility which is possibly basic in Dr Albert Schweitzer's reverence for life, through which even the lowly ants at Lambarene were protected. The vast society of the universe in this view leaves a place for the most humble forms of life and matter no less than for the crowning glory of the human soul. To conceive of the universe as only matter is to deny its life-giving and soul-forming potencies. To see it only as spirit, above and beyond matter and apart from it, is to indulge in anthropomorphism, which may be pleasing to our vanity, but in reality detracts from the richness and variety of life.

This world, in the noble language of Keats, is indeed the valley of soul-making, but it could not be that if the valley itself consisted of nothing but souls. "To those who have the deepest experience of life," writes Smuts, "this world is not only the upward path of the soul, but a very hard and flinty one. To attempt to pave that rugged way with the roses of the spiritual order would be a profound mistake from every point of view."[13]

But in saying this he does not mean that there is anything antagonistic between the human soul and the forces of nature. There is not only poetic value but profound truth in the spiritual interpretation of nature to which Wordsworth and other great poets of nature have accustomed us. That truth is not merely due to the creative part which the mind plays in the shaping and fashioning of nature. It is also not merely because we invest nature with our own emotional attributes. It is in fact to be traced to far deeper sources in our human origins.

In a striking passage Smuts discussed this intimate contact which he himself had with nature. It is a passage of beauty and truth which, perhaps more than his philosophical explanations, reveals the working of his mind.

"For we are indeed one with Nature, her genetic fibres run through all our being, our physical organs connect us with millions of years of her history; our minds are full of immemorial paths of pre-human experience.

"Our ear for music, our eye for art carry us back to the early beginnings of animal life on this globe. Press but a button in our brain and the gaunt spectres of the dim forgotten past rise once more before us; the ghostly dreaded forms of the primeval Fear loom before us and we tremble all over with inexplicable fright. And then again some distant sound, some call of bird or smell of wild plants, or some sunrise or sunset glow in the distant clouds, some mixture of light and shade on the mountains may suddenly throw an unearthly spell over the spirit, lead it forth from the deep chambers and set it panting and wondering with inexpressible emotion. For the overwrought mind there is no peace like nature's, for the wounded spirit there is no healing like hers. There are indeed times when human companionship becomes unbearable, and we fly to nature for that silent sympathy and communion which she alone can give.

"Some of the deepest emotional experiences of my life have come to me on the many nights I have spent under the open African sky, and I am sure my case has not been singular in this respect.

"The intimate rapport with nature is one of the most precious things in life. Nature is indeed very close to us; sometimes closer than hands and feet, of which in truth she is but the extension. The emotional appeal of nature is tremendous, sometimes almost more than one can bear."[14]

The key to this view is the scientific truth that there is no dichotomy between mind and matter. They are related, they are a unity.

There is a second truth to be grasped before we can finally look beyond the finite world. Having established the existence of a series of "wholes" in matter, life, mind and personality, are we justified in conceiving a Supreme Whole in the universe? If there are such wholes must they be conceived by way of analogy of mind as a Supreme Personality? Smuts shows that neither view is correct, from the viewpoint of either science or philosophy. A whole cannot be constructed from its parts because our entire inquiry has shown that it is always more than the mere aggregate of its parts. We can therefore not construct a Supreme Personality from the parts of nature and mind as we know them. If such a Personality exists or comes into being it must necessarily, from our own scientific point of view, be something entirely different from the sum of these parts with which we endow it. We cannot, therefore, construct or shape a Supreme Personality or a Supreme Divine Being on the analogy of our own finite world and its forces. This was also what Kant meant when he wrote that from the facts of nature no inference of God is justified.

But this does not mean that Smuts denies the existence of God. He merely warns against the idea of thinking of God in terms of an analogy of nature or of seeing God as an extension of the human Personality. We are here before the great mystery of the Divine Being and he points out that the belief in God rests, and necessarily must rest, on quite different grounds. With our limited insights and our imperfect minds we cannot rationally solve this incomprehensible mystery. He himself has called it the "immensity, the profundity and the unutterable mystery of the universe".[15]

His thinking here is in line with modern theology. God is not a mere extension of our being.

It is clear, however, from the vast amount of letters, notes, memoirs and other personal material which he left behind, that he had a deep and abiding belief in God as the Father of all. His religion was real to him, but it was not a formal religion of creed and doctrine. He regarded religion not as an end but as a quest, a search for the ultimate truth, which is in the finite no less than in the infinite world. It was here too that he placed such a high value on science because he regarded science in the quest for truth – as "perhaps the clearest revelation of God to our age". In its selfless pursuit of truth, in its vision of order and beauty, he saw it as partaking of the quality of both art and religion, and he invested it with a profound aesthetic and religious appeal to thinking people.

He saw as one of the greatest tasks before the human race, precisely this linking up of science with ethical values, thus to bridge the gaps between the disciplines of religion, art and science. This is undoubtedly one field where he might have sought to make a contribution, as he was continually thinking of ways and means of uniting these lines of human endeavour which so far have remained separate and largely antagonistic and conflicting.

Another field to which he extended his holistic ideas was the development of the sense of the spiritual in nature. We have already noted his own appreciation of the influence of nature on the human soul. As life went on he became even more interested in this. He himself was progressively finding greater spiritual stimulation in his communion with nature. It was not only for exercise that he went for his long walks over mountains and through the African veld. He found something deep and spiritual in nature, and as he walked at a steady pace, mentally browsing, talking about botany and philosophy, he felt at one with nature. It was this that he worshipped. Mrs Gillett told me that this was explicit in his letters, but also in quiet conversations with his friends.

"He was continually writing and talking about the mountains, about the bush and about sleeping under the stars, and through this he revealed his interest in the sense of the inner life, the sense of the spiritual in nature, and it was along these lines that he was extending his holistic ideas. This was evident both in his letters and in his private conversations," she said.

"It was the inwardness of nature in deepest harmony with the inner soul of human beings which he wanted to develop further in his second book," was her explanation.[16]

But there is a further and deeper interest which occupied his thoughts equally. This was the extension of his idea of personality.

As I have shown in dealing with personality he regarded our present stage of development as incomplete. One result of this is that individual personalities still show discordance of elements, which creates tensions and confusions in itself and so lies at the root of our present uncertainties. Personality is still a growing factor in the universe and is merely in its infancy. But at the same time there is ample evidence that the level of its power and activity is gradually rising. More and more it is exercising effective central control in greater numbers of individuals over the entire world, and often it wins in even the most discouraging circumstances those moral victories which form the landmarks of personal and human progress. From the depths of moral and spiritual aberration it guides the weak steps of the wanderer to conscious manhood and moral control.

In a striking passage Smuts indicated in his *Holism and Evolution* how a personality often saves and purifies itself and moves onto a higher plane by means of the sins and excesses of which it has been guilty, but he regarded this as beyond the scope of his "introductory" book.

But what is important for us is that here he reveals the extension in the application of his holistic ideas. He was in fact trying to think beyond our present incomplete and imperfect personalities to those ideal persons who would be whole in the sense that they would not have in them anything which is not at peace with themselves or which is alien or external to themselves.

Such a personality must be free in the highest sense of the word, it must be pure and it must be fully conscious of its powers, its limitations, its purpose and its values.[17]

If the interest of Smuts in figures like Goethe, Shakespeare, Whitman, Roosevelt, Gandhi, President Kruger, Lord Kitchener, Dr A. W. Roberts,

Cecil Rhodes, Charles John Anderson, Livingstone and others reveals anything, it is that he was for ever looking for the ideal personality in actual life. It may be said that in his view Goethe as a person probably approximated nearest to that ideal. But to him the greatest of all personalities that have walked this earth was Jesus.

Jannie tells how his father preferred to read the New Testament in the original Greek. Indeed, few people have studied the New Testament more meticulously, and hence few, in the opinion of Smuts himself, realized just how short the active phase of Jesus' career was. In his study there were many books dealing with the life of Jesus and with the New Testament, and many names of books and authors dealing with this subject also appear in the list of books supplied to him by Mrs Gillett. He preferred to read the New Testament in the original Greek so as to be able to better understand what the original authors tried to express. That it must have been a long and difficult study is clear from all the evidence, and it took him many years to unravel the details to his satisfaction.

In dealing with this, Jannie states: "That Christ actually lived, he had no doubt, but he thought of Him as a very remarkable gifted young man, rather than as the Immaculate Son of God."

This was not the impression of Mrs Gillett, who was probably nearer to Smuts and his religion than his son Jannie.

But whatever his ideas about the divinity of Jesus, even Jannie records that his father was forever thinking of the problem of personality "and of Christ as the Greatest Personality". He sums up his father's thought as follows:

"The world could only advance through the efforts of the Greatest Personalities and he pondered over the genius of Christ continually."[18]

How did he in reality see the figure of Christ as the highest embodiment of Personality and therefore as the Ideal Person?

When I discussed this aspect of his thoughts with Mrs Gillett she mentioned the great influence of the Friends upon him. Like the Friends, he preferred to worship in silence and like them he found the indwelling Spirit of God in human beings. They believe that the Spirit of God speaks in the human heart. They also believe that the Spirit of Jesus Christ is in the world today and always, and speaking to people. She said she knew the kind of religion Smuts was interested in.

The figure and the personality of Jesus had tremendous influence over him and as his life went on, he felt the power of the personality of Jesus more and more intensely. "Jesus Christ was to him about, now and here," was how she expressed it.

She was convinced that it was wrong to think that to him Christ was only a human person. Jesus was a person and so are we, but at the same time we are part of the whole of God, the Father of us all. God is in all of us, how much more then is God in Christ. In Jesus is the culmination of divinity. He is human and He is divine. To say Jesus is only human is wrong. To say He is only divine is equally wrong. He is human and divine in one, and that is what Smuts, according to her interpretation, wanted to express in his later work.

"With his holistic ideas he found the deeper unity and synthesis in all existence as in all life. Applied to religion this holistic synthesis could equally explain the Personality of Christ as the unity, the synthesis, the bridge between suffering mankind and the loving and merciful Father which is God. He is human and He is Divine. He is the Son of Man and also the Son of the Father, the Great Redeemer who has come to reveal not force and might but righteousness, tenderness, love and mercy. He became the Word which was made flesh and dwelt among us," she explained to me when I talked to her under a mulberry tree at her home in Street.[19]

What appealed to Smuts especially was the uniqueness of the teaching of Jesus which, in the words of Hugh Montefiore, consisted not in novelty but in Personality. Smuts never believed in systems of thought or a *Weltanschauung*. As we know, Christianity is not a system or a world outlook, but a faith in a living Person that is grounded in historical events.

Here we touch the essence of the influence of Christianity on Smuts and what he had in mind as his final contribution to mankind as revealed in many letters and messages which he left as a legacy to posterity.

He might have differed from many Christians of various denominations over certain special doctrinal features which differentiate Christianity from the universal human standpoint. Similarly he confessed that he never could make up his mind how much of the early story of Christ is fact or is perhaps the result of Christian faith and piety and tradition.

But whatever one may think of these matters and however much his view may differ from certain ecclesiastical doctrines, he always saw the figure of Christ as of the greatest historic importance.

In defending the idealism of Woodrow Wilson against the intelligentsia – the people who, admiring only their own cleverness, despise real goodness, real thought, real wisdom – Smuts wrote to a friend:

"I can't help remembering that if it depended on the intelligentsia of the day, our knowledge of Christ would be a casual and contemptuous remark in Tacitus. A few fishermen in Galilee prevented it."

Again, writing to a friend in New York and later to a bishop elsewhere he repeated his strong conviction:

"Christ remains as the outstanding miracle of our human story. And the more one gathers experience of life and sees the pitiable lot of mankind, the more one is drawn to the Figure and the message He delivered and stands for in our human story."[20]

It is in this sense that the Man of Galilee came to be for him the Summit and the Crowning Glory of Personality. As we follow in the footsteps of Jesus, as we apply His teachings in our lives, and as we approximate to His spirit of love, we come nearer to that which is deepest and highest in us – our noblest self and our purest personality.

It is against this background of philosophy and religion combined that Smuts has left a legacy to mankind as well as a memory of his own striking holistic personality. He himself in a beautiful letter to Lady Moore, wrote how he regarded memory as often greater and richer than the presence itself.

"I find something very beautiful in the gospel story in St John (St John 14:16-18, 26) where Jesus tells the distressed disciples that He is going but he will send the Comforter, the Holy Spirit, to make up for His going.

"Memory is in many respects the Holy Spirit of friendship. The friend goes but the immortal memory remains. It is in some ways more effective and goes deeper than the presence itself. The presence is so absorbing, in a sense so disturbing; its emotional appeal is so terrific and almost shattering. The memory is gentler, more spiritual, more of a Holy Spirit, and softens and sublimates the actualities of the presence. At bottom we are more spiritual than physical in our nature – the inmost core of our being is spirit and not body.

"And so in physical absence the spiritual memory comes into play, and we can ponder over things in their real meaning, undisturbed by the bodily pulls. The great meaning behind it all stands out more clearly."[21]

It may be that in this sense we are now able to understand and evaluate Smuts better than while he was alive and with us. On this basis he emerges as one of the greatest that has lived and walked this earth.

In my evaluation of Smuts, his most significant contribution to mankind was his realization that we live in a friendly world where co-operation rather than strife forms the core of our beings. As I have pointed out in Chapter 9, to his way of thinking Holism as a pattern in evolution not only reconciles the inner and external factors stressed by Darwin but also accounts for the creative unity of life.

It was on this basis that to him life does not become merely a struggle for survival as the end and purpose. It is rather a creative growing unity which makes all the diverse elements of existence the co-operative members of an essentially friendly universe. We are here to nourish and protect all nature, and in co-operating with the deepest forces in all nature, we achieve order, harmony, beauty, happiness and blessedness. In this way we are capable of realizing our highest and noblest personalities to the glory of the Creator of all life.

His last letter to Queen Frederica written on May 7 1950, almost as a valedictory – he had his first heart attack on his 80th birthday on May 24 and died on September 8 – contains the essence of his beliefs, his religion and his philosophy. I have already quoted one passage from the letter in discussing his religion, but the letter is of much beauty and so revealing that it is worthwhile to quote it here more fully as a final summing up. Writing about a glorious

Transvaal day after good rains which made "the earth look a picture", he continues, "It is at such times that one becomes aware of the Divine, not as something beyond, but as the soul and essence of nature and oneself. Language fails one to express the joy of it, and of the unity which goes with it, as if it were one glory, one life, one love. I think it is at such times that we realize more fully than at other times the divine whole in which we share and of which we are part. And is that not the truth too?

"And we are truly one with all things, but one realizes this at such great moments of inspiration, when the self merges into the Whole, and all life and consciousness becomes as today a great act of marriage in which the love at the heart of things finds its supreme consummation. It is only occasionally that the real Truth is revealed to us as a flash of light in our happiest experiences.

"A day like today is like a real marriage feast in which we partake, not only of love but of the Highest. There is the Great Presence of nature, and there is the great feast which is consummated in it. This mystery of things should be an abiding impression and accompany us all the time. But it would be too much for us. It is only on the mountain summit of our experience that we have this sense and realization of the meaning of it all, and feel ourselves of the Great Company at the great Feast. If this experience were too long continued it might be too much for us as we would be drunk of it and undone by it. So we get it in small short doses. But those short moments of vital experience reveal the real truth and reality of things to us, and are perhaps all our little strength can bear. The mystic whole is all the time with us and in us, but we understand it only in flashes of high experience."[22]

References

CHAPTER 1

1. P. J. Cillié: *Tydgenote*. Tafelberg-Uitgewers 1981. On page 28, Piet Cillié, former Editor of *Die Burger*, characterized Smuts as follows:
   "In die politiek het hy die brandpunt geword van magtige en soms onbeheerbare gevoelens en spanninge binne die wordende nasie. Geloof en hoop was op hom gekonsentreer en van die ander kant hewige afkeer en vyandigheid. Vir sommige was sy meteoriese glans soos 'n lig op die pad, vir ander soos 'n gloed van onheil oor ons staatkundige lewe."

   (In politics he became the focus of powerful and sometimes uncontrollable emotions and tensions within the nascent nation. Trust and hope were concentrated on him, and conversely, strong aversion and enmity. For some his meteoric brilliance was like a light on the road; for others, like a blaze of disaster over our political life.)
2. H. C. Armstrong: *Grey Steel, A Study in Arrogance*. Page 375
3. Sarah Gertrude Millin: *General Smuts*.
4. J. C. Smuts Jnr.: *Jan Christiaan Smuts*.
5. F. C. Kolbe: *Holism and Evolution* – privately assembled manuscript in possession of the author. Kolbe attacks Smuts's materialistic outlook but "Much as we shall have to differ from him here and there, we admit from the first his high spiritual aim."
6. J. C. Smuts: *Holism and Evolution*. Pages 341 and 342.
7. F. C. Kolbe: *Holism and Evolution* – privately assembled manuscript. Page 5.
8. See *Time* of March 16, 1981. Pages 56 and 57.
   Even today according to the well-known American news magazine there is a tendency among the public to regard the acceptance of evolution as proof of atheism and the rejection of the Bible. In the USA those who favour evolution are called evolutionists and those who reject evolution and accept the Bible are called creationists. According to *Time* a fierce struggle is raging in the American educational system between the evolutionists and the creationists.
   During his presidential campaign swing through Texas, Mr Ronald Reagan was asked his view on the teaching of evolution. His answer was as follows:
   "It is a scientific theory only, and it is not believed in the scientific community to be as infallible as it once was believed. But if it is going to be taught in the schools, then I think the Biblical story of creation should also be taught."
   Quoted in *Time, page 56.*

CHAPTER 2

1. J. C. Smuts: *Holism and Evolution*. Pages 284-289.
2. Prof. James Ward: *Psychological Principles*. Page 431.
3. J. C. Smuts: *Holism and Evolution*. Page 283.

4. J. C. Smuts: *Holism and Evolution.* Page 285.
5. N. Levi: *Jan Smuts.*
6. *Smuts Papers – Volume III.* Page 693.
7. H. C. Armstrong: *Grey Steel: A Study in Arrogance.* Smuts in a letter to Mrs Gillett on September 21 1939 refers to this biography in scathing terms.
"The image of *Grey Steel* is continually before their minds (his political opponents). I have not read the book, but I gather that it sets out the record of the deep political schemer who manages somehow – often by unorthodox means – to get the better of his opponents. Sarah Gertrude Millin is furious with the author – says he stole his facts from her and then proceeded to twist them so as to paint a sinister picture which has nothing to do with reality." *Smuts Papers – Volume VI.* Page 194.
8. Sarah Gertrude Millin: *General Smuts.*
9. Sarah Gertrude Millin: *The Measure of my Days.*
10. P. B. Blanckenberg: *The Thoughts of General Smuts.* From a letter of Smuts to a friend quoted on page 33.
11. Ditto: From a letter to a friend, September 1938, page 27.
12. F. S. Crafford: *Jan Smuts: A Biography.*
13. *Smuts Papers – Volume VI.* Page 489.
14. René Kraus: *Old Master: The Life of Jan Christiaan Smuts.*
15. R. H. Kiernan: *General Smuts.*
Dorothy F. Wilson: *Smuts of South Africa.*
16. Walter Bargatzky: *Smuts: Sieg eines Besiegten.*
17. Horace Shipp: *Lives that Moved the World.* Chapter on Smuts under the title: "The enemy who became a friend."
18. J. C. Smuts Jnr.: *Jan Christiaan Smuts.*
19. P. B. Blanckenberg: *The Thoughts of General Smuts.*
20. W. K. Hancock: *Smuts: (I) The Sanguine Years, 1870-1919. (II) The Fields of Force, 1919-1950.*
21. Jean van der Poel: Article on the Smuts collection in *The Bluestocking* published by the University Women's Association.
22. Piet Meiring: *Smuts the Patriot.*
23. J. C. Smuts: *Holism and Evolution.* Pages 286-287.
24. J. C. Smuts: *Holism and Evolution.* Page 288.
25. J. C. Smuts: *Holism and Evolution.* Page 301.

CHAPTER 3

1. Alan Paton: Article in *The Forum*, September 1952. Page 4.
2. Jannie Smuts (the son) gives interesting information on the early life of his father in his biography *Jan Christiaan Smuts.*
3. W. K. Hancock: *Smuts.* Page 13 tells of a mystic experience the boy Smuts had on the summit of a steep crag of the mountain Riebeek Kasteel.
4. M. K. Gandhi in an *Autobiography* laid great emphasis on the spiritual quality of life. In their earlier years he and Smuts pitted their legal brains as well as their spiritual resources against one another.
5. W. K. Hancock: *Smuts (Volume I).* Page 13.
6. W. K. Hancock: *Smuts (Volume I).* Page 28 reveals that his Latin and Greek notebooks with their vocabularies are still to be seen at Stellenbosch.
7. *Encyclopaedia Britannica*: Article on Smuts. Volume XVI. Pages 909-910.
8. W. K. Hancock: *Smuts (Volume I).* Page 46.
9. After the death of Smuts, his wife, Mrs Isie Smuts, showed me his big collection of grasses in presses in a special room in their farmhouse at Irene.

10. J. C. Smuts Jnr.: *Jan Christiaan Smuts*. Page 340.
11. J. C. Smuts Jnr.: *Jan Christiaan Smuts*. Page 23.
12. H. C. Armstrong: *Grey Steel*. Page 300.
13. Lloyd George in his *War Memoirs* refers to Smuts's intellectual powers in glowing terms.
14. Viscount Chandos as Oliver Lyttelton worked very closely with Smuts in the Middle East during the Second World War.
15. W. K. Hancock: *Smuts (Volume II)*. Page 234.
16. Alan Paton: article in *The Forum*, September, 1952. Page 5.
17. W. K. Hancock: *Smuts (Volume II)*. Page 483.
18. Alan Paton: article in *The Forum*, September 1952. Page 5.
19. *The Student*, edition of 1895 kept at the University of Stellenbosch, contains the poem.
20. Quoted from an article by Smuts in *The London Spectator* on the Jubilee of King George V, May, 1935.
21. Sarah Gertrude Millin: *General Smuts*. Page 41.
22. Alan Paton: Article in *The Forum*, September 1952. Page 6.

CHAPTER 4

1. Dr. E. G. Malherbe in a personal letter to the author written on November 27 1980 gives this intimate account of Smuts's religion:

"Vanweë die intieme verwantskap (vanaf hul kinderjare) met my ouers was Genl. Smuts se verhouding teenoor my soos die van 'n vader teenoor 'n seun en ons het dikwels oor godsdienstige en filosofiese probleme gesels. Dit het my altoos tot groot verontwaardiging gestem toe sy teenstanders en veral sommige koerante die indruk probeer skep het dat Genl. Smuts 'n ateïs was. Ek kan persoonlik getuig van sy *diepe* godsdienssin. Dit was meer as vorm-godsdiens wat meestal gepaard gaan met ritueel en niks meer nie.

"Tog het hy respek gehad vir die Kerk as instelling. Dit was die rede waarom hy my destyds verbied het om die name van die Broeders te publiseer. Hy het gevrees dat dit onenigheid in ons kerk sou meebring."

(Owing to the intimate relationship between him and my parents from childhood days, General Smuts's attitude to me was that of a father to a son, and we often discussed religious and philosophical questions. I always felt great indignation when his opponents, and in particular certain newspapers, tried to create the impression that General Smuts was an atheist. I can personally vouch for his deep piety. It was more than formal worship which mostly involves mere ritual and nothing more.

Yet he respected the Church as an institution. That was why he forbade me at that time to publish the names of the Broeders (Broederbond). He feared that it would cause dissension in our church.)

2. W. K. Hancock: *Smuts (Volume I)*. Page 4.
3. Ibid. Page 10.
4. Ibid. Page 14.
5. Ibid. Page 18.
6. Ibid. Page 17.
7. Ibid. Page 34.
8. Ibid. Page 48.
9. Ibid. Pages 47-51.
10. W. K. Hancock: *Smuts (Volume I)*. Page 133.
11. *Smuts Papers – Volume I*. Page 513.
12. *Smuts Papers – Volume I*. Page 533.
13. N. Levi: *Jan Smuts*. Page 70.
14. J. C. Smuts: *Greater South Africa*.

15. Sarah Gertrude Millin: *General Smuts (Volume I).* Page 23.
16. "Freedom", the rectorial address delivered at St Andrews University on October 17 1934 and published as a booklet.
17. P. B. Blanckenberg: *The Thoughts of General Smuts.* Page 71.
18. Sarah Gertrude Millin: *General Smuts.* Page 202.
19. Sarah Gertrude Millin: *World Black Out.* Page 70.
20. J. C. Smuts Jnr.: *Jan Christiaan Smuts.* Page 439.
21. Scott Haigh: *Strangers May Be Present.* Page 16.
22. Told to the author by the late Senator A. M. Conroy, shortly after he persuaded Smuts to continue his political leadership of the United Party.
23. J. C. Smuts Jnr.: *Jan Christiaan Smuts.* Page 515.
24. Piet Beukes: Article in *Mense*, May 1955. Page 6.
25. Sarah Gertrude Millin: *The Measure of My Days.* Page 322.
26. Sarah Gertrude Millin: *The Measure of My Days.* Page 321.
27. Queen Frederica: *A Measure of Understanding.* Page 70.

CHAPTER 5

1. Sarah Gertrude Millin: *General Smuts.* Page 60.
2. J. C. Smuts Jnr.: *Jan Christiaan Smuts.* Page 20.
3. W. K. Hancock: *Smuts (Volume I).* Page 29.
4. P. B. Blanckenberg: *The Thoughts of General Smuts.* Pages 17 and 18.
5. Sarah Gertrude Millin: *General Smuts (I).* Page 22.
6. Walt Whitman: *Leaves of Grass.*
7. J. C. Smuts: The manuscript of *Walt Whitman – A Study in the Evolution of Personality*, forms part of the *Smuts Papers.*
8. J. C. Smuts: *Holism and Evolution.* Page 185.
9. J. C. Smuts: *Holism and Evolution.* Page 187.
10. J. C. Smuts: *The Theory of Holism.* Copy of speech in *The Star*, September 21 1927.

CHAPTER 6

1. F. V. Engelenburg: *General Louis Botha.* Page 99.
2. F. V. Engelenburg: *General Louis Botha.* Introduction by J. C. Smuts. Pages 15-20.
3. *Smuts Papers – Volume III.* Pages 84, 85, 88 and 91.
4. W. K. Hancock: *Smuts (Volume I).* Page 180.
5. *Glasgow High School Magazine.* Campbell-Bannerman Centenary edition, June 1948, contains an article by Smuts on how self-government was obtained and the results that flowed from it for South Africa and for himself.
6. F. V. Engelenburg: *General Louis Botha.* Page 332.
7. Sarah Gertrude Millin: *General Smuts (I).* Page 41.
8. F. V. Engelenburg: *General Louis Botha.* Pages 322-333.
9. Quoted by W. K. Hancock: *Smuts (Volume I).* Page 592.

CHAPTER 7

1. Mrs Margaret Gillett showed me the private diary kept by her mother which recorded the arrival of Smuts in England in January 1906 and his stay with the Clark family in Street, Somersetshire. The diary now forms part of the *Smuts Papers.*
2. Personal reminiscence of Mrs Margaret Gillett describing how she decided to go to South Africa. I recorded her reminiscences when I visited her in 1954.
3. Ditto.
4. Ditto.

5. Related by Mrs Gillett to me in 1954.
6. W. K. Hancock: *Smuts (Volume I)*. Page 44. H. J. Wolstenholme is described by Hancock as a radical don who had set out to become a Congregational minister but had succumbed to doubts and had become a teacher of German at Cambridge. Smuts took German lessons from him and Wolstenholme became Smuts's best friend at Cambridge and kept up his friendship until his death in 1919.
7. Mrs Gillett showed me the notebook in 1954 and allowed me to copy the names of books and authors from it. The notebook now forms part of the *Smuts Papers*.
8. Quoted from an interview with Mrs Gillett in 1954.

CHAPTER 8

1. J. C. Smuts Jnr.: *Jan Christiaan Smuts*. Page 25.
2. W. K. Hancock: *Smuts (Volume I)*. Page 10.
3. W. K. Hancock: *Smuts (Volume I)*. Pages 56-58 show how Smuts at first aligned himself with Cecil John Rhodes and how disillusioned he was after the Jameson Raid.
4. Letter from Smuts to Emily Hobhouse quoted from the *Smuts Papers – Volume II*. Page 155.
5. J. C. Smuts. *Een Eeuw van Onrecht*, translated as *A Century of Wrong*. Although Smuts was indisputably the author of this treatise against British rule, he was inclined in later years for political purposes to disclaim exclusive authorship.
6. Quoted from the Foreword by Smuts to Constance Lowry: *Life of Frederick Charles Kolbe*.
7. Quoted from Dorothy Wilson: *Smuts of South Africa: Soldier and Peacemaker*.
8. Quoted from W. Bargatzsky: *Smuts, Sieg eines Besiegten*. Page 37.
9. J. C. Smuts: *Holism and Evolution*. Pages 314-316.
10. J. C. Smuts: *Holism and Evolution*. Page 315.
11. Alan Paton: *Jan Smuts – The Second Anniversary*. Page 5.
12. N. Levi: *Jan Smuts*. Page 78.
13. Ibid. Page 295.
14. Ibid. Page 304.
15. Quoted from A. C. Benson, Master of Magdalene College, Cambridge: *The Happy Warrior: A Sight of General Smuts at Cambridge*, which appeared in the *Church Family Newspaper*.
16. Alan Paton: *Jan Smuts – The Second Anniversary*. Page 4.
17. Ibid. Page 4.
18. Ibid. Page 5.
19. Ibid. Page 6.
20. Quoted from James Lees-Milne: *Harold Nicolson: A Biography (I)*.

CHAPTER 9

1. Quoted from the foreword by Smuts of F. C. Kolbe: *A Catholic view of Holism*.
2. Quoted from an essay on "The Dramatic Character of Sir John Falstaff" by Maurice Morgan.
3. R. G. Collingwood in his philosophical book *The First Mate's Log*, 1940, like Smuts, also stressed the importance of returning to the teachings of Socrates as "the father of a genuine 'Geisteswissenschaft'", combining philosophy and religion.
4. J. C. Smuts: *Holism and Evolution*. Page 102.
5. F. C. Kolbe: *A Catholic View of Holism*.
6. F. C. Kolbe in his articles in *The Southern Cross "which were privately assembled under the title Holism and Evolution"* gives an interesting history of Christian leaders, starting with St Paul, who endowed matter with creative qualities, thereby paving the way to the concept of evolution in nature.
7. F. C. Kolbe: *Holism and Evolution*. Page 2 of assembled articles.
8. J. C. Smuts: *Holism and Evolution*. Pages 9-15. He states his viewpoint as follows:

"We believe in Evolution, but it is no more the mechanical Evolution of a generation or two ago, but a creative Evolution."

9. J. C. Smuts: *Holism and Evolution.* Pages 16 and 17.
10. J. B. S. Haldane: *Is Evolution a Myth?* Smuts also drew upon Haldane's book *Organism and Environment* to illustrate the power of co-ordination in nature.
11. J. C. Smuts: *Holism and Evolution.* Page 185, where Smuts evaluates Darwin as even more epoch-making than Newton.
12. Ibid. Page 189.
13. Ibid. Page 198.
14. Smuts devotes an entire chapter in his *Holism and Evolution* to Mind as an organ of wholes and thus as a vital element in his theory of Holism. See chapter 9.
15. J. C. Smuts: *Holism and Evolution.* Page 222.
16. Ibid. Page 223.
17. In 1929, three years after the appearance of *Holism and Evolution*, *The Times Literary Supplement* carried an article on "The Dethronement of Descartes", edition of September 9 1929. Pages 585 and 586.
18. W. K. Hancock: *Smuts (Volume I).* Pages 232-234.
19. A. D. Ritchie: *Essays in Philosophy and Other Pieces.*

CHAPTER 10

1. W. K. Hancock: *Smuts (Volume I).*
2. N. Levi: *Jan Smuts.* Page 13.
3. W. K. Hancock: *Smuts (Volume I).* On page 23 he writes: "In *Homo Sum* (written when Smuts was 19), as in the verses addressed to Isie Krige, we see foreshadowed his philosophy of Holism."
4. W. K. Hancock: *Smuts (Volume I).* Pages 38-39.
5. Sarah Gertrude Millin: *General Smuts.* Page 39.
6. J. C. Smuts: *Holism and Evolution.* Page 6 of Preface.
7. *Smuts Papers – Volume III.* Page 69.
8. Smuts in 1927 explained the importance of patterns in modern scientific thinking to the students at the University of the Witwatersrand as follows, stating that the only constant things which scientists worked with now are ratios; he explained that there has been a complete change in their point of view. Matter has gone; it has disappeared into energy. All we could see now were patterns and structures. "If you take patterns as the ultimate structure of the world, if it is arrangements and not stuff that make up the world, the new concept leads you to the concept of wholes. Wholes have no stuff; they are arrangements. Science has come around to the view that the world consists of patterns, and I construe that to be that the world consists of wholes." See report in *The Star*, Johannesburg, September 21 1927.
9. J. C. Smuts: *Holism and Evolution.* Page 183.
10. Ibid. Page 183.
11. *Encyclopaedia Britannica* (1955 edition). Page 641.
12. Ibid. Page 642.
13. J. C. Smuts: *Holism and Evolution.* Page 336.

CHAPTER 11

1. J. C. Smuts: *Een Eeuw van Onrecht* (*A Century of Wrong*).
2. *Smuts Papers – Volume III.* Page 189. In a letter to Sir A. J. Murray, Smuts wrote that Ministers in the Botha cabinet were being pressed to take active steps in German South West Africa.
3. J. C. Smuts: *Holism and Evolution.* Page 119.
4. Ibid. Page 138.

5. Ibid. Page 139.
6. Ibid. Pages 307-311.
7. Ibid. Page 312.
8. J. C. Smuts: "Freedom", rectorial address delivered at St Andrews on October 17 1934.

CHAPTER 12

1. W. K. Hancock: *Smuts (Volume I).* Pages 160-161.
2. J. C. Smuts: Preface to the German edition of *Holism and Evolution*, written in April 1938.
3. J. C. Smuts: *Holism and Evolution.* Pages 267-273.
4. Ibid. Page 229.
5. Ibid. Pages 265-267.
6. Ibid. Page 266.
7. Ibid. Page 283.
8. Ibid. Pages 273-276.
9. Ibid. Chapter 11 under the heading Functions and Ideals emphasizes the importance of freedom, purity and creativeness in the shaping of a personality.
10. J. C. Smuts: *Holism and Evolution.* Page 297.
11. Ibid. Page 296.
12. Ibid. Page 315.

CHAPTER 13

1. W. K. Hancock: *Smuts (Volume I).* Page 158.
2. Ibid. Pages 215-216.
3. J. C. Smuts: *Holism and Evolution.* Page 106.
4. M. K. Gandhi: *An Autobiography.* Gandhi is absolutely honest with himself in all his revelations, which makes this a truly remarkable autobiography.
5. W. K. Hancock: *Smuts (Volume I).* Pages 333-347.
6. *Smuts Papers (Volume II).* Page 251. In his letter of March 3 1908 to Merriman, Smuts discussed the alternative facing the four provinces in their plans to unite. His many letters to leading figures of the time reveal his vast preparations to achieve unification.

   In a letter to Mrs Gillett on August 24 1908 he tells her how hard he worked "to prepare for the ordeal". *Smuts Papers – Volume II.* Page 456.
7. E. Walton: *The Inner History of the National Convention of South Africa* emphasizes the importance Smuts placed on mutual trust as a prerequisite for a successful convention.
8. *Smuts Papers – Volume II* contains the complete Draft Constitution of South Africa, a neat typescript marked in Smuts's handwriting and signed August, 1908 J.C.S. Pages 457-487.
9. W. K. Hancock: *Smuts (Volume I).* Page 366 gives a graphic description of the humiliation Smuts suffered especially as Merriman continued to rub it in in letter after letter to Smuts.
10. Smuts called in his Boer War friend, General Koos de la Rey, to put down the miners and thereafter deported the leaders.
11. J. Meintjes: *General Louis Botha.* Page 217.
12. F. V. Engelenburg: *General Louis Botha*, from the Preface by Smuts.
13. *Smuts Papers – Volume III.* Page 202. In a letter to Mrs Gillett on September 27 1914, Smuts spoke of his anguish that the British Government had asked Botha and him to attack South West Africa. "Many valuable lives will be lost there. But such was the wish of the English Government and Botha and I are not the men to desert England in this dark hour. Many Boers cannot forget the past and bitterly disapprove our action. But I think we are doing our duty."
14. *Smuts Papers – Volume VI.* Page 190. In the midst of the crisis Smuts found time to visit Kirstenbosch to look at the flowers and to write a number of letters to his wife, and to

T. W. Lamont, his American friend.

"It is a curious circumstance that just 25 years ago – to the month and the week – I had to be responsible for a resolution in Parliament declaring war on Germany. I never dreamt that I would have to face the same situation in my lifetime; but here it is."

15. Thomas: *Abraham Lincoln, A Biography.* Page 324.
16. P. B. Blanckenberg: *The Thoughts of General Smuts.* Pages 11-12.
17. *Smuts Papers – Volume I.* Pages 80-100 contain his first important political speech.
18. J. C. Smuts: *Africa and Some World Problems* contains the Oxford lectures Smuts gave in 1929. One of the lectures dealt specifically with the so-called Native Problem in South Africa. It is reprinted in *Groter Suid-Afrika.* Pages 39-62.
19. W. K. Hancock: *Smuts (Volume II).* Page 113.
20. Quoted from my notes on an interview with Mrs Gillett in 1954 in Street, Somersetshire.
21. *Sunday Times*, 1988.

CHAPTER 14

1. W. K. Hancock: *Smuts (Volume II).* Pages 151-154.
2. *Smuts Papers – Volume VI.* Page 191 contains a cablegram Churchill sent Smuts on September 7 1939. "I rejoice to feel that we are once again on commando together."
3. W. K. Hancock: *Smuts (Volume II).* Page 467.
4. Ibid. Page 468.
5. *Smuts Papers – Volume VII.* Page 116.
6. Ibid. Page 194. Letter to Lady Moore April 8 1948. "The indications are that we shall win elections once more," was his confident prediction, but in the event he lost, which was a tremendous blow to him.

CHAPTER 15

1. *Smuts Papers – Volume I.* Pages 464-493.
2. *Smuts Papers – Volume II.* Page 171.
3. W. K. Hancock: *Smuts (Volume I).* Page 204.
4. Ibid. Page 310.
5. *Smuts Papers – Volume III.* Pages 506-517.
6. Ibid. Page 506.
7. Ibid. Page 513.
8. Ibid. Page 514.
9. W. K. Hancock: *Smuts (Volume II).* Page 521.
10. *Smuts Papers – Volume VII.* Pages 296-298.

Churchill had cabled him under the name Colonel Warden. Smuts replied under the name Henry Cooper and then wrote his letter objecting to the decision to allow republics in the Commonwealth. Churchill differed from him on this important issue and said so in a letter to "Henry Cooper" on May 22 1949 – *Smuts Papers – Volume VII.* Page 298.

CHAPTER 16

1. *Smuts Papers – Volume III.* Page 334.
2. Ibid. Pages 337-338.
3. Ibid. Pages 361-362.
4. Ibid. Pages 407-409.
5. Ibid. pages 459-460.
6. Ibid. Page 477.
7. Ibid. Page 478.
8. *Smuts Papers – Volume IV.* Page 30.

9. Ibid. Page 43.
10. Ibid. Page 43.
11. Ibid. Page 48.
12. Ibid. Page 49.
13. Ibid. Page 71.
14. Ibid. Pages 83-87.
15. Ibid. Pages 87-88.
16. Ibid. Page 89.
17. Ibid. Page 135.
18. Ibid. Page 142.
19. Ibid. Page 145.
20. Ibid. Pages 148-150.
21. Ibid. Page 247.
22. Ibid. Pages 256-259.
23. *Smuts Papers – Volume V.* Pages 605-607.
24. J. C. Smuts: *Groter Suid-Afrika.* Page 73.
25. *Smuts Papers – Volume VI.* Page 459.
26. Ibid. Page 527.
27. *Smuts Papers – Volume VII.* Pages 13-19.
28. *Smuts Papers – Volume VI.* Pages 209-212.
29. Ibid. Pages 129-130.

CHAPTER 17

1. *Smuts Papers – Volume III.* Page 528.
2. Sen. A. M. Conroy reported this to me after he had spoken to Smuts after his defeat in the election of May 1948.
3. Lady D. Moore: *South African Diary, 1943.* Page 15.
4. Queen Frederica: *A Measure of Understanding.* Page 65.
5. W. K. Hancock: *Smuts (Volume I).* Page 483.
6. Ibid. Page 588.
7. *Smuts Papers – Volume VII.* Page 126.
8. Quoted from copy of Lady Moore's letter of April 4 1947 (in possession of author).
9. Ibid. Copy of letter of July 25 1943.
10. Ibid. Copy of letter of April 2 1947.
11. Ibid. Copy of letter of April 26 1947.
12. *Smuts Papers – Volume VII.* Page 193.
13. W. K. Hancock: *Smuts (Volume II).* Page 437.
14. W. K. Hancock: *Smuts (Volume II).* Pages 311-312.
15. *Smuts Papers – Volume II* contains letters which passed between Smuts and Merriman regarding the so-called Native Question.
16. *Smuts Papers – Volume II.* Page 242.
17. W. K. Hancock: *Smuts (Volume I).* Page 345.
18. Ibid. Page 346.
19. Ibid. Page 347.
20. *Smuts Papers – Volume VII.* Page 121.
21. Copy of letter from Lady Moore to Smuts written on April 4 1947 from Ceylon (in possession of author).
22. *Smuts Papers – Volume VII.* Page 117.

CHAPTER 18

1. J. C. Smuts: *Theory of Holism in Greater South Africa.* Page 147.
2. Lionel Rubinoff: My Professor at Oxford similarly evaluated Socrates in this light. He wrote: "The important thing about Socrates, the first not only to have answered the call but to have become aware of what it meant to have done so, was that in becoming a philosopher he ceased to act solely in his private capacity. He had become at Apollo's bidding the organ by which the corporate consciousness of the Greeks examined and criticized itself, and in doing so, according to Collingwood, Socrates defined for all times the calling of philosophers, which is to re-affirm the covenant first made by Socrates, and to bear witness thereafter. The philosopher sets out to redeem himself by contributing toward the redemption of his fellows. In more secular terms, the philosopher is one who criticizes his generation's ideas of itself, and what it is doing, in order thereby to criticize his own idea of what he is and what he is doing – thereby amending his idea of himself in order to amend further his neighbours' ideas of themselves." Quoted from "Religion and the Rapprochement between Thought and Action" by Lionel Rubinoff in M. Krausz: *Critical Essays on the Philosophy of R. G. Collingwood.*
3. F. C. Kolbe: *A Catholic View of Holism* with a foreword by Smuts in which he compares his views on Holism with the views expounded by Kolbe.
4. J. C. Smuts: *Holism and Evolution.* Page 6 of Preface.
5. *Smuts Papers – Volume 48.* No. 49. Letter to Mrs Lamont, June 21 1931.
6. *Smuts Papers*: Letter to Mrs Gillett, October 14 1940.
7. *Smuts Papers – Volume 77.* No. 128. Letter to C. E. Raven, January 3 1945.
8. *Smuts Papers – Volume 88.* No. 258. Letter to Mrs Gillett, September 8 1948.
9. W. K. Hancock: *Smuts (Volume II).* Page 395.
10. *Smuts Papers – Volume VII.* Pages 193-194.
11. *Smuts Papers – Volume VII.* Pages 219-220.
12. J. C. Smuts: *Holism and Evolution.* Pages 280-281.
13. Ibid. Page 336.
14. Ibid. Pages 336-337.
15. J. C. Smuts Jnr.: *Jan Christiaan Smuts.* Page 322.
16. Quoted from my notes of an interview with Mrs Gillett at Street, Somersetshire in 1954.
17. J. C. Smuts: *The Theory of Holism, Envisaged New Forms of Life in Future.* "What forms of life there will be in millions of years to come it is impossible to conceive. They will, at any rate, be far higher than they are today. Far greater advances in evolution will be made in the future. Life is only young; it is an infant in this universe, and we are only getting into our stride now. I don't believe that we, the human beings, are the acme of the universe. I believe there will be evolved far higher forms of spiritual wholes than we see before us today." Page 155 of *Greater South Africa.*
18. J. C. Smuts Jnr.: *Jan Christiaan Smuts.* Page 292.
19. Quoted from my notes of an interview with Mrs Gillett in 1954.
20. P. B. Blanckenberg: *The Thoughts of General Smuts.* Page 71.
21. *Smuts Papers.* Page 125.
22. Queen Frederica: *A Measure of Understanding.* Pages 70-71.

Bibliography

Armstrong, Harold Courtenay: *Grey Steel: J. C. Smuts, A Study in Arrogance*. London, Barker, 1938.

Bargatzsky, Walter: *Smuts: Sieg eines Besiegten*. München, Biederstein, 1948.

Benson, A. C.: *The Happy Warrior: A Sight of General Smuts at Cambridge, May 1917. The Church Family Newspaper*, Cambridge University Press, 1917.

Bernstein, Edgar: *The Legacy of General Smuts*. (Four essays reprinted from *Forward*.) Johannesburg, Eagle Press, 1950.

Beukes, Piet: *Generaal Smuts se Persoonlike Godsdiens*. From *Die Beste*. Cape Town, Citadel Press, September 1954.

Blanckenberg, Pieter Botha: *The Thoughts of General Smuts*. Cape Town, Juta, 1951.

Boydell, Thomas: *My Luck's Still In*. Cape Town, Stewart, 1948.

Campbell, A.: *Smuts and Swastika*. London, Gollancz, 1943.

Carlyle, Thomas: *Sartor Resartus: The Life and Opinions of Herr Teufelsdröckh*. London, Chapman and Hall, 1849. 3rd Edition.

Cillié, P. J.: *Tydgenote*. Kaapstad, Tafelberg, 1981.

Collyer, John Johnston: *Die Suid-Afrikaners met Generaal Smuts in Duits Oos-Afrika, 1916*. Pretoria, Staatsdrukker, 1939.

Crafford, F. S.: *Jan Smuts: A Biography*. New York, Doubleday, Doran and Co., 1943.

Crowe, J. H. V.: *General Smuts' Campaign in East Africa*. Introduction by Smuts, pp. v-xvii. London, John Murray, 1918.

Darwin, Charles Robert: *On the Origin of Species*. London, John Murray, 1926. Reprint of 6th Edition.

Doornkloof Society: *Laaste Dae van Smuts deur Een van Sy Geneeshere*. Irene Genootskap, 1965.

Duffus, Louis: *Beyond the Laager*. Foreword by Smuts. London, Hurst and Blackett, 1947.

Eksteen, Terence Arnold: *The Statesmen*. Cape Town, Don Nelson, 1978.

Encyclopaedia Britannica: Volume XVI.

Engelenburg, Frans V.: *General Louis Botha*. Introduction by Smuts, pp. 15-20. Pretoria, Van Schaik, 1929.

Fagan, H. A.: *Co-Existence in South Africa*. Cape Town, Juta, 1963.

Frederica, Queen: *A Measure of Understanding*. London, Macmillan, 1971.

Friedlander, Zelda: *Jan Smuts Remembered: A Centennial Tribute*. Cape Town, Timmins, 1970.

Friedman, Bernard: *Smuts: A Reappraisal*. Johannesburg, Keartland, 1975.

Gandhi, M. K.: *An Autobiography: The Story of My Experience with Truth*. London, Phoenix Press, 1949.

Goethe, Johann Wolfgang von: *Novels and Tales*. London, George Bell and Sons, 1883.

Gregory, Theodore: *Ernest Oppenheimer and the Economic Development of Southern Africa*. Cape Town, Oxford University Press, 1962.

Haarhoff, T. J.: *Smuts the Humanist: A Personal Reminiscence*. Oxford, Blackwell, 1970.
Haigh, Scott: *Strangers May Be Present*. Cape Town, Timmins, 1951.
Haldane, J. B. S.: *Is Evolution a Myth?* Chapter: Organism and Environment. 1917.
Hancock, W. K.: *Smuts, Two Volumes: The Sanguine Years, 1870-1919; The Fields of Force, 1919-1950*. Cambridge University Press, 1962, 1968.
Hancock, W. K. and Van der Poel, J.: *Selections from the Smuts Papers. (June 1886-October 1950.)* Seven Volumes. Cambridge University Press, 1966-1973.
Inner Light: A Devotional Anthology. London, George Allen and Unwin, 1953. Note: This book was sent by Mrs M. C. Gillett of Street, Somersetshire, to the author with a personal letter in 1955. The passages on wholeness as the essence of personality give a clue to Smuts's ideas for his contemplated second book on Holism.
Kant, Immanuel: *Fundamental Principles of the Metaphysics of Ethics*. London, Longmans Green, 1937.
Kiernan, Reginald H.: *General Smuts*. London, Harrap, 1943.
Kolbe, Frederick Charles: *A Catholic View of Holism*. A criticism of the theory put forward by General Smuts in his book, *Holism and Evolution*. Foreword by Smuts pp. v-viii. London, Macmillan, 1928.
– *Mightier than the Sword*. Chapter 25. Cape Town, Catholic Newspaper and Publishing Co., 1954.
– Cuttings from *The Southern Cross* as well as a typed chapter privately assembled and never published.
Kraus, Rene: *Old Master: The Life of Jan Christiaan Smuts*. New York, Dutton and Co., 1944.
Krausz, Michael: *Critical Essays on the Philosophy of R. G. Collingwood*. Oxford, Clarendon Press, 1972.
Krige, Jan: *American Sympathy in the Boer War*. Published privately with no reference to any publisher or date.
Lees-Milne, James: *Harold Nicolson: A Biography*. Volume 1. London, Chatto and Windus, 1980.
Levi, N.: *Jan Smuts*. London, Longmans Green, 1917.
Lippman, Walter: *The Method of Freedom*. London, George Allen and Unwin, 1934.
Lowry, Constance: *Life of Frederick Charles Kolbe*. Foreword by Smuts.
Meintjes, Johannes: *General Louis Botha: A Biography*. London, Cassell, 1970.
Meiring, P. G. J.: *Ons Eerste Ses Premiers: 'n Persoonlike Terugblik*. Kaapstad, Tafelberg, 1972.
– *Smuts the Patriot*. Kaapstad, Tafelberg, 1975.
Millin, Sarah Gertrude: *General Smuts*. Two Volumes. London, Faber and Faber, 1936.
– *The Measure of My Days*. Johannesburg, CNA, 1955.
– *World Black Out*. London, Faber and Faber, 1944.
Mincher, Kathleen: *I Lived in his Shadow: My Life with General Smuts*. Cape Town, Timmins, 1965.
Moore, Lady Daphne: *South African Diary, 1943*. In possession of Mr Paddy O'Neill, Newlands, Cape.
Pakenham, Thomas: *The Boer War*. Johannesburg. Jonathan Ball in association with Weidenfeld and Nicolson, London, 1979.
Paton, Alan: *Jan Smuts – The Second Anniversary*. From *Forum*. September 1952. pp. 4-6.
Pyper, P. A.: *Smuts en die Tweede Vryheidsoorlog*. Proefskrif (MA). Potchefstroom, 1960.
Reitz, Deneys: *Commando*. A Boer Journal of the Boer War with Preface by Smuts. London, Penguin Books in association with Faber and Faber, 1938.
Ritchie, A. D.: *Essays in Philosophy and Other Pieces*. London, Longmans Green, 1948.
Sencourt, Robert: *Winston Churchill*. London, Faber and Faber, 1940.
Shipp, Horace: *Lives that Moved the World: Stories of Men and Women who Dared*. London,

Evans, 1948. pp. 66-74.
Smuts, General, the Right Hon. J. C.: *Holism and Evolution*. London, Macmillan, 1926.
- *Greater South Africa, Plans for a Better World*. Speeches of Field Marshall J. C. Smuts. London, Hodder and Stoughton, 1942.

Smuts, General J. C.: *Groter Suid-Afrika, Planne vir 'n Beter Wêreld.* Toesprake deur die Hoogedelagbare J. C. Smuts. Johannesburg, Waarheidsleer, 1941.
- *Africa and Some World Problems.* Oxford University Press, 1930.
- *Een Eeuw van Onrecht.* Published under auspices of President F. W. Reitz, Transvaal Republic, 1899.
- *Freedom.* Being the rectorial address delivered by General Smuts at St Andrews University on October 17 1934 at his installation. London, Alexander Maclehose and Co., 1934. pp. 7-36.
- Three Kings. From *The Spectator*. Friday, May 3 1935. p. 723.

Smuts, J. C. Jnr.: *Jan Christiaan Smuts.* Cape Town, Heinemann and Cassell, 1952.
Time News Periodical. March 16 1981.
Van der Merwe, N. J.: *Marthinus Theunis Steyn, 'n Lewensbeskrywing.* Twee Dele. Kaapstad, Nasionale Pers, 1921.
Walton, Sir Edgar: *The Inner History of the National Convention of South Africa.* Cape Town, Maskew Miller, 1912.
Whitman, Walt: *Leaves of Grass.* New York, Caldwell and Co., 1900.
Williams, A. F. B.: *Botha, Smuts and South Africa.* London, Hodder and Stoughton, 1946.
Wilson, Dorothy F.: *Smuts of South Africa: Soldier and Peacemaker.* London, S.C.M. Press, 1946.
Zimmern, Alfred: *The Greek Commonwealth.* Oxford, Clarendon Press, 1931.

More recent works

Friedman, Bernard: *Smuts. A Reappraisal.* 1975.
Ingham, Kenneth: *Jan Christiaan Smuts. The Conscience of a South African.* 1986.